THE REPORT OF THE
DEMOCRACY COMMISSION

TASC: think tank for action on social change

TASC is an independent think tank committed to progressive social change in Ireland. It aims to provide a space for innovative thinking where dialogue between citizens, researchers and politicians is facilitated. It is dedicated to seeking out new evidence based ideas and policy solutions which will inform strategies and campaigns for change as it works towards a society where equality is a human right. TASC is funded through independent consultancy work, donations and trusts. For more information on TASC visit www.tascnet.ie

Democratic Dialogue

Democratic Dialogue is a think tank based in Belfast but with links across Ireland, Britain and beyond. Its twin focus is: the continuing change of political accommodation in Northern Ireland, and the social and economic issues neglected during the region's 'troubles'. Its vision is of an egalitarian society, at ease with itself and its evolving context. Democratic Dialogue organsises its work around projects, for which it welcomes commissions. It facilitates dialogue to generate publications, with a view to concrete policy outcomes. Further information on Democratic Dialoge can be found at www.democraticdialogue.org

The Report of the Democracy Commission

ENGAGING CITIZENS

The Case for Democratic Renewal in Ireland

EDITED BY Clodagh Harris
David Begg
Ivana Bacik • Ruth Barrington • John Hanafin • Tony Kennedy
Bernadette MacMahon • Mark Mortell • Elizabeth Meehan
Nora Owen • Donal Toolan • Caroline Wilson

The Report of the Democracy Commission
First published 2005
by tasc at New Island
an imprint of New Island Press
2 Brookside
Dundrum Road
Dublin 14

www.newisland.ie

The authors have asserted their moral rights.

ISBN 1-904301 96 7.

Typeset by Ashfield Press
Cover design by Susan Waine

Printed in Ireland by
Betaprint Limited, Dublin

Table of Contents

Welcome the Report of the Democracy Commission

We established the Democracy Commission because we believe that collective participation in political decision-making is key to achieving equality in Irish society. We wanted to tackle the increasing disconnection from even the most basic forms of democratic participation in decision making for large groups of people, and to make public engagement the cornerstone of the process. We asked a number of people from across the spectrum of Irish society to form an independent commission, working in a voluntary capacity, to consider this question as they thought best and to give us their views and recommendations.

At an early stage, the Joseph Rowntree Charitable Trust, which has an established record of work on democratic issues, supported the proposal and generously provided the main funding. In the meantime TASC initiated the Democratic Audit Ireland project, a complementary research project on democracy. Though this work will take another year, it has already produced information for use by the Commission.

The Commission's work is contained in these pages. The comprehensive consultation undertaken in both parts of the island of Ireland and the depth and range of its conclusions and recommendations cannot fail to impress. We owe them our deepest gratitude.

PAULA CLANCY Director, TASC
ROBIN WILSON Director, *Democratic Dialogue*

Foreword by David Begg

Winston Churchill is supposed to have said of democracy "It is *a terrible bad system until you consider the alternatives*". Any review of the state of our democracy is unlikely to give it an absolutely clean bill of health. The question is rather if it can be improved to make it more responsive to the needs of the population and the common good. We conclude that it can and should and this report contains a number of recommendations which will, we think, allow for a more engaged and active citizenry which should in turn lead to a greater empowerment of people. Our hope is that some or all of these ideas will be debated and ultimately adopted by practitioners of politics and the public at large.

In a national and international context this is a time of great change. The recent IRA statement has gone someway towards removing the greatest threat to democracy on this island, the existence of private armies and of armed political factions that do not recognise the authority of democratically elected governments. The Commission is aware that despite this statement, or even because of some of the reactions to it in government and elsewhere, devolution in Northern Ireland is unlikely to be restored in the weeks and months ahead. In the course of our enquiry we sensed a growing public concern about the way the region is becoming increasingly polarised against a backdrop of sectarian violence and intimidation. Indeed, this is being written at a time of an extraordinary upsurge of violence in loyalist communities. We share these concerns and hope that if and when devolution is restored in Northern Ireland it is more stably embedded than hitherto in the democratic norms of non-violence, human rights and the rule of law. We urge the British and Irish government, all parties in Northern Ireland and all civic actors there to focus their minds on a resolution of the current impasse in the spirit of the Belfast agreement and its various Irish, British and European contexts. Any resolution needs to promote genuine reciprocity between Protestant and Catholic. In particular we believe, taking our cue from the IDEA standard of democratic assessment, that the twin principles of equality and accountability are essential to the well being of democracy on the entire island of Ireland.

For its part, the Commission suggests that, in advance of further rounds of political negotiation, the parties and interested civic actors in Northern Ireland should get around a table to discuss 'the establishment over time of a normal, civic society, in which all individuals are considered as equals, where differences are resolved through dialogue in the public sphere and where all people are treated impartially', as outlined in the recent policy document A Shared Future by the Northern Ireland Office. Such a forum could be convened by a neutral broker and could ease public concerns that MLAs continue to be paid in the absence of the assembly, as well as lending a sense of direction amid the current worrying drift. Ideally, as a consequence of this forum the parties would then themselves be able to present to the Governments a position over which they had ownership, and which commanded civic endorsement, as to the way in which democratic structures in Northern Ireland can be stably re-established.

Internationally, the United States is pursuing a foreign relations policy of trying to impose democracy by force in Iraq, itself an anti-democratic action. This has provoked an effort to subvert democracy by Islamist terrorists who, presumably, hope to provoke restrictions on human rights and an even harsher security response. This cycle of violence is approaching Samuel Huntington's sphere of "A Clash of Civilizations".

The draft European Union constitution has been derailed by a strong and well informed vote by the people of France and the Netherlands. Writing in the Financial Times on 26 July, 2005 Mikhail Gorbachev opined that Europe is now in crisis due to the arrogance of its political elites who he blames for isolating themselves from the people:

> "The EU crises could destablise political systems in Europe. After all, democracy – government reflecting the will of the people – is

the main value of the European order. The attempt by elites to exclude the people from the decision-making process could lead to the rejection of those very elites by society. In the worst-case scenario, forces that have until recently been marginalized could return to the centre of political life. It is notable that the almost forgotten "Internationale" became the victory song of some of some of the constitution's opponents in France".

This over-eggs the pudding. It is one of the ironies of the rejection of the draft Constitution that it proposed greater democratic accountability to the EU, not less. It can equally be argued that, given the chance, the electorate in France and the Netherlands used democracy very effectively to enforce its will on the so called elites. Nevertheless, his analysis does make an important point about the consequences of not promoting the political facilitation of an engaged citizenry.

It is this objective of political facilitation which has dominated the work of the Democracy Commission. Indeed, the setting-up of the Democracy Commission by the two think-tanks TASC and Democratic Dialogue, was in response to widespread concerns about the capacity of democracy in Ireland to be inclusive, participatory and egalitarian.

We have gone to considerable lengths to solicit the views of society as can be seen from the methodologies listed in the report. Our work has also been informed by the emerging findings from the Democratic Audit, a parallel research project which is currently underway and is due for completion next year. As a result we think we have come as close as is possible to getting a clear picture of the health of democracy in both parts of Ireland.

What the Commission has not done is to offer a political analysis. We were too broad a church to accomplish this because, in order to ensure a dispassionate approach to democracy per se, a conscious decision was made to constitute the commission on the basis of a diversity of political belief. The problem, of course, is that it is hard to segregate the issues completely for it is certain that political philosophies do affect the level of political engagement. This is most apparent in the conflicting values of Civic Republicanism and Liberal Democracy.

What I mean by this is that if you trace the evolution of politics since the last war some discernible trends emerge from which Ireland is not immune. General improvements in living standards have changed class perceptions. From the 1960s onwards, increasing prosperity affected social mobility increasing the size of the middle class. People became more consumer orientated, less interested in social solidarity and more conscious of the burden of taxation.

The emergence of Ronald Reagan in the United States, Margaret Thatcher in Britain and Roger Douglas in New Zealand together shifted the balance of the post war settlement at least in the Anglo-Saxon world, of which Ireland is a part. But in reality they were the logical outcome of a trend already evident. The collapse of the Soviet Union and the communist regimes of Eastern Europe appeared to reinforce liberal capitalism as the one true faith.

This conclusion is, of course, hotly contested by Social Democrats and there is now a serious ideological battle for the soul of Europe between free market Liberals and Social Democrats. So, while people often say that there are no ideological differences anymore it is not quite true. The picture is confused, of course, in a European context by the fact that the leading protagonists appear to be in a role reversal. Tony Blair, nominally a Socialist, is the champion of free markets while Jacques Chirac, from the centre right, is fighting the battle for Social Europe.

As a personal observation I would say that the Anglo-Saxon free market model has shown itself better at creating wealth but has failed to stem the rise in inequality both in the developed and the developing world.

The fact that the Commission did not get into this territory does not mean that we did not appreciate the importance of it. Indeed, we do from time to time in the report comment on the mistaken perception that politics is only about marginalism. We realise that the citizen will not be engaged unless he/she believes in something. This is where political leadership comes in.

It is assumed that disillusionment is experienced only by the electorate. Perhaps the most unexpected outcome of our enquiry is the extent of disillusionment among politicians. Voters see – because the media shows them – that our politicians are full time professionals but most of them can do very little that directly impacts on the lives of voters. They also endure trivialising of their efforts by media. Much of their power has gone to Brussels or to the European Central Bank in Frankfurt. Judges circumscribe the limit of public inquiry they can make. The increasing centralisation of responsibility for services that impact on the lives of people has reduced the scope for political leadership at local and regional level. The voter claims to want better public services, but objects to paying the taxes that would make them feasible. It is a difficult but noble profession. In my opinion it is a huge personal achievement on the part of anyone who gets elected.

The overriding aim of the Commission is to strengthen democracy and to support those who make it work. Hopefully, our conclusions will, in the course of time, contribute to those objectives.

Acknowledgements

This project drew on the input of numerous people and organisations. First and foremost our profound thanks goes to all the citizens who engaged with us through written submissions and attendances at our public meetings. Without them this report would never have happened. We would like to thank the principle funder of this project the Joseph Rowntree Charitable Trust and Mr. Stephen Pittam and Mr. Nick Perks in particular. Mrs. Mary Robinson, in her role as international counsellor, lent her invaluable support and expertise to the project and we are very grateful to her.

Many issues arose during our inquiry which required more detailed research and we would like to thank Dr. John Baker, Mr. Gerard Colleran, Mr. Seamus Dooley, Dr. Garret FitzGerald, Professor Iseult Honohan, Ms. Geraldine Kennedy, Mr. Patrick Kinsella and Mr. Philip Watt for sharing their knowledge and experiences with us. We are particularly grateful to Ms. Fiona Buckley, Professor Neil Collins, Dr. Adrian Kavanagh, Mr. Patrick Kinsella, Dr. Aodh Quinlivan, Dr. Theresa Reidy and Dr. Eilis Ward for casting a friendly but expert eye over the various chapters in this report.

Public meetings were a critical part of the process and we wish to thank all those who accepted our invitation to address these meetings. We are most grateful to Ms. Mary Hanafin, TD, Minister for Education and Science, Mr. Dick Roche, TD Minister for the Environment, Heritage and Local Government, Mr. Pat Cox (Former President of the European Parliament) and Mr. Fintan O'Toole, who provided keynote addresses.

A number of people and organisations have been supportive of the Commission's work. Thanks are particularly due to those who assisted in the organisation of our public meetings and other events. Ms. Frances McCandless at NICVA deserves a special mention for co hosting Commission events in Belfast. We are also grateful to the Vincentian Partnership for Social Justice, Community Action Network, Disability Action, the Irish Centre for the unemployed, the Department of Government, University College Cork, and the Irish Social Forum. We are grateful to ICTU for providing a room for the Commission meetings.

We wish to thank all at TASC who provided the Secretariat to the Commission and their co-partner in the initiative, Democratic Dialogue for their enormous commitment to this project from its inception in 2002. Ms. Paula Clancy and Mr. Robin Wilson were constant in their support throughout. Over the course of the project, many TASC staff, interns and volunteers made a valuable contribution in a variety of ways, among whom are - Ms. Sarah Benson, Ms. Elizabeth Harrington, Dr. Ian Hughes, Ms. Phill McCaughey, Ms. Grainne Murphy, Ms. Josephine Murtagh and Ms. Dolores Whelan and we would like to thank them all. We are particularly grateful to Ms. Fiona Ryan and Ms. Eithne McManus for their work in establishing and launching the Commission.

For her professionalism, dedication and unerring ability to keep us focused throughout a complex and demanding process we are deeply grateful to Dr. Clodagh Harris, Secretary to the Commission and coordinator of all its activities.

Finally, although we have benefited from all these people, the views expressed in this Report are solely those of the Commissioners.

List of Acronyms

AMS	Additional Member System
BBC	British Broadcasting Corporation
BCI	Broadcasting Commission of Ireland
CCEA	Council for the Curriculum, Examinations and Assessment
CDU-CDVEC	Curriculum Development Unit of the City of Dublin Vocational Education Committee
CLRAE	Congress of Local and Regional Authorities of Europe
CPG	Corporate Policy Group
CSO	Central Statistics Office
CSPE	Civic, Social and Political Education
EU	European Union
FF	Fianna Fáil
FG	Fine Gael
FOI	Freedom of Information
GCSE	General Certificate of Secondary Education
HSE	Health Service Executive
ICCL	Irish Council for Civil Liberties
IRTC	Irish Radio and Television Commission
IULA	International Union of Local Authorities
MLA	Member of the Legislative Assembly in Northern Ireland
MP	Member of Parliament
NCCA	National Council for Curriculum and Assessment
NCCRI	National Consultative Committee on Racism and Interculturalism

NCO	National Children's Office
NCPP	National Centre for Partnership and Performance
NESC	National Economic and Social Council
NESF	National Economic and Social Forum
NIO	Northern Ireland Office
NNI	National Newspapers of Ireland
NUJ	National Union of Journalists
NYF	National Youth Federation
NYCI	National Youth Council of Ireland
OFMDFM	Office of First Minister and Deputy First Minister
PD	Progressive Democrats
PPS Number	Personal Public Service Number
PR (STV)	Proportional Representation (Single Transferable Vote)
RTÉ	Radio Telefis Éireann
SF	Sinn Fein
SPC	Strategic Policy Committees
TD	Teachta Dála
UK	United Kingdom
VVAT	Voter Verified Audit Trail

Glossary

Accountability – Those who hold office or a position of authority are required to give progress reports and regular accounts. These authorities are subject to the scrutiny of an appropriate body.

Additional Member System – A type of electoral system that mixes elements of the first past the post electoral system with the list PR system. In effect this means that a number of seats are filled on the basis of first past the post elections to single seat constituencies while the remaining seats are allocated on the basis of a list PR election.

Bunreacht Na hÉireann – The Constitution of Ireland

Backbencher – A member of parliament who does not hold governmental office and is not a front bench spokesperson for the opposition party. Backbenchers individually do not carry much power to influence Government policy, but are important in providing services to their constituencies.

Belfast Agreement – This is also known as the Good Friday Agreement. It was signed in Belfast on April 10, 1998 (Good Friday) by the British and Irish governments and endorsed by most Northern Ireland political parties. It was endorsed by the voters of Northern Ireland and Ireland in separate referenda on May 23, 1998. There are three strands to the agreement. Strand One involves devolved government to Northern Ireland. Strand Two involves building links between Northern Ireland and Ireland. Strand Three involves establishing links between Ireland and Great Britain.

Citizen – There are several aspects to this concept. At its most basic level, it means that an individual is a member of a state. This endows an individual with certain civil, social and political rights. Being a citizen, however, also brings with it certain responsibilities such as supporting the public good and participating in the political decision-making process.

Civic Republicanism – Civic republicanism is an approach to citizenship which emphasises freedom in self-government. Under this approach, citizens, who do not necessarily share cultural or ethnic identity but are interdependent in terms of a common fate, form an involuntary community to act in solidarity, share common goods and jointly exercise some collective direction over their lives.

Dáil Éireann – The lower house of the Oireachtas. Members are directly elected at least once in every five years under the system of Proportional Representation (Single Transferable Vote).

Defamation – This is publication of a false statement about a person, which tends to lower the reputation of that individual in the eyes of a right thinking person. There are two forms of defamation: libel and slander. Traditionally, libel was the written form of defamation while slander was the spoken form. However, the advent of the television, radio and Internet has altered this understanding of libel and slander so that today a defamatory statement on any of these mediums would be regarded as libellous, rather than slanderous.

Direct Initiative – A proposal may go directly to a public vote (referendum) when a required number of citizen signatures are collected.

Electoral Commission – A committee dedicated to electoral politics and affairs that may advise or oversee issues such as electoral law, determining boundaries of constituencies, ensuring free and fair elections, and increasing democratic participation.

Electoral System – This governs how votes are cast at election time.

E-voting – Electronic voting allows the electorate to cast ballots by means of electronics such as a wired kiosk, the internet, telephone, punch card and optical scan ballot.

Fianna Fáil – Currently is the largest political party in Ireland. The party formed out of the anti-Anglo-Irish treaty side.

Fine Gael – Currently the second largest political party in Ireland. It was formed out of the pro-treaty side in Ireland's civil war.

Freedom of Information – This principle, as expressed in legislation, obliges government departments, local authorities and a range of other statutory agencies to publish information on their activities and to make personal information available to citizens, though certain restrictions are imposed.

Garda Siochana – The police force of Ireland.

GCSE – The General Certificate of Secondary Education (GCSE) is the compulsory State examination in the UK and is a means of testing a student's knowledge at the end of secondary school. Students normally sit the exam between the ages of 15 and 17.

Green Party – The Green party in Ireland was founded in 1981. Its policies are informed by environmental issues.

Indirect Initiative – A proposal that goes to the legislature after a certain number of citizen signatures is collected. If the legislature fails to approve the proposal, then a popular vote (referendum) may take place if the necessary number of citizen' signatures are collected.

Ireland – The official name of the Irish state

Junior Certificate – This is a State examination held at the end of the junior cycle in secondary school. Students normally sit the exam between the ages of 15 and 16.

Labour Party – The Irish Labour party was founded in 1912 and is currently the third largest party in Ireland. It is a left wing party committed to the ideals of social democracy.

Leaving Certificate – The Leaving Certificate is the state examination at the end of secondary school in Ireland. It is a two year programme. There is a choice of three Leaving Certificate programmes, namely the Established Leaving Certificate, the Leaving Certificate Applied and the Leaving Certificate Vocational Programme. Students normally sit the exam between the ages of 17 and 18.

Northern Ireland – The official name for the part of the island of Ireland that is a constituent part of the United Kingdom of Great Britain and Northern Ireland.

Oireachtas – The national parliament of Ireland. The Oireachtas consists of the President of Ireland, Dáil Éireann and Seanad Éireann.

Parliamentary Systems – A form of democratic government where the majority party often chooses the executive branch. No clear separation of powers exists between the legislative and executive branches. The head of state in a parliamentary system has mostly ceremonial functions and is often separate from the head of government.

Progressive Democrats – This political party was founded in 1985. The party is right wing on most economic matters but is regarded as being liberal on social policy issues.

PRSTV – This is a type of electoral system. PRSTV stands for proportional representation by means of the single transferable vote. In essence, PRSTV means that the voter indicates his/her first and subsequent choices for the candidates on the ballot paper in multi seat constituencies. Ireland and Malta are the only countries that employ this type of electoral system for elections to their lower houses of parliament.

Public Service Broadcasting – This concept is based on the principles of universality of service and diversity of programming and perspectives. It is designed to educate, inform and entertain by providing a wide range of programmes. A public service broadcaster should be independent from government. Traditionally, public service broadcasting is funded through a licence fee. However, Ireland's public broadcasting service is unusual in the sense that RTE is funded by a licence fee and commercial funding.

Referendum – This is a form of direct democracy in which the entire electorate is asked to vote to either accept or reject a particular proposal. In Ireland, in order for the government to amend the Constitution, it is mandatory that the constitutional amendment first be put to the people in the form of a referendum.

Seanad Éireann – This body forms the upper house or Senate of the Oireachtas. The Senate has no veto power but can delay decisions of the Dáil. Members of the Senate are not directly elected but are chosen by a variety of different methods. Eleven members are appointed by the Taoiseach, six are elected by graduates of Dublin University and the National University of Ireland, and forty-three are elected from five panels by members of the county and major city councils, the Dáil and the outgoing Seanad. The five panels are Agriculture, Culture and Education, Industry and Commerce, Labour, and Public Administration.

Sinn Féin – mainly northern-based but island-wide political party, linked to the IRA, which seeks a British withdrawal from Ireland. It is left of centre on social and economic issues.

Subsidiarity – This principle involves handling matters at the lowest possible level, with the central government department performing only those tasks that cannot be performed effectively at a more local level.

Supplementary Register – A method to allow people who are qualified to vote but have missed the deadline to include their name on the electoral register.

Tánaiste – Deputy Prime Minister of Ireland. The Tánaiste acts in place of the Taoiseach during his or her temporary absence, and until a successor has been appointed, in the event of the Taoiseach's death or permanent incapacitation.

Taoiseach – The head of Government of Ireland and the leader of the Irish Cabinet. The President upon nomination of the Dáil appoints the Taoiseach.

TD (Teachta Dála) – Member of the lower house, Dáil Éireann, of the Irish Oireachtas.

Think Tanks – organizations which provide a bridge between academics, politicians and civil society to produce new policy options.

Voter Verified Audit Trail – Paper ballots that have been verified by individual voters so that if a recount was called counters could refer back to those ballots.

Executive Summary

The Democracy Commission was set up to respond to widespread concerns about the nature of democracy on the island of Ireland.

It is an initiative of two think tanks, TASC and Democratic Dialogue, both of which are concerned with issues of equality and social justice.

Launched in June 2003, the Commission was asked to consider the capacity of our democracy to be inclusive, participatory and egalitarian in the 21st century.

Eleven people committed to this work, acting in a voluntary capacity and supported by a Secretariat provided by TASC. The Commission's members are:

- **Mr. David Begg,** *General Secretary of the Irish Congress of Trade Unions;*
- **Dr. Ruth Barrington,** *senior public servant;*
- **Professor Ivana Bacik,** *Reid Professor of Criminal Law, Criminology and Penology at Trinity College Dublin and practising barrister;*
- **Senator John Hanafin,** *Fianna Fáil Senator and former Deputy Lord Mayor of North Tipperary;*
- **Sr. Bernadette MacMahon DC,** *coordinator of the Vincentian Partnership for Social Justice;*
- **Professor Elizabeth Meehan,** *Director of the Institute of Governance, Public Policy and Social Research at Queen's University Belfast;*
- **Mrs. Nora Owen,** *former Minister for Justice and former deputy leader of Fine Gael;*
- **Mr. Donal Toolan,** *disability rights activist, actor and award-winning journalist;*
- **Mr. Tony Kennedy,** *Chief Executive of Co-operation Ireland;*
- **Mr. Mark Mortell,** *Company Director and head of FH consulting at Fleishman Hillard, International Communications Consultants;* and
- **Ms. Caroline Wilson,** *Good Relations Officer, Belfast City Council.*

1

Ms. Kim Bartley, Ms. Leanne Hyland and Mr. Stewart Kenny had to withdraw during the course of the project due to pressure of other commitments. Their contribution was much appreciated.

The Commission is chaired by Mr. David Begg and is funded by the Joseph Rowntree Charitable Trust. It is indebted to Mrs. Mary Robinson, former President of Ireland and ex-United Nations High Commissioner for Human Rights, who acted as International Counsellor to the Commission.

Dr. Clodagh Harris is the Coordinator of the Democracy Commission project and is Secretary to the Commission.

The Commission was charged with:

- gathering available information on opportunities for and barriers to real participative democracy within Irish political institutions, with particular emphasis on social inclusion and the under 25s;
- reviewing international best practice and identifying options for new forms of democratic political institutions; and
- assessing alternative forms of citizen participation and political representation.

In carrying out its work the Commission held public meetings across the island; met with political representatives North and South; consulted with community activists, journalists, students, academics, retired political representatives, trade unionists and members of the community and voluntary sector, among others; and took part in meetings and conferences organised by other groups addressing issues relevant to its work. In addition, the Commission placed advertisements in the national newspapers requesting written submissions from the public. Over 100 submissions were received from interested parties.

In May 2004 the Commission launched its progress report 'Disempowered and disillusioned but not disengaged – Democracy in Ireland' which contained a preliminary overview of the soundings it had taken at that time and outlined the agenda for a number of public consultation events.

These public events included a one day public event in Dublin in November 2004 entitled 'Standing at the crossroads - what path should Ireland take in the 21st century?' which drew over 250 participants, and two National Consultative Conferences entitled 'New Directions for Irish Democracy' which were held in Dublin and Belfast in June and July 2005. During the National Consultative Conferences, the Commission presented its findings on the six themes addressed in the chapters of this report and sought feedback from attendees.

The Commission has recognised the need for additional research to

> During the National Consultative Conferences, the Commission presented its findings on the six themes addressed in the chapters of this report.

supplement the findings obtained through public consultation. Experts on active citizenship, equality and the media were invited to present papers to the Commission. These presentations also inform the findings herein. The Commission has also been a key driver of the initiative to undertake an audit of the state of democracy in Ireland. The democratic audit project was initiated in July 2004. The Commission acts as an advisory body to the project and has been able to draw on its work in the course of its deliberations.

The Commission has worked on an all-island basis, but with a primary focus on democracy in Ireland. As a result, some of the issues raised in this report will not have parallels in Northern Ireland. Nonetheless, where relevant, the Commission has highlighted issues with the potential for North-South co-operation and mutual lesson learning.

The summary findings are presented under the headings Citizenship; Voter Participation; Representation; Accountability and Transparency; Local Democracy; and Media.

1. Citizenship

Concepts of citizenship have become more relevant in the context of recent social, economic and demographic changes in Irish society. For the first time in living memory, we are experiencing significant immigration and an estimated 160 different nationalities are now living in Ireland. Modern Irish citizens no longer necessarily share common ethnic or cultural backgrounds, and there is more diversity around moral, religious and ethical perspectives. Other developments, such as the Belfast Agreement and Ireland's membership of the European Union have challenged traditional concepts of Irish citizenship. The Commission believes that citizenship of the future is likely to rely more on loyalty to democratic institutions and the rule of law than on an identity based on birth, language and religion.

While recognising that much of what is contestable about citizenship stems from its legal definition, the Commission wishes to encourage a discussion on what citizenship should mean in 21st century Ireland. In particular, the Commission is persuaded by the value of 'active democratic citizenship' whose core principles include an active approach to tolerance, interdependency, civic self-restraint, responsibility and openness to deliberative argument.

Active democratic citizenship requires democratic citizenship education as well as accessible opportunities and mechanisms for participation.

Democratic citizenship education, which includes a non-partisan political dimension, is required to provide citizens with information and facilitate their participation in the political discussions and decisions that affect their everyday lives. The Democracy Commission takes its definition of citizenship education from Will Kymlicka who states that citizenship education involves learning the basic facts about the institutions and procedures of political life and '*acquiring a range of dispositions, virtues and loyalties that are immediately bound up with the practice of democratic citizenship*' (1999:79).

At present, neither democratic citizenship nor political education is offered as an independent subject to senior cycle in Ireland. This leaves Ireland out of step with most of its European neighbours in this regard, a situation which the Commission believes should change.

In Northern Ireland, the local and global citizenship programme is part of the core curriculum subject, Learning for Life and Work. While yet to be formally incorporated into the curriculum, citizenship classes have been piloted in a growing number of schools and materials are currently being drafted. The work so far has rooted citizenship education in notions of human rights. To date political education has been found to be popular among young people in Northern Ireland but there is resistance, particularly among grammar schools, to democratic citizenship education, on the grounds that this is a parental responsibility and/or a distraction from conventional academic education. The Commission wishes to emphasise the importance of democratic citizenship education in Northern Ireland and believes it needs to be underpinned by the aim to build a shared future. To achieve this it needs to address issues of interculturalism, separateness and sectarianism.

Any discussion on democratic citizenship education needs to address the role played by school culture in preparing students for citizenship and democratic participation. The Democracy Commission believes that student councils can, if effectively established, provide a key forum for young people to actively experience democratic processes. In addition, the Commission argues that mechanisms within schools to teach democratic citizenship education need to be supported within the wider community. This is particularly vital in communities which have no experience of or have encountered problems to political participation.

> Democratic citizenship education in Northern Ireland needs to be underpinned by the aim to build a shared future.

Recommendations

The Democracy Commission calls for:

- The extension of social and political education to senior cycle. The Commission favours the introduction of citizenship studies as defined by Eilis Ward as a full optional subject to Leaving Certificate and supports the provision of citizenship education short courses and transition year units. Care should be taken that this is tackled in a planned and properly resourced way.

- Democratic citizenship education in Northern Ireland to be underpinned by the aim to build a shared future.
- Targeted spending on citizenship education and voter awareness programmes.
- Promoting citizenship issues in primary schools.
- Promoting greater democracy within school structures.
- Promoting democratic citizenship education within community education programmes.
- Provision of training and materials to support teachers of democratic citizenship education.

2. Voter Participation

Popular participation lies at the core of any democratic society. The Commission has been particularly concerned with examining the reasons for disconnection from the political process by the under 25s and those living in socially disadvantaged areas.

Disconnection is best exemplified in the declining rates of electoral participation. Ireland has been experiencing falling electoral turnout in recent decades. Over a 25 year period, turnout in Irish general elections has dropped from 76% in 1977 to around 63% in 2002. In the recent general election, Northern Ireland was the only region within the UK to experience a drop in turnout.

The Commission has sought to identify the causes leading to low turnout, particularly amongst the under 25s and the less well off in society.

Young People

In Ireland just over 40% of young adult respondents aged 18-19, and only 53% of those aged 20-24 indicated that they voted in the 2002 general election. (CSO, 2003:1) In the 1999 local and European elections almost 67% of young people (aged 18-25) did not vote.

The same is true for young people in Northern Ireland. In the 2003 Assembly elections it is estimated that 49% of voters aged between 18-24 voted compared to an estimated 80% turnout amongst the over 55s. (Electoral Commission (NI), 2004:96)

It would be wrong, however, to assume that apathy and a lack of interest lie behind low youth turnout. The Commission's findings show that of non voters in the 20-24 age category, 47% didn't vote because of procedural obstacles ('not registered', 'away' 'no polling card') as opposed to the 39% who didn't vote due to 'no interest', 'disillusionment', 'lack of information/knowledge' and 'my vote would make no difference'.

Procedural issues such as registration and the day of polling thus appear to be the major block to youth participation.

People living in socially disadvantaged areas

Electoral turnout also tends to be lower amongst the less affluent in society. The link between the level of formal education received and the likelihood of voting has been well established. In the 2003 Northern Ireland Assembly elections 61% of unskilled manual workers, the unemployed and those in receipt of long term state benefits voted, compared with 79% of middle class or professional voters. (Electoral Commission (NI), 2004: 96)

Recent research however reveals the positive impact of community based voter education programmes on turnout. This is evident for example in the 2004 local and European elections when areas such as Mulhuddart, Clondalkin and Tallaght South, where there had been such programmes, experienced increases of 138%, 82% and 77% respectively in turnout. Nonetheless even with the improved participation rates all wards in disadvantaged areas were still lower than the national average of 58.7%, with many well below the 50% mark.

Recommendations

The Democracy Commission recommends:

- Automatic Registration through Personal Public Service (PPS) / National Insurance Number.
- Reducing the candidacy age for elections to Dáil Eireann.
- Extending the postal voting option to all registered voters, including prisoners, in Ireland.
- Introducing electronic voting for all elections in Ireland and Northern Ireland. The Commission believes that despite the bad experience Ireland had with the first attempts at E-Voting it is a system well worth introducing for the benefits it will bring. The new e-voting system should consider innovations that permit people to vote not only at polling stations but in supermarkets, post offices, public libraries or on their personal computers or mobile phones. All sites would have to be accessible for disabled people. It is imperative that such a system is introduced in a way that promotes confidence in the integrity of the system. In Ireland, it is also essential that the system staggers the counts, which are part of Irish political culture and play a role in generating interest in politics and elections, and preserves the information provided by them.
- That all political parties should be conscious of the need to be seen to be active across all sectors of Irish society. The perceived absence of cross party activity in socially disadvantaged areas presents a

Introduce electronic voting for all elections in Ireland and Northern Ireland

threat to Irish democracy. It risks contributing to a belief that people living in socially disadvantaged areas have only one, or at the most two, political parties to choose from. Choice is central to democracy. If a section of Irish society believes that it is not presented with political choice in its area then this poses a serious challenge to the future state of democracy in Ireland.

- Introducing legislation which gives homeless people, travellers and others with a transitory lifestyle the right to register using an address near a place where they 'commonly spend' their time.

- Introducing legislation in Ireland and Northern Ireland that permits proposals, which do not contravene existing rights, to come before the legislature when the necessary number of citizen signatures is gathered (indirect initiative).

- Establishing an Independent Electoral Commission in Ireland.
  An Irish Electoral Commission could, for example:
  - Provide outreach programmes and public awareness campaigns on the democratic process in Ireland and encourage people to get involved in elections.
  - support voter education programmes, particularly in disadvantaged areas, through targeted spending and resource materials.
  - Co-operate and collaborate with the Electoral Commission in Northern Ireland on issues of research, education, awareness campaigns etc.
  - Ensure that everyone has equal opportunity to vote by monitoring the physical accessibility of voting sites and mechanisms to transcend communication barriers through the provision of accessible information and facilities such as Braille, large print, and sign language in all aspects of the electoral process.
  - Provide evidence-based research to help politicians, the media, academics, and policy makers understand the nature of political engagement among certain audiences and to develop strategies and policies in response.

Choice is central to democracy.

3. Representation

Around the world governments and parliaments rarely mirror the composition of their society. Ireland and Northern Ireland are no exception.

Issues of representation, particularly under-representation amongst the disadvantaged and marginalised in society by virtue of class, disability, gender, sexual orientation, race, creed, or age, are essentially equality issues. Equality underpins democracy. Inequalities in political participation lead to inequalities in political representation which reinforces wider social inequalities and in turn deepens inequalities in political participation.

Recognising the under-representation of all those categories of the population covered by the nine grounds of the equality legislation in Irish political institutions, the Commission, as a consequence of its consultations, has focused on gender, age and socio-economic class.

The introduction of party candidate quotas is necessary to achieve gender balance in politics.

Gender

Women account for approximately 50% of Irish society yet remain heavily underrepresented. Of the 166 deputies elected to the 29th Dáil, 22 of them were women (13%). Furthermore, of the 157 people who held full Ministerial positions from 1922-2002, only 9.6% of them were women (Galligan, 2005:273). Compared with its fellow member states in the EU, Ireland languishes at 19th place out of 25 in terms of the percentage of women in its national parliament (www.ipu.org)

In Northern Ireland the picture is no different. The assemblies elected in 1998 and 2003 were also overwhelmingly male. Interestingly, women in Northern Ireland fare much better, proportionately, in appointments to the boards of public bodies rather than election. This is in no small measure due to the public competitive system of public appointments in the UK which includes attention to gender balance.

The Irish government has made commitments to improve the position of women by signing up to the Beijing Platform for Action (1995) and the Convention on the Elimination of All Forms of Discrimination against Women (1979). Yet Ireland's record continues to be one of deep and systematic inequality.

In the 2002 general election only 61 women candidates ran for election accounting for 19% of all candidates. This was a drop on the 1997 figures. The Commission believes that the introduction of party candidate quotas is necessary to redress this glaring democratic deficit in Ireland's parliament. More than 80 countries around the world have already adopted quotas of women candidates as a means of achieving a greater gender balance. (Lovenduski, 2005:90) The Commission believes that Ireland must now do the same.

Age

The unrepresentative nature of politics may impact on voter apathy. An examination of the age profile of Irish national political representatives shows that it is not representative of young people. According to the 2002 census, 21.2% of the Irish population is aged between 18 and 30, and

41.7% of the population is aged between 18 and 44. All the political parties are under-representative of this age category. Thirty year olds and under are, however, grossly underrepresented. Only six TDs aged 30 and under, were elected in 2002. This accounted for 3.6% of the total number of deputies in Dáil Éireann and reinforces young peoples' perceptions that politicians are 'old and grey'. Ironically, people aged 65 and over are also under represented in Dáil Éireann. Only five of the 166 deputies elected in the 2002 general election were aged 65 or over in the year of the election, even though this age group accounts for over 11% of the population (www.cso.ie).

Socio-economic class

Not only are Irish politicians predominantly middle aged, they also tend to be largely middle class. Almost half (47%) of the TDs in the 29th Dáil come from the lower and higher professional classes. In Irish society as a whole, only 15% of the total population are lower and higher professionals (Galligan, 2005:287 and the 2002 census www.cso.ie). The over representation of the higher and lower professional classes in Irish political institutions reinforces public perceptions of politics as being the preserve of the educated and the wealthy. This is harmful to the health of Irish democracy as it excludes sections of Irish society from the decision-making process and reinforces perceptions within these areas/communities that politics is not for them.

> Thirty year olds and under are, however, grossly underrepresented [in the Dáil]

Recommendations

The Democracy Commission

- Calls for the introduction of obligatory gender quotas (50:50) for the candidates put forward by political parties in Ireland and Northern Ireland[*].
- Calls for increased spending to support the self-organisation of marginalised groups. Financial, training, and capacity-building supports are required for the self organisation of marginalised groups. Targeted spending on community education programmes in disadvantaged areas would be one concrete step in developing the political capacity of marginalised groups who are limited by the inequalities that structure their lives and opportunities.
- The introduction of family-friendly working hours in political institutions in Ireland and Northern Ireland.

---

[*] Within the Commission there was one dissenting member on the use of this method to redress the gender imbalance.

4. Accountability and Transparency

In its consultations the Commission has noted a number of issues related to accountability and transparency in Ireland and Northern Ireland.

Increase in the number of non-departmental public bodies

A noticeable feature of the governmental system in Ireland is the growth in the number of non departmental public bodies, which have been described as all bodies responsible for developing, managing or delivering public services or policies, or for performing public functions, under governing bodies with a plural membership of wholly or largely appointed or 'self-appointing' persons. Research currently being conducted by the Democratic Audit Ireland project puts the number of these bodies in Ireland at national level at approximately 500, and with a further 400 operating at regional and local level. Data suggest that up to half of those at national level and a majority of those at local level have come into existence in the past ten years.

Since the early 1990s, successive Irish governments have introduced measures to provide for a more effective governance of national public bodies in Ireland. These measures include Comptroller and Auditor General Act, 1993, Ethics in Public Office Act, 1995, Freedom of Information Act, 1997 and 2003, Ombudsman for Children Act, 2002 and the Code of Practice for the Governance of State Bodies 2002. These Acts have done much to improve the transparency and governance of non-departmental public bodies. Yet they are not sufficient in a democracy.

> Democratic Audit Ireland research indicates that non-departmental public bodies have been developed in an unplanned manner

Democratic Audit Ireland research indicates that non-departmental public bodies have been developed in an unplanned manner and in the absence of an over-arching rationale or coherent system of accountability. This raises a number of issues in terms of transparency, democratic accountability and freedom from political/elite patronage. Their sheer growth and number contributes to the degree to which modern government is opaque and impenetrable to: the average citizen; to many advocacy and civil society groups; and in some cases to the officials and public servants which are charged with an oversight role.

Currently Ministers are responsible for appointing the majority of members to these bodies. There is no clearly defined mechanism in Ireland to ensure that appointments are free from undue political or other influence.

Another source of concern is the number of these bodies which fall outside the scope of the Freedom of Information (FOI) Act and the office of the Comptroller and Auditor General.

The increasing use of the private sector to provide essential services

The increasing use of the private sector to provide essential services such as hospital and nursing home care, in the absence of adequate systems of regulation and protection, raises strong concerns regarding accountability and the adequate provision of quality services.

Due to privatisation and changes in EU law, many largely State-owned companies in the energy and transport sectors have witnessed the transfer of regulatory responsibility from the relevant Minster to independent regulators in recent years. The current regulatory system has come under criticism for lacking accountability.

In addition, the increasing tendency of government to use private legal firms to draft legislation threatens transparency and democratic accountability. This practice could lead to conflicts of interest that could prove detrimental to Irish democracy.

Relative Weakness of the Dáil and Seanad

In democratic theory, parliament plays an important role in making government accountable for its actions. In practice, however, the Oireachtas has little control over government and little power to influence legislation. The dominant role of political parties and the strength of the party whip in Irish politics are the main reasons for this. The Commission recognises that the value placed on strong government is high within Irish political culture. Nonetheless, the Commission believes Irish democracy would be strengthened by an increase in the law making role of the Oireachtas and its powers of scrutiny and investigation, both of domestic and EU affairs.

In practice, however, the Oireachtas has little control over government and little power to influence legislation.

Recommendations

The Democracy Commission

- Calls on the Government to extend the remit of the Standards in Public Office Commission[*].

   The Standards in Public Office Commission should be given powers to draft guidelines for appointments to the boards of non departmental public bodies. The parent Department would then be responsible for advertising positions and recruiting through open competition, while recognising the need for balance. This process should be subject to the scrutiny of the Oireachtas. Similarly the appointment of the chair of each commercial state body and of the larger non-commercial bodies should be subject to ratification by the Seanad or relevant Oireachtas committee.

- Calls for urgent clarification of those bodies to which the Freedom of Information Act applies.
- Calls for the extension of the provisions of the FOI Act and the remit

---

[*]   One member of the Commission disagreed with this recommendation.

of the Comptroller and Auditor General to all non-departmental public bodies.

* Calls on the parties and interested civic actors in Northern Ireland to get around a table, in advance of further rounds of political negotiation, to discuss 'the establishment over time of a normal, civic society, in which all individuals are considered as equals, where differences are resolved through dialogue in the public sphere and where all people are treated impartially', as outlined in the recent policy document A Shared Future by the Northern Ireland Office.

5. Local Democracy

Local democracy allows local citizens themselves or through their directly elected representatives to settle local affairs and permits local communities to control local services, as well as participate in the processes and responsibilities of government. It is the level of government most accessible to citizens and provides the most opportunities for participating in public affairs. For most citizens and their political representatives, local government is often their first experience of democratic institutions and systems. In this regard, local government is an important arena for the political education of citizens and their representatives.

There have been a number of changes to local government in Ireland since the early 1990s. The Local Government Act 1991 established eight regional authorities to monitor the implementation of EU structural fund spending and gave local authorities increased general powers of competence. In 1999 a specific provision for local government was included in the Irish Constitution for the first time. Legislation on local government was consolidated under the Local Government Act 2001, and two years later the dual mandate, which had permitted members of the Oireachtas to serve on local authorities, was removed. Recent changes in local government structures, such as the formation of Strategic Policy Committees, have been influenced by Ireland's experience of social partnership and have increased the involvement of civil society in local decision-making processes. At the same time, however, powers have been removed from the responsibility of local government and in a number of controversial areas, responsibility for decisions have been removed from the elected representatives and transferred to city and county managers.

Local authorities in Northern Ireland have even weaker powers than their counterparts in Ireland. Local government in Northern Ireland is also weaker than in the rest of the UK.

In comparison with other EU states, local government in both Ireland and Northern Ireland has a high level of control from central government, weak financial independence, and narrow range of powers and fewer elected representatives. In fact, in our analysis, Ireland comes third from bottom, ahead of only Greece and Portugal, in terms of the power of local government across 15 European countries studied.

The principle of subsidiarity, that public services should be devolved to the lowest practicable level at which they can be discharged efficiently and effectively, is one of the cornerstones of EU governance. From our analysis it is clear that Ireland at present adheres to a minimal interpretation of this principle.

The Commission echoes a question posed in the Barrington report, '... does the current distribution of functions as between local government and other central public agencies give the best use of public resources and level of service, taking account of cost, social and other relevant factors?' (1991:13) The Commission believes it currently does not, and favours devolving powers from the centre across a range of policy areas. The Commission stresses however that devolution of powers to the local or regional levels can only be effective if accompanied by some measure of devolution of tax-raising functions to the same local or regional level.

Central government to increase local democracy by devolving more powers from the centre to local government

Central Recommendations

The Commission wishes to restate the case for strong local government and the role of democratically elected councillors within it. To this end it calls for:

• Research and public debate into the most appropriate level for revenue raising and for the planning, organisation and delivery of public services.

• Central government to increase local democracy by devolving more powers from the centre to local government. The Commission stresses that this must be done in tandem with decentralization of revenue raising powers. A progressive local tax regime, which would not pose additional burdens on the disadvantaged, could be used to fund local services[*]. Equalisation across areas that are disadvantaged due to their peripheral status etc. would be necessary.

• Strategic Policy Committees (SPCs) should be given the power to consider issues which have a local dimension but are outside their current brief, and Corporate Policy Groups (CPGs) should be given a more executive role in managing local affairs. Local authorities should have the same legal authority to plan the economic, social and cultural development of the communities for which they are responsible as they have to plan physical development.

---

[*] One member of the Commission disagreed with this recommendation.

13

- The election of delegates from popular assemblies to SPCs to enhance the participatory structures of local democracy in Ireland.
- The Review of Public Administration in Northern Ireland to reflect the principles of subsidiarity and power sharing in its recommendations. As far as possible the Review's recommendations should be compatible with local government structures in Ireland in order to maximise cross border co-operation.
- The direct election of Mayors to local authorities in Ireland, as provided in the Local Government Act 2001 but not implemented, to bring a new dynamism to local democracy and provide a focus for local leadership.
- The introduction of legislation to place a cap on the spending of candidates in local elections.

6. Media

A free, diverse and vibrant media lie at the heart of a healthy democratic society. By disseminating information on the actions of Government into the public domain, the media not only report on matters of public interest but act as a watchdog over Government.

Concerns have been expressed in Ireland in recent years that this diversity of views has been undermined by the concentration of media ownership. Within the radio sector, the Government has recently moved to protect diversity by imposing a cap on ownership and control so that no one company can own and control more than 17.9% of the sector.

By way of contrast, around 80% of Irish newspapers sold in Ireland are sold by companies which are fully or partially owned by Independent News and Media. The Commission on the Newspaper Industry report in 1996 cautioned that 'any further reduction of titles or increase in concentration of ownership in the indigenous industry could severely curtail the diversity requisite to maintain a vigorous democracy' (1996:34). Since then Independent News and Media has acquired additional regional papers, the Belfast Telegraph group and a controlling share of the Sunday Tribune. The Commission believes that the concentration of media ownership in Ireland is a cause of grave concern.

The media in Ireland have been constrained in their ability to act as watchdog by out-dated libel laws and recent amendments to the Freedom of Information Act

The media in Ireland have been constrained in their ability to act as watchdog by out-dated libel laws and recent amendments to the Freedom of Information Act. Irish defamation laws are currently under review in a draft Bill proposed by the Minister for Justice, Equality and Law Reform Michael McDowell, which proposes the establishment of a statutory but independently appointed press council and ombudsman.

The Commission believes that it is crucial that any future press council should be independent, a tool neither of the industry nor the

Government but of the public's right to and need for a free and responsible press and should have statutory protection. The Commission does not believe in a state appointed regulatory body but supports the establishment of an independent press ombudsman and a press council recognised in law. The press council should be established by the press industry but should have an independent chair and should take the majority of its members from civil society. One of its preliminary tasks should be to draft a code of editorial ethics. The Commission believes that the council should be recognised in law and its deliberations legally privileged. This will strengthen freedom of expression by making it possible to cite compliance with the Press Council's standards as proof of "reasonable publication" in libel actions. It will also provide quicker and more effective redress for people who feel they have been misrepresented. The Commission does not support the recommendation from the Legal Advisory Group that people who use the press council's machinery should be legally debarred from pursuing a libel action in the courts. Recourse to the courts should still be available to citizens.

The press council should be established by the press industry but should have an independent chair and should take the majority of its members from civil society.

Central Recommendations
The Democracy Commission
- Supports the establishment of an independent press ombudsman and press council recognised by law.
- Calls for the draft bill which proposes establishing a press council to be amended to address the lack of diversity of media ownership in Ireland. The concerns expressed by the Commission on the Newspaper Industry in 1996 have been realised and need to be addressed. Immediate action is required to:
  - guarantee plurality of ownership in the newspaper industry to maintain the diversity of editorial viewpoints necessary for a vigorous democracy and to promote cultural diversity in the industry;
  - address the concentration of ownership in the media generally, on a media-wide basis as well as on a single media basis.
- Calls for recent amendments to Freedom of Information Act to be reversed[*].
- Contends that the exclusively public service broadcasting role for RTE should be reinforced and supports a definition of public service broadcasting that focuses on the service rather than on a type of programming.
- Suggests televising tribunals.

---

[*] One member of the Commission disagreed with this recommendation.

Conclusion

D emocracy has been described as critical and contestable. It is critical to the extent that is not perfect in practice and contestable because it is open to reflection, reform and renewal. Accepting the former, the Commission has endeavoured through its consultation process and the recommendations outlined in this report to achieve the latter.

At the outset it quickly became clear that people, although disillusioned and disenchanted, were not disengaged. This raised a number of concerns. Firstly there was the concern that if the disillusionment and disenchantment were not addressed then people would become disengaged. Secondly the Commission was aware that there were many who were already disengaged by virtue of a lack of information, a lack of experience, a lack of opportunity to participate in issues that affected them and so forth. Thirdly the Commission had heard from those who tried to engage but faced obstacles in doing so. Finally in its discussions with those at the helm of Irish democracy, the political representatives, the Commission realised that they too were often disillusioned and disenchanted.

The Commission hopes that its recommendations not only facilitate and mobilise citizens but assist those whose job is to strengthen democracy in Ireland and Northern Ireland on a day to day basis.

Time will tell if the Commission has succeeded in this task. It hopes that through the public reflection it stimulated and the reforms it recommended that it has helped to renew and revitalise democracy on the island of Ireland.

...renew and revitalise democracy on the island of Ireland

References

Advisory Expert Committee, 1991: *Local Government Reorganisation and Reform*. Dublin: Government publications.

CSO, 2003: *Quarterly National Household Survey, Voter Participation and Abstention*. Cork: CSO.

CSO, 2003. *Census 2002*, www.cso.ie

The Electoral Commission (NI), 2004: *The Northern Ireland Assembly Elections 2003*. Belfast: The Electoral Commission NI.

Galligan, Yvonne, 2005: 'Women in politics' in Coakley, John and Michael Gallagher, (eds) *Politics in the Republic of Ireland*. Oxon: Routledge and PSAI Press.

Inter-Parliamentary Union www.ipu.org

Kymlicka, Will, 1999: 'Education for Citizenship' in Halstead, J.M. and McLaughlin T.H. (ed) *Education and Morality*. London: Routledge.

Lovenduski, Joni, 2005: *Feminizing Politics*. Cambridge: Polity Press.

National Women's Council of Ireland, 2002: *Irish politics Jobs for the Boys! Recommendations on Increasing the Number of Women in Decision Making*. Dublin: National Women's Council of Ireland.

Report of the Commission on the Newspaper Industry, 1996. Dublin: Government Stationery Office.

Introduction

The Democracy Commission was set up to respond to widespread concerns about the nature of democracy in Ireland and Northern Ireland.

An initiative of two think tanks, TASC and Democratic Dialogue, both of which are concerned with issues of equality and social justice, the Commission was asked to consider the question of the capacity of our democracy to be inclusive, participatory and egalitarian in the 21st century.

Eleven people committed to this work, acting in a voluntary capacity and supported by a Secretariat provided by TASC. The Commission's members are:

- Mr. David Begg, *General Secretary of the Irish Congress of Trade Unions;*
- Dr. Ruth Barrington, *senior public servant;*
- Professor Ivana Bacik, *Reid Professor of Criminal Law, Criminology and Penology at Trinity College Dublin and practising barrister;*
- Senator John Hanafin, *Fianna Fáil Senator and former Deputy Lord Mayor of North Tipperary;*
- Sr. Bernadette MacMahon DC, *coordinator of the Vincentian Partnership for Social Justice;*
- Professor Elizabeth Meehan, *Director of the Institute of Governance, Public Policy and Social Research at Queen's University Belfast;*
- Mrs. Nora Owen, *former Minister for Justice and former deputy leader of Fine Gael;*
- Mr. Donal Toolan, *disability rights activist, actor and award-winning journalist;*
- Mr. Tony Kennedy *Chief Executive of Co-operation Ireland;*

- Mr. Mark Mortell, *Company Director and head of FH consulting at Fleishman Hillard, International Communications Consultants*; and
- Ms. Caroline Wilson, *Good Relations Officer, Belfast City Council.*

Ms. Kim Bartley, Ms. Leanne Hyland and Mr. Stewart Kenny had to withdraw during the course of the project due to pressure of other commitments. Their contribution was much appreciated.

The Commission is chaired by Mr. David Begg and is funded by the Joseph Rowntree Charitable Trust. It is indebted to Mrs. Mary Robinson, former President of Ireland and ex-United Nations High Commissioner for Human Rights, who acted as International Counsellor to the Commission.

Dr. Clodagh Harris is the Coordinator of the Democracy Commission project and is Secretary to the Commission.

Launched in June 2003, the Commission was charged with:
- gathering available information on opportunities for and barriers to real participative democracy within Irish political institutions, with particular emphasis on social inclusion and the under 25s;
- reviewing international best practice and identifying options for new forms of democratic political institutions; and
- assessing alternative forms of citizen participation and political representation.

In its approach it was asked to take account of the following issues:
- the reasons for disconnection from the political process, concentrating on the under 25s and those living in socially disadvantaged areas;
- the role of 'civil society' and the possibility to effect change outside formal political involvement;
- the potential for North-South co-operation and mutual lesson-learning;
- the role of the media as a channel for and a creator of the values shaping our political participation;
- multi-level governance and the relationship between public and private bodies at the local, regional, and supranational levels; and
- the debate surrounding rights-based culture which hinges on

extending rights from the political and civil sphere to encompass the social, economic and cultural.

In its work the Commission

- held public meetings across the island;
- met with political representatives North and South;
- consulted with community activists, students, academics, retired political representatives, journalists, trade unionists, members of the community and voluntary sector and others;
- placed advertisements in the national newspapers requesting written submissions from the public and received over 100 submissions from individuals, political parties, interest groups, non-governmental organisations etc;
- took part in meetings and conferences organised by other groups addressing issues relevant to its work and others; and
- conducted exploratory primary research.

"politics is not for me" – a scene from the Commission's Forum theatre piece in November 2004.

A detailed list of the activities of the Commission and the written submissions it received can be found in Appendices One and Two.

In May 2004 the Commission launched its progress report 'Disempowered and disillusioned but not disengaged – Democracy in Ireland' which contained a preliminary overview of the soundings it had taken at that time and outlined its agenda going forward.

In November 2004 the Commission held a one day public event in Dublin entitled 'Standing at the crossroads - what path should Ireland take in the 21st century?' at which there were over 250 participants. This event concentrated on themes which had emerged from previous consultations and submissions namely: active democratic citizenship, local democracy, representation in political institutions and the role of the media. Information gathered from round table discussions on these issues informed the focus and content of this report.

National Consultative Conferences entitled 'New Directions for Irish Democracy' were held in Dublin and Belfast in June and July 2005 at which the Commission presented its findings and perspectives on the six themes addressed in the chapters of this report. Feedback received from participants, who included members of the public, political representatives, civil servants, academics, community activists and members of NGOS, was incorporated into this report.

In its approach the Commission employed a diverse array of mechanisms to encourage engagement with its work. A lively forum theatre piece on active citizenship during the one-day public event in Dublin was successful in securing the participation of a broad range of delegates. At the National Consultative Conferences participants were asked to express their interpretations of the themes discussed in an interactive art piece 'the tapestry of thought'. In this they were facilitated by a community artist. Many of the images in this report come from this art piece.

The Commission recognised the need for research to supplement the information gathered at public consultations. It invited experts on active citizenship, equality and the media to present papers to the Commission to inform its findings. These papers are included in Appendix Five. The Commission has also been a key driver of the initiative to undertake an audit of the state of democracy in Ireland. The democratic audit project was initiated in July 2004. The Commission acts as an advisory body to the project and has been able

"The Art of Democracy", Mrs Nora Owen with artist-in-residence Ms Genevieve Harden contributes to the "tapestry of thought".

to draw on its work in the course of its deliberations.

The Commission worked on an all-Island basis with a primary focus on democracy in Ireland. As a result some of the issues raised in this report will not have parallels in Northern Ireland. Nonetheless, where relevant, the Commission has highlighted issues with the potential for North-South co-operation and mutual lesson learning.

The soundings gathered by the Commission and its findings and recommendations that emerged in the course of its consultations are presented under the six headings: Citizenship; Voter Participation; Representation; Accountability and Transparency; Local Democracy; and Media.

Citizenship

1

Discussions with the Commission on active democratic citizenship and citizenship education stressed:

- 'Citizenship and political education needs to be extended to senior cycle'
- 'Schools should not be seen as a cure all. People, particularly young people, need to be given constant opportunities to participate'
- 'We need to challenge our notions of Irishness'
- 'The citizenship referendum shut down debate on citizenship. This debate needs to be restarted'
- 'Those who are granted Irish citizenship receive no information or education on what it means'
- 'How can we expect students to be interested in participation and democracy when schools themselves are not democratic?'
- 'Student councils give young people a voice but not a say'
- 'The work in schools needs to be supported within the community.'
- 'Government needs to meet the promises it made on political and voter education programmes'
- 'Is there the political will to make people living in socially disadvantaged areas politically active?'
- 'Is there the political will to educate the new immigrant communities in their political rights?'

In recent years the concept of Irish citizenship has become controversial in terms of who is entitled to be a citizen and who is not. Never was this truer than in the run up to, and indeed the aftermath of, the citizenship referendum in June 2004.

While recognising that much of what is contestable about citizenship in the Irish sense stems from its legal definition, and

> *Citizenship of the future is likely to rely more on loyalty to democratic institutions and the rule of law than to an identity based on birth, language and religion.*

acknowledging that the debate around citizenship law is of vital national significance, the Commission now wishes to encourage discussion on what citizenship should mean in 21st Century Ireland. This means moving beyond the narrow definition of whom, in Ireland, is or is not entitled to Irish citizenship or, in Northern Ireland, to issues of allegiance to the State. The Commission believes that there is a need to recognise that the contemporary world requires a much broader view of what it means to be a citizen. In particular, the Commission is persuaded by the value of 'active democratic citizenship' and stresses that citizenship of the future is likely to rely more on loyalty to democratic institutions and the rule of law than to an identity based on birth, language and religion.

Democracy does not require that everyone is the author of every decision. It does require, however, that people can have their say on matters that affect them. An active democratic citizenry ensures broad deliberative participation and can strengthen democracy as decisions to which more people contribute are likely to be better and ones which people are more likely to adhere to (Honohan, 2005:4). This is only possible if they are provided with accessible opportunities and mechanisms for participation.

Citizenship is *'a political concept, defined by a package of rights and responsibilities that express the form of social membership in a given political community. It is both a dynamic and contested concept as rights and responsibilities change over time'*. (Faulks, 2005: 2). It tends to be discussed in terms of the relationship between the State and the citizen where rights and responsibilities are confined to territorial boundaries. Globalisation – the growing interdependence of peoples, cultures and economies – means that the rights and responsibilities of citizenship must stretch beyond state boundaries. We live in a world where we all need to be aware of planetary issues such as wide scale poverty, global warming, global terrorism and international crime. No one State can deal with these alone. Everyone is affected by them.

The Commission is conscious that the days when there was a simple dominant national identity in any Western European state are coming to an end. Both immigration and emigration involving all these states is ensuring that there is a diverse range of ethnicities and religions. It is also conscious that concepts of citizenship have become more relevant in the context of recent social, economic and demographic changes in Irish society. For the first time in living memory, we are experiencing an increasing diversity in Ireland, with significant immigration including the return of many Irish citizens from abroad. According to the National Consultative Committee on Racism and Interculturalism (NCCRI), there are now approximately 160 different nationalities living in Ireland (2005:5). This means that modern Irish citizens do not necessarily share common ethnic or cultural backgrounds, and that there is more diversity around moral, religious and ethical perspectives.

The Commission supports moving beyond what has come to be known as the politics of recognition or multiculturalism (basic or passive tolerance) to an active approach to tolerance, often described as an intercultural approach. Multiculturalism *'seeks to acknowledge and celebrate diversity without necessarily promoting interaction or equality'* (Watt, 2005:2). It is based on the recognition of diverse ethnic communities who have different types of links into society. It recognises different ways of being a citizen. It has been criticised for it weakness in promoting interaction and equality and for permitting a notion of separateness that lends itself to stereotypes.

Interculturalism, on the other hand, is *'essentially about interaction, understanding, and respect, ...about ensuring that cultural diversity should be acknowledged and catered for ... about inclusion for minority ethnic groups by design and planning, not as a default or add-on. .... (and) acknowledges that people should have the freedom to keep alive, enhance and share their cultural heritage'* (NCCRI submission to the Democracy Commission).

Interculturalism takes an active approach to tolerance, which along with interdependency, civic self-restraint and openness to deliberative argument is one of the core principles of active democratic citizenship.

Iseult Honohan outlines two dimensions to active democratic citizenship[1], status and practice. Legal status grants certain rights, such as equality before the law, freedom of speech and association, etc., and certain duties or obligations, such as obeying the law, paying taxes, etc. In this sense being a citizen is essentially a matter of laws, and of fixed rights and obligations. The practice of citizenship on the other hand involves such things as participating in self-

There are now approximately 160 different nationalities living in Ireland.

---

[1] The Commission distinguishes between active democratic citizenship which involves a political dimension as opposed to active citizenship in terms of involvement in neighbourhood watch schemes, walking the neighbour's dog etc.

government, sitting on juries, informing oneself about the democratic process, supporting the public good and defending one's country, and refers to people's attitudes and behaviour (Honohan, 2005: 2).

The Commission believes that active democratic citizenship involves:

All groups and individuals in Irish and Northern Irish society are dependent on one another.

- An awareness of interdependence, that is all groups and individuals in Irish and Northern Irish society are dependent on one another no matter how weak or strong. This involves a sense of a broader social concern and acknowledging responsibilities not only to oneself but to those with whom we are interdependent. As a society we share public goods that can only be 'realised if there is a significant body of citizens who have a sense of common concerns and who are prepared to take into account in their actions the common good or wider interests of, for example, the environment and culture that they share with others' (Honohan, 2005:3).

- Civic self-restraint, that is taking on responsibility for what happens in society such as recycling waste, voting, taking part in jury duty etc.

- Openness to deliberative argument. This refers to how we engage in politics. We should challenge authority, where necessary, not only for our own interests but in the interests of other sections of society when these are threatened. A commitment to tolerance underpins this to the extent that we need to accept that there is a multiplicity of perspectives, respect them and take them into account (Honohan, 2005:3). The Commission sees tolerance as essential in order to cope with and benefit from the ethnic/cultural/moral diversity of our social world. It regards tolerance as emanating from an empathy for others, based on a common sense of humanity. But tolerance goes beyond mere indifference to difference. Essentially, intolerance of intolerance is required.

- A growing awareness and acceptance of the compatibility of Irish and EU citizenship.

- An acceptance in Northern Ireland that Irish, British and EU citizenship are all compatible and provided for under the terms of the Belfast Agreement.

Active democratic citizenship can be encouraged through education

26

we are all interdependent

processes and through institutional mechanisms. This chapter focuses primarily on democratic citizenship education, as institutional mechanisms and experiments are discussed in the chapters on voter participation and representation.

Active Democratic Citizenship Education

Democratic citizenship education focuses on the rights, responsibilities and roles of the citizen, locally, nationally and globally, and on the concept of human interdependence. It provides citizens with non-partisan political information to facilitate their participation in the political discussions and decisions that affect their every day lives.

The Democracy Commission takes its definition of citizenship education from Will Kymlicka who states that citizenship education involves learning the basic facts about the institutions and procedures of political life and *'acquiring a range of dispositions, virtues and loyalties that are immediately bound up with the practice of democratic citizenship'* (1999:79).

Political literacy, a critical understanding of democracy and democratic political institutions and systems are key components of democratic citizenship education. However in addition to providing information on political systems, democratic citizenship education should *'foster respect for law, justice, democracy and nurture common good at the same time as encouraging independence of thought. It should develop skills of reflection, enquiry and debate'* (British Advisory Group on Citizenship, 1998:11). It should develop through knowledge, values and dispositions the five elements of active democratic citizenship outlined above.

Since the foundation of the Irish state, citizenship education has been a contentious issue. The Catholic Church did not favour the creation of a separate single school subject on citizenship as it believed that moral education and personal development were best taught through religious education (Gleeson and Munnelly, 2004:3). In 1966 the establishment of free second level education coincided with the 50th anniversary of the 1916 Easter Rising and introduced a new mandatory but non-examined secondary school subject, Civics. Its primary aims were *'to inculcate values such as civic responsibility, moral virtue, patriotism, and law abidingness'* (Gleeson and Munnelly, 2004:3). In 1967, in a document entitled 'The Rules and Programme for Teachers', the Department of Education described Civics as *'teaching the young citizen to recognise and obey lawful authority, to help preserve law, order and discipline, to respect private and public right to property and to be ready to defend the national territory should the need arise'* (Gleeson and Munnelly, 2003:3).

After an enthusiastic start, Civics was, by the end of the 1970s, a dying subject due to a shortage of trained teachers in the subject; a lack of teaching and learning resources; and a perception that it was less important than other subjects as it was unexamined and only given one hour a week in the school timetable. In 1993, however, at the request of the then Minister for Education Mary O'Rourke, the National Council for Curriculum and Assessment introduced a pilot programme on Civic, Social and Political Education (CSPE) to Junior Certificate.

CSPE was introduced as a mandatory subject in the junior cycle in 1997, replacing Civics. Its aim is *'to prepare students for active participatory citizenship... through comprehensive exploration of the civic, social and political dimensions of their lives at a time when pupils are developing from* dependent children into independent young adults. It should produce knowledgeable pupils who can explore, analyse and evaluate, who are skilled and practised in moral and critical appraisal, and capable of making decisions and judgements through a reflective citizenship, based on human rights and social responsibilities. Such pupils should be better prepared for living in a world where traditional structures and values are being challenged, and where pupils are being confronted with conflicting interests, impermanent structures and constant questioning' (CSPE syllabus). The course's central concepts include democracy, rights and responsibilities, human dignity, interdependence, development, and law and stewardship. The course is allocated one class period per week or around 70 hours total teaching over the three-year junior cycle.

Since its introduction, CSPE has encountered a number of problems, namely the allocation of teachers; the amount of time given to the subject; the status of the subject; the level of assessment; teacher support/professional development; and resourcing of the subject and management support (Coleman, Gray and Harrison, 2004:4). As the subject is not currently taught to Leaving Certificate and has no weighting in the 'points race', it is not viewed seriously by some students. In a survey of 732 upper secondary school pupils in the academic year 2001/02, Gleeson and Munnelly found that 34% of respondents stated that CSPE was 'not important' while 25% of those survey claimed that it was the least important subject in their school (2004:7). Nonetheless, the authors found that 72% of the students questioned felt that CSPE had made them more aware of how government works and 80% of respondents said that they would like to vote (Gleeson & Munnelly, 2004: 8).

One of the challenges faced by CSPE is that in some schools it is taught by teachers who have little interest in it or are uncomfortable teaching it due a lack of knowledge of the area but who have been given the task of doing so because of a gap in their timetable or because it is their 'turn' to do so. In a postal survey of principals and CSPE teachers, Annette Honan found that in relation to the teaching of CSPE, school principals stated that their main problem was finding staff willing or suitably qualified to teach it. Moreover, the turnover rate of CSPE teachers was very high. Only 41% of the teacher respondents had taken the same class group from first year to third year. Finally, most of the teachers who responded were not teaching CSPE by choice (Gleeson & Munnelly, 2004:13).

Since its introduction, CSPE has encountered a number of problems.

At present neither democratic citizenship nor political education is taught as an independent subject to senior cycle. In this regard Ireland has been seriously out of line with most of its European neighbours. For instance in the UK it is possible to take A levels in sociology, media studies and politics. No such offerings exist in the Leaving Certificate (Established) in Ireland at present. This situation is currently under examination as part of the National Council for Curriculum and Assessment's (NCCA) review of senior cycle post primary education. In current discussions on the review of the senior cycle, three options have been posited by the NCCA for extending social and political education, the generic term allocated in Irish education circles to democratic citizenship education. Firstly, it could be offered as part of a 40-hour transition year unit. Secondly, it could become a short course of 80 teaching hours in one year, which could be examined at the end of fifth year (the year before the Leaving Certificate) (2004:16). Unlike transition year units, short courses would be examined externally by the State and would be allocated points for entry to third level institutions. Finally, social and political education could be offered as a full optional Leaving Certificate subject.

> In Ireland democratic citizenship education is not taught to senior cycle.

The Commission believes that social and political education should be offered in all three. To make it available in transition year alone would be insufficient as not all students take the transition year. Similarly, to offer it solely as a short course would not be acceptable as under the NCCA's proposals the two-year route to Leaving Certificate will not have a short course as a minimum requirement. In keeping with good practice elsewhere, social and political/ democratic citizenship education should be a full Leaving Certificate subject.

In its curricular proposal for social and political education for the Leaving Certificate (established), the Curriculum Development Unit (CDU) of the City of Dublin Vocational Educational Committee (CDVEC) speaks of citizenship studies. This proposal takes the arena of citizenship from citizenship education, which involves developing values, skills and understanding, and moves it nearer to the academic disciplines of politics, philosophy and sociology. It can be described as extracting the 'best of theory and practice from both disciplines' (Ward, 2002:15). Democratic deliberation is suggested as the political theory to underpin citizenship studies.

Democratic deliberation aims to 'reinvigorate our understanding and practice of democracy in a pluralist and complicated world through emphasising democracy itself as a process that requires constant deliberation or dialogue' (Ward, 2002:20). It requires acceptance of the following principles:

- Human relations are characterised by interdependence.
- All individuals are equal.
- Dialogue can only occur where there is respect for difference and recognition of the right to hold different views and opinions.
- Dialogue is characterised by the idea of reciprocity.
- Participants in the dialogue must be genuine, open and transparent and interested in resolving difficulty.
- Agreement that conflict will be resolved by non-violent means (Ward, 2002: 37).

In Northern Ireland democratic citizenship education has developed within the education framework of the review of the Northern Ireland curriculum. The Council for the Curriculum, Examinations and Assessment (CCEA) has proposed that democratic citizenship education will be provided across the four key stages of student education from primary to post-primary within two specific programmes, personal development and citizenship.

The personal development programme will be taught from key stages one to four. It endeavours to personally, socially and emotionally empower pupils so that they can make informed and responsible choices and decisions. Within this programme, citizenship education is contained within the Living in the Local and Wider Community objective and taught to primary school students.

The local and global citizenship programme is part of the core curriculum subject Learning for Life and Work. Its central concepts include diversity and inclusion; democracy and active participation; human rights and social responsibilities; and equality and social justice. While yet to be formally incorporated into the curriculum, citizenship classes have been piloted in a growing number of schools and materials are currently being drafted. The work so far has rooted citizenship education in notions of human rights. It is intended that by September 2005 citizenship education as part of Learning for Life and Work will be taught at key stage three level (11- 14) in all schools in Northern Ireland and that it will be rolled out to key stage four across all schools by 2007. Survey and focus-group evidence to date has found political education to be popular among young people in Northern Ireland but there is resistance, particularly among grammar schools, to democratic citizenship education, on the grounds that this is a parental responsibility and/or a distraction from conventional academic education and accreditation (Wilson and Wilford, forthcoming). The Commission wishes to emphasise the importance of democratic citizenship education in Northern Ireland and believes it needs to be underpinned by the aim to build a shared future. To achieve this it needs to address issues of interculturalism, separateness and sectarianism.

The Commission also believes that it is imperative that teachers of citizenship education on the island of Ireland are properly supported in terms of training and materials. Evidence in England has highlighted the danger that poorly provided citizenship education can reinforce the idea that citizenship and politics are not relevant to peoples' lives.

Teachers of citizenship education should be properly supported in terms of training and materials.

School Culture and Student Councils

Any discussion on democratic citizenship education needs to address the role played by school culture in preparing students for citizenship and democratic participation. This begs the question as to whether schools, institutions not renowned for their democratic structures, are the best arena in which to learn about democracy. This was recognised by the British Advisory Group on Citizenship which stated that 'it is obvious that all formal preparation for citizenship in adult life can be helped or hindered by the ethos and organisation of a school, whether pupils are given opportunities for exercising responsibilities and initiatives or not; and also whether they are consulted realistically on matters where their opinions can prove relevant both to the efficient running of a school and to their general motivation for learning' (1998:25).

In its review of the senior cycle, the NCCA has expressed 'a concern to find the right balance between independence and structure in the learning environment for 16-19 year olds' (2004:6) and is focusing on 'the importance of developing a school culture conducive to teaching and learning in the post-compulsory period of education' (2004:23). Recognising that the NCCA is currently reviewing the senior cycle and acknowledging differences between junior and senior students, the Commission believes that students need to be provided with opportunities to be consulted and to exercise responsibilities in matters that affect them throughout their schooling. Student councils are the primary mechanism to achieve this. These opportunities could even be extended to primary schools where children, as part of Social, Personal and Health Education, learn the rudiments of media, political and citizenship education. This is in keeping with the National Children's Strategy which states that *'children will have a voice in matters which affect them and their views will be given due weight in accordance with their age and maturity'* (2000:8).

The Education Act 1998 legislated for the establishment of student councils in secondary schools. Although some schools have been effective in meeting this requirement others have yet to do so. Research conducted by the Department of Education and Science shows that out of 743 secondary schools in Ireland, 559 have student councils in operation and 181 do not (National Youth Council of Ireland submission to the Democracy Commission). In its consultations, the Commission has heard that in some of the schools where student councils have been established they have proven to be little more than talking shops wherein students are given limited powers to tackle the litter problem or organise a charity fund raising event. In some schools student representatives are appointed to councils by school staff rather than through direct election by their classmates. One individual summarised the situation by saying 'student councils give students a voice but not a say'. Student councils need to be granted the powers outlined by the National Children's Office if students are to experience the value of participation. If not, they risk reinforcing the idea that politics is not relevant to their lives.

> "Student councils give students a voice but not a say."

The Democracy Commission believes that student councils can, if effectively established, provide a key forum for young people to actively experience democratic processes. In addition, the Commission argues that mechanisms within schools to teach democratic citizenship education need to be supported within the wider community. This is particularly vital in communities which have no experience of or have encountered problems to political participation.

Most Irish adults, depending on their age, have received citizenship education either through Civics or through CSPE. Yet the never-ending nature of citizenship, which is both lifelong and lifewide and

in permanent construction, means that democratic citizenship education should not stop at 16 or 18 (Keogh, 2003:11). One of the strongest concerns raised with the Commission in its consultations was that people were not provided with basic information on political institutions and processes and how to access them. Community education programmes are one way of addressing this problem and can also be used to provide people, not originally from Ireland, with information on Irish politics and society.

In Ireland community education has provided a forum for 'listening to the voices of otherwise silenced people' and has 'supplied the wherewithal for disparate groups to engage with empowering processes and become active agents in their communities' (Connolly, 2003:9). It has been defined as 'education and learning which is rooted in a process of empowerment, social justice, change, challenge, respect and collective consciousness. It is within the community and of the community, reflecting the developing needs of individuals and their locale' (Aontas, 2004:18-19).

Targeted spending on citizenship education within community

education programmes in disadvantaged and marginalised communities is necessary to develop a community's capacity to participate and strengthen the measures taken within the formal education sector.

Commission Recommendations

The Commission recommends:

- The extension of social and political education to senior cycle. The Commission favours the introduction of citizenship studies as defined by Eilis Ward as a full optional subject to Leaving Certificate and supports the provision of citizenship education short courses and transition year units.
- Targeting spending on citizenship education and voter awareness programmes.
- Promoting citizenship issues in primary schools.
- Promoting greater democracy within school structures.
- That democratic citizenship education in Northern Ireland be rooted in the goal to build a shared future and address issues of sectarianism, interculturalism and separateness
- Promoting democratic citizenship education within community education programmes.
- Provision of training and materials to support teachers of democratic citizenship education.

References

Aontas, 2004: Community Education 2004. Dublin: Aontas.

Baker, John, Kathleen Lynch, Sara Cantillon and Judy Walsh, 2004: Equality from Theory to Action. London: Palgrave MacMillan.

British Advisory Group on Citizenship, 1998: 'Education for Citizenship and the teaching of democracy in schools'. London: Qualifications and Curriculum Authority.

Coleman, Eileen, Gray, Eileen and Conor Harrison, 2004: Submission of the Civic Social and Political Education (CSPE) Support Team of the Second Level Support Service to the Democracy Commission.

Connolly, Brid, 2003: 'Community Education: Listening to the voices', Adult Learner. Dublin: Aontas.

CSPE Junior Certificate Syllabus.

Faulks, Keith, 2005: 'Rethinking citizenship education in England: some lessons from contemporary social and political theory' paper presented at Citizenship Education and Social Justice seminar in Queen's University Belfast 2005. http://www.qub.ac.uk/edu/seminar/seminar_paper_faulks2.doc.

Gleeson, Jim and Jarlath Munnelly, 2004: 'Developments in citizenship education in Ireland: context, rhetoric and reality'.
http://civiced.indiana.edu/papers/2003/1053010537.pdf.

Honohan, Iseult, 2005: Active Citizenship in contemporary Democracy – presentation made to the Democracy Commission.

Keogh, Helen, 2003: 'Learning for Citizenship in Ireland: the Role of Adult Education' in Medel-Anonuevo, Carolyn & Mitchell, Gordon (ed) Citizenship, Democracy, and Lifelong Learning. Philippines: UNESCO.

Kymlicka, Will, 1999: 'Education for Citizenship' in Halstead, J.M. and McLaughlin T.H. (ed) Education and Morality. London: Routledge.

National Youth Council of Ireland, 2004: Submission to the Democracy Commission.

NCCA, 2004: Proposals for the future of Senior Cycle Education in Ireland.

NCCRI, 2005. Submission to the Democracy Commission.

NCO, 2000: National Children's Strategy.

Ward, Eilis, 2002: 'Citizenship Studies', a curricular proposal for Social and Political Education in the Leaving Certificate (Established). Dublin: CDVEC CDU.

Watt, Philip, 2005: Approaches to Cultural and Ethnic Diversity and the role of citizenship in promoting a more inclusive intercultural society in Ireland. Paper presented to the Democracy Commission.

Wilson, Robin and Wilford, Rick, forthcoming: Democratic Audit of Northern Ireland – work in progress, Democratic Audit Ireland project. Dublin: Tasc.

Voter Participation

2

I f democracy is 'government of the people for the people by the people' then popular participation lies at the core of any democratic society. This has been one of the key areas of focus for the Commission, which has been particularly concerned with examining the reasons for disconnection from the political process by the under 25s and those living in socially disadvantaged areas.

The Commission has received an impression of disempowerment and disillusionment from many of those it has engaged with.

- 'Why should I vote? It won't make any difference to my life'.
- 'Politicians are all the same, middle aged men in suits... they don't represent me'.
- 'Young people see government as something that happens to them, not for them.'
- 'Voting is not an option for those who do not have an address'.
- From people living in socially disadvantaged areas the Commission heard 'from what I can see there is only one party doing anything in my area'.

Disconnection is best exemplified in the declining rates of electoral participation. Similar to other Western democracies, Ireland has been experiencing falling electoral turnout in recent decades. In a 25 year period, turnout in Irish general elections dropped from 76.3 % (1977) to 62.7% (2002). This trend was unexpectedly reversed when turnout for the 2004 local and European elections increased by 8.6 percentage points.

It remains to be seen whether the recent increase in turnout was a once off event or the beginning of a trend in increased participation. Speculation as to the causes of the increase touched on the role of Sinn Féin in mobilising the vote, the level of interest in the citizenship referendum, disgruntlement with the government of the day, voter education programmes and extended polling hours.

In Northern Ireland, which has until recently enjoyed high turnout, the trend is towards declining electoral participation. In the 2005 Westminster election, Northern Ireland was the only region within the UK to experience a drop in turnout. Overall turnout for the UK increased by two percentage points. In comparison Northern Ireland witnessed a 5.5 percentage point decrease. This drop mirrors the decline in turnout at the European elections in Northern Ireland in June 2004. On that occasion turnout was down by more than five percentage points on the 1999 poll.

Declining levels of electoral participation can weaken democratic systems.

Over a sustained period of time, declining levels of electoral participation can weaken democratic systems by eroding mandates, damaging legitimacy, reducing political equality and the diversity of dialogue. Evidence shows that low and declining turnouts often involve a class bias that leaves the less well off in society and certain age groups significantly under-represented (Lijphart, 1997).

It in its investigations the Commission has sought to identify the causes leading to low turnout, particularly amongst the under 25s and the less well off in society with a view to making specific recommendations to address them.

Yet it is mindful that electoral participation is but one form of political participation. Other forms of political activity include:

- Pressure activity - attending demonstrations, signing petitions, lobbying elected representatives, sending letters or postcards to elected representatives and donating resources to campaign bodies.
- Consultation activity – citizens' panels, focus groups, public forums, Internet consultation and partnership bodies.
- Do It Yourself Activity - mutual associations, credit unions or co-operatives, and campaigning to influence personal behaviour.

The Commission, for the most part, has focused its attention on electoral and pressure activities.

Young People

Research undertaken by the National Youth Council of Ireland (NYCI) shows that youth participation in the electoral process is declining. In the 1999 local and European elections, almost 67% of young people (aged 18-25) did not vote (www.youth.ie). This is supported by the quarterly national household survey of spring 2003 which revealed that 'just over 40% of young adult respondents aged 18-19, and only 53% of those aged 20-24 indicated that they voted in the [2002 general election]' (CSO, 2003:1). In contrast, almost 90% of those aged 65-74 said they had voted.

The same is true for young people in Northern Ireland. In the 2003 Assembly elections it is estimated that 49% of those aged between 18-24 voted compared with an estimated 80% turnout amongst the over 55s (Electoral Commission (NI), 2004:96).

It would be wrong, however, to assume that apathy and a lack of interest lie behind low youth turnout. Of the young non-voters aged between 18-19, there is a large gap between those who did not vote because they were not registered (39%) and those who did not vote because that they were not interested (24%).

An examination of non-voters in the 20-24 age category shows that 47% of them did not vote because of procedural obstacles ('not registered', 'away', 'no polling card') as opposed to the 39 % who did not vote due to 'no interest', 'disillusionment', 'lack of information/ knowledge' and 'my vote would make no difference'.

It would be wrong to assume that apathy and a lack of interest lie behind low youth turnout.

Table 1. Non-voters in the May 2002 general election classified by reasons for not voting (18-19, 20-24)

Age Group	18-19	20-24
No Interest	24.0	25.8
Disillusionment	4.6	5.8
Lack of Knowledge/Information	2.6	4.5
My vote would make no difference	4.0	2.6
Illness/Disability	0	0.9
Away	9.0	17.3
Too Busy	5.8	9.6
Not Registered	39.4	25.5
No Polling Card	6.3	4.3
Lack of Transport	0.7	0.3
Other	3.6	3.5

(CSO, 2003:5)

Table 2. Non-voters in the May 2002 general election classified by reasons for not voting (students)

	Student
No interest	14.7
Disillusioned	6.1
Lack of knowledge /information	4.6
My vote would make no difference	3.7
Illness/disability	0.1
Away	18.0
Too busy	6.4
Not Registered	38.4
No polling card	4.5
Lack of transport	0.6
Other	2.9

(CSO, 2003: 5)

This research also reveals that student non-voters are over two and half times more likely not to vote because they are not registered than a lack of interest. Again, if this data is examined in terms of voter facilitation (ability to vote) rather than voter mobilisation (interest/motivation to vote), it shows that 61% cite procedural obstacles ('not registered', 'away', 'no polling card') to voting compared with the 29% who highlight motivational barriers ('no interest', 'disillusioned', 'lack of knowledge/information', 'my vote would make no difference').

Procedural issues also influenced turnout in the Northern Ireland Assembly election 2003 amongst certain sections of Northern Irish society. This election was the first at which changes brought about by the Electoral Fraud (Northern Ireland) Act 2002 were implemented in full[2]. Registration subsequently declined and was concentrated among disadvantaged and hard-to-reach groups like young people and students (Electoral Commission (NI),

---

2   This Act brought about significant change replacing the household registration system with individual registration. Under the new system individuals wishing to register to vote must on an annual basis: give personal details (date of birth and national insurance number); a signature upon registration (previously only the head of the household signed the form which only otherwise included the names of eligible voters living there); a statement of residence in Northern Ireland for the whole of the three month period prior to the date of their application; and details of any other addresses at which they have registered. Under the provisions of this Act a voter is also required to present photographic ID (a special electoral identity card was made available for those lacking a passport or driver's licence) upon voting.

2004:23). Measures to prevent voter fraud are required to protect democracy. Care needs to be taken, however, that they are not counterproductive to democratic participation.

Barriers to youth participation are a concern as international research has shown that voting is habit forming, that is, voting in one election increases a person's likelihood of voting in future elections. This is reinforced by the CSO's analysis of the 2002 general election which indicated that over 80% of those who voted participate in most elections. More worryingly, the CSO survey revealed that over 55% of those aged 25 and under indicated that they had not voted in any election since they became eligible to do so (CSO, 2003:2).

Procedural issues such as registration and the day of polling may be the bigger blocks to youth participation. Yet factors such as a lack of interest, disillusionment and a shortage of knowledge/information cannot be overlooked.

Recent Democratic Audit Ireland survey results reveal that young peoples' belief in their ability to influence decisions is weaker than their parents and grandparents. Only half of the 15-24 year olds questioned believed that 'ordinary citizens could influence decisions when they made an effort' compared with over two thirds of older respondents. Only one fifth of the young respondents disagreed strongly with the statement that 'citizens being active in politics is a waste of time' compared with one third of older respondents. Young people are also far less inclined to discuss politics or political news with someone else. Their parents and grandparents are twice as likely to take part in a political discussion with someone else than they are (Clancy et al, 2005).

This is in keeping with the National Youth Federation's national youth poll of young people aged between 15 and 17 which found that 45% of the respondents had no interest in politics, 55% (small majority) said they did and 8% said that they were very interested (www.nyf.ie).

In 2004 the Northern Ireland Young Life and Times survey of 16 year olds found that 45% of the respondents said that people should only vote if they care who wins, 35% said that it is everyone's duty to vote and 12% answered that it is really not worth voting. In the same survey 26% of the respondents said they did not have much interest in politics, 38% said they had none at all and 20% had some interest (http://www.ark.ac.uk/ylt/2004).

Young people are less inclined to discuss politics than their parents and grandparents.

In its official report on the 2003 Northern Ireland assembly elections, the Electoral Commission (NI) found that only 19% of 18-24 years olds said they had a 'great deal' or 'quite a lot of' interest in politics compared with 37% of 55-64 year olds and 27% of those in the 35-44 age bracket (Electoral Commission (NI), 2004:100).

If our definition of participation is broadened to include pressure activity we find that young people aged between 15 and 24 are less likely than those older than they to sign petitions, discuss political news or take and active part in a political campaign. They are, however, more likely or equally as likely to take part in a picket or demonstration (Clancy et al 2005).

People living in socially disadvantaged areas

Electoral turnout also tends to be lower amongst the less affluent in society. Adrian Kavanagh notes that *'class related factors have a large bearing on the geography of turnouts in Dublin and other large urban areas, with large differences in turnout rates generally existing between middle class and working class areas'* (2005:3)

In the 1999 local elections in Ireland, turnout reached dismally low levels in the less well off areas of Dublin failing to reach 30% in Clondalkin and Mulhuddart as outlined in Table 3.

Table 3. % Turnout in Local Authority Elections of 1999 and 2004 in less affluent wards in Dublin.

Ward	%Turnout 2004	% Turnout 1999
Artane	54.8	32.6
Ballyfermot	50.3	33
Crumlin / Kimmage	53.5	34.2
Donaghmede	57.2	34.4
Dublin North Inner City	42.27	30.6
Dublin South East Inner City	44.7	32
Dublin South West Inner City	43.6	31
Finglas	54.4	38.7
Mulhuddart	50	29.7
Tallaght Central	54.39	39.8
Tallaght South	45.89	32.3

Source: Department of the Environment, Heritage and Local Government

This was dramatically reversed in the 2004 local and European elections when Mulhuddart, Clondalkin and Tallaght South experienced phenomenal increases of 138%, 82% and 77% respectively.

Table 4. Percentage increase in Number of Voters 1999-2004

Ward	% Increase
Mulhuddart	138
Clondalkin	82
Tallaght South	77
Tallaght Central	76
Ballyfermot	71.5
Donaghmede	62
Artane	61
Crumlin/Kimmage	49
Dublin South West Inner City	41
Dublin South East Inner City	39
Dublin North Inner City	37
Finglas	36

This increase was undoubtedly a welcome development. Nonetheless, even with the improved participation rates, all wards listed in Table 4 were still lower than the national average of 58.7% and many were below the 50% mark.

In the 2003 Northern Ireland Assembly elections, 61% of

unskilled manual workers, the unemployed and those in receipt of state benefits in the long term (DE category) voted compared with 79% of middle class or professional voters (AB category), and 69% of lower middle class or junior management (C1) (Electoral Commission (NI), 2004: 96). When the same socio-economic categories are assessed in terms of having a 'great deal' or 'quite a lot' of interest in politics only 19% of those in the DE group agreed as opposed to 43% of those in the AB group and 32% of people in the C1 group (Electoral Commission (NI), 2004:100).

Recent academic analysis, however, shows that turnout figures may not be a true reflection of socio-economic participation in a ward. Kavanagh notes that in the 1999 and 2004 local elections low turnouts in the predominantly middle class private 'gated' apartments in Dublin Inner City push down the average turnout in these wards and lead to a perception of low political and electoral engagement among the local, mainly working class, inner city population. Information gathered from the marked registered analysis, he asserts, puts 'such perceptions to the lie' (2005:14).

research reveals the positive impact of community based voter education programmes on turnout.

Turnout levels in rural areas tend to be higher than in urban ones. A variety of explanations including stronger sense of community, stronger political organisations and traditions as well as an older population have been put forward. High population mobility in the new commuter belts around Dublin, however, has a negative impact on turnout in these areas.

The link between the level of formal education received and the likelihood of voting has been well established. Recent research reveals the impact of community based voter education programmes on turnout. In Fatima Mansions, turnout levels have increased steadily as a consequence of locally based voter education programmes and urban regeneration programmes. Voter education programmes run by the Vincentian partnership for social justice were also one of the factors contributing to the high turnout rate for non-EU nationals in the 2004 local elections in the Portlaoise region (Kavanagh, 2005:24).

Recent Democratic Audit Ireland survey findings support Kavanagh's research as 68% of the C2DEs surveyed said they had voted in the last general election compared with 67% of ABC1s. Similarly, the gap between the two social groups was negligible for the last local election with 66% of people in the C2DE group saying they had voted. This was two percentage points lower than the number of ABC1 respondents who said they had voted (Clancy et al, 2005).

Yet there were differences across the social groups with respect to their perceptions of politics. When asked to respond to a statement that 'citizens being active in politics is a waste of time', 27% of those in the DE category said yes, a figure that contrasts sharply with the 11% of those classified as ABs who thought so. In fact, 68% of the AB respondents believed being active in politics was worthwhile compared with 48% of DE respondents. Furthermore, 75% of those surveyed in the AB category believed ordinary citizens can influence political decisions when they make an effort while only 59% of the DE respondents thought so (Clancy et al, 2005).

The survey also found that over half of the middle class and professional respondents were more likely to discuss political news and views with someone else compared with 35% of the less affluent respondents.

In terms of pressure activities, the survey data reveals little difference in participation across socio-economic groups. The only striking comparison that emerged was that almost half of those in the ABC1 group have discussed politics or political news with someone else compared with one third of those in the C2DE group (Clancy et al, 2005).

These findings reinforce the sense of disempowerment and disillusionment amongst those in disadvantaged communities that the Commission came across in its consultations and is a source of concern.

The perceived absence of cross party activity in socially disadvantaged areas also presents a threat to Irish democracy. It risks contributing to a belief that people living in socially disadvantaged areas have only one, or at the most two, political parties to choose from. Choice is central to democracy. If a section of Irish society believes that it is not presented with political choice in its area then this poses a serious challenge to the future state of democracy in Ireland.

Prisoners

Prisoners represent the group in society for whom the capacity to vote is most severely restricted. The current legal position is that prisoners are legally entitled to vote, but are physically unable to exercise this right because they are incarcerated. A series of cases taken by prisoners have established that they have a right to be registered in the constituency in which they are normally resident, but have no right to be given physical access to a ballot box, or to a postal vote, while they are in custody. This means that only those prisoners who happen to be on parole or temporary release on the day of any election may exercise their right to vote wherever they are registered. This position is legally anomalous and has no logical justification. There is no reason why prisoners cannot be enabled to exercise their established right to vote through a postal vote mechanism. The Commission accordingly recommends that the right to vote through postal means be extended to prisoners in custody.

Possible methods to promote participation

- **Automatic Registration through Personal Public Service (PPS) / National Insurance Number** to tackle register inaccuracies which prevent people from voting and distort actual turnout in a given area. Currently the Government issues a PPS number to young people at 16 for taxation purposes. The Commission suggests introducing a system whereby there could be automatic registration of 18 years olds on their birthday through their PPS or National Insurance number[3].

At present every local authority in Ireland is responsible for compiling and publishing a register of electors each year for its area. This draft register is published each year on 1 November and can be inspected by anyone in public places such as local authority offices, the post office, Garda stations and public libraries. Those qualified to vote have until 25 November to make a correction to or have their name included on the register. The amended register of electors is then published in February of the following year and runs for twelve months.

Automatic registration through PPS number in Ireland and National Insurance Number in Northern Ireland would remove one of the largest procedural obstacles to voting.

- **Week-end voting**
  Although 60% of the CSO's respondents (voters and non-voters) did not indicate a preference for the day of the week on which polling occurs, it is worth highlighting that Saturday was the preferred polling day for 51% of voting students and 41% of non-voting students. Of young non-voters, 30% of 18-19 year olds preferred Saturday voting and 58% said it didn't matter. In the case of the 18-19 year olds who did vote, 40% indicated a preference for Saturday voting while 43% said it did not matter. Of the 20-24 year olds who voted, 36% chose Saturday voting and 46% said it did not matter. The younger the voter the more likely the day of polling mattered. The Commission believes that the possibility of and support for week-end or multiple day voting should be investigated by an independent electoral commission.

- **Reduce Candidacy Age**
  The current age of majority in Ireland is 18 years of age. At 18 years of age an individual can run for Local Government, marry, serve on jury duty and vote in local, general and

---

3   PPS numbers are automatically issued to people who: were born in Ireland in or after 1971; started work in Ireland after 1979; are in receipt of a social welfare payment; are taking part in the drugs payment scheme. In the UK, a person is automatically registered and sent an NI number before their 16th birthday if they live in the UK or their parents or guardians are getting child benefit for them.

European elections. Yet, he/she cannot be a candidate for election to Dáil Éireann until they reach 21. The Democracy Commission favours lowering the candidacy age to 18.

- **Lower the voting age**

  The Commission has heard from groups and individuals calling for the extension of the franchise to 16 year olds. It acknowledges their argument that if a 16 year old can leave school, seek full-time employment, be liable for tax and obtain a licence to drive a small motorcycle then they should be given the vote.

  In its consultations, however, the Commission did not come across popular support for the proposal. It is also mindful of division amongst young people themselves on this issue as is reflected in the National Youth Federation's national youth poll. This surveyed 1,014 young people (59% were 16, 28% were 17 and 13% were 15 and younger) and found that 63% of them favoured giving a vote to 16 years olds (www.nyf.ie). When assessed according to the respondents' ages, it was found that only a bare majority of 17 year olds (51%) favoured extending the franchise compared with 68% of 16 year olds and 71% of those aged 15 and under (www.nyf.ie).

  The Commission is also concerned that lowering the minimum voting age would adversely impact on future turnout levels. The Commission does, however, recognise that the context could change in the future and would suggest a formal review of the minimum voting age by an independent electoral commission in the near future.

- **Compulsory Voting**

  A number of people who engaged with the Commission called for compulsory voting. They highlighted the citizen's duty to vote and the need to protect democracy through strong turnout and mandates.

  There are, however, strong arguments against mandatory voting as it undermines the freedoms associated with democracy, can be contrary to a country's political culture and be unpopular with the general public. It is also difficult and expensive to enforce. For these reasons the Commission does not favour compulsory voting.

- **Postal Voting**

  Postal voting facilitates participation by expanding the time frame for voting and allows electors access to voting who may not be able to attend a polling station in person either through illness, a physical disability or absence from the locality on election day.

  In Ireland, voters are required to cast their ballot at an official voting centre. Postal votes are granted to members of the Defence Forces, the Gardai and to Irish diplomats posted abroad and their spouses. People with a physical illness or disability that prevents them from going to the polling station and those in full time education away from their address of registration who are likely to be unable to attend their designated polling station may also be eligible for postal votes.

  All postal voting pilot schemes were used by many local authorities in the UK in May 2000, 2002 and 2003. In May 2003, 35 local authorities used all postal voting in their local elections. Following the success of these pilot schemes, in some places turnout doubled, the Electoral Commission (UK) recommended that all postal voting should be adopted as the normal method of voting at local elections in the UK.

  In the May 2004 local and European elections in the UK, all postal voting trials took place across four regions: North East, North West, East Midlands, and Yorkshire and Humber. It was a success to the extent that in the European elections the turnout in the four all postal regions doubled compared to 1999. In other regions, turnout increased by half.

  Yet postal voting is not without its difficulties. One of the biggest challenges it faces is the prevention of voter fraud.

  The Commission favours the extension of the postal voting option to all, including prisoners, on the electoral register as a means of facilitating participation. Recognising that a balance must be struck between the facilitation of participation and protecting and maintaining the integrity of and public confidence in the voting system the Commission calls for measures to prevent voter fraud.

- **Electronic Voting**

  Electronic voting is put forward as a mechanism to increase

turnout as it can make voting more convenient and attractive by using of different technologies to make voting more accessible.

E-voting was used for the first time in Ireland in the 2002 general election. Three pilot constituencies, Dublin North, Dublin West and Meath, were chosen and the Government's aim was to use the system across the country for the 2004 local and European parliament elections. In its proposals the Government promoted electronic voting as improving electoral administration, providing earlier and more accurate results, and easier voting for the public. In particular it would make spoilt votes a thing of the past. It is worth highlighting that in the 2002 pilot schemes and the proposals for the 2004 elections the e-voting machines were (to be) located in polling stations. Increasing convenience was not a factor in the Irish e-voting experiment. Instead emphasis lay on efficiency in terms of saving time and money.

E-voting was not used in the local and European parliament elections in 2004. When the Commission on electronic voting, set up by the Government to examine the proposed e-voting system, found that it was unable to verify the accuracy and secrecy of the proposed system the Government postponed introducing widespread e-voting.

Public confidence in electronic voting has been damaged by this initiative and the Commission would question the rationale of introducing a system of voting which not only fails to guarantee increased participation but also risks the overall integrity of the process.

Yet any action that encourages more people to engage in the electoral process is worth pursuing and the Commission believes that despite the bad experience Ireland had with the first attempts at E-Voting it is a system well worth introducing for the benefits it will bring. The Commission believes that future e-voting initiatives need to have a voter verified audit trail (VVAT) to secure the trust of the electorate and they should also look to innovations that make voting more convenient by allowing, for example, voters to cast their ballots in public libraries, post offices, supermarkets etc.

In keeping with its desire to facilitate participation across all sectors of society, the Commission believes that electronic voting should be used for all elections in Ireland and Northern Ireland. Any new e-voting system should look to innovations that permit people to vote not only at polling stations but in supermarkets, post offices, public libraries or on their personal computers or mobile phones. All sites would have to be accessible for disabled people. It is imperative that such a system is introduced in a way that promotes confidence in the integrity of the system. In Ireland, it is also essential that the system staggers the counts, which are part of Irish political culture and play a role in generating interest in politics and elections, and preserves the information provided by them.

- **Introduction of legislation** which gives homeless people, travellers and others with a transitory lifestyle the right to register using an address near a place where they 'commonly spend' their time (e.g. community centre or hostel).

- **Develop new participatory structures**
  In its consultations the Commission heard that people need 'to be provided with opportunities for meaningful participation'. Deliberative polling, citizen juries, preferendum, and the Porto Alegre model of participatory budgeting as outlined in the boxes below are but a number of mechanisms through which this can be achieved.

Box 1 Deliberative Polls

Deliberative Polls, as developed by Professor James Fishkin at the University of Texas, were designed to measure what public opinion on major issues would be like if citizens had the time and resources to become better informed. In this process, a random, representative sample of the public (approx 250 to 500 citizens) gather in one place for a weekend to participate in face-to-face small group discussions and to pose questions to opposing experts and political leaders. At the outset, each individual completes an opinion poll. Then, over the course of 2-3 days, citizens hear evidence from experts and discuss the particular policy issue in small groups. At the end of the event, a second poll is taken i.e. the deliberative poll. The process has shown that frequently, once a citizen has been informed of the facts surrounding a policy issue, he/she will change his/her opinion. Deliberative polls provide citizens with the opportunity to become more knowledgeable about current issues and give them a public space in which to express their opinions. They also give politicians valuable insight into citizens' priorities and the values that shape public opinion.

Box 2 Citizen Juries

Citizen juries bring together a small group of citizens (usually between 12-24 people) to discuss and deliberate on a particular policy issue and issue a series of recommendations. Individuals are selected through a stratified random selection process to ensure representation of different groups in society. Juries usually run for 3-4 days. The idea of citizen juries first originated in the United States in the 1970s, but has been used in the UK since the mid-1990s. Evidence suggests that citizen juries are a positive way of engaging citizens in the formulation of policy, though it should be noted that citizen juries can be expensive to run and only a limited number of citizens get the opportunity to participate in the process.

Box 3 Preferendum

A preferendum is a form of a multi-choice referendum and is based on a modified points system of voting. It is a means by which people may seek their best possible compromise on a contentious issue, or their collective wisdom on a less controversial matter.

There are three stages to the process: debate; vote and analysis of vote.

In the first stage, all those concerned with a particular issue nominate their preferred option. Following debate, these options form the choices on the ballot paper.

During the second stage, voters are asked to state their preference on all options on just one ballot paper (say there are 5 options), giving 5 points to their most preferred option, 4 points to their next option, 3 points to their third option and so on.

The analysis of the vote is the third and final stage. The winning option is the one with the most points. If the outcome has a certain minimum average preference from all participants that outcome may then be adopted. But if the highest scoring is below the minimum average preference, then it may be necessary for the chair to ask for the debate to be resumed and the process repeated until the required level of consensus is reached.

This method has several merits. Firstly, it is very difficult to manipulate and it is usually an accurate measure of the collective will of all those voting. Secondly, it allows for the participation of everyone, including the more extreme elements in society and can be used to identify a consensus opinion. Finally, advocates of the preferendum argue that it is particularly effective in situations of contentious social change, like, for instance, that experienced in Northern Ireland.

Box 4 Porto Alegre model of participatory budgeting

Participatory budgeting, first developed in Porto Alegre, Brazil in 1989, combines popular engagement at the local level with the development and monitoring of a city wide budget and mixes open
assemblies with representative bodies.

Under this model, the annual participatory budget cycle involves three levels of citizen engagement:

(1) Popular Assemblies

In March assemblies/meetings are held in each of the city's 16 districts at which the previous year's
budget allocation is reviewed. After this initial district meeting, smaller neighbourhood assemblies
come together and draw up lists of investment priorities for their locality. These are formally
presented at the second district assembly/meeting. At this second meeting, delegates are elected to
district budget forums (the number of delegates elected is proportional to the number of citizens
attending the first district assembly). Two councillors are also voted onto the municipal budget
council from each district.

(2) District Budget Forums

Every district has a district budget forum in which delegates work together with the city administration to translate neighbourhood priority lists into an overall list of investment priorities for
the district. This involves a process of negotiation with neighbourhood representatives.

(3) Municipal Budget Council

This contains two councillors per district chosen at the second popular assembly. It is in charge
of deciding the relative distribution of resources across the various districts within the city. Its
decisions are informed by priority lists and needs-based criteria developed by the district budget
forums. The Municipal Budget Council presents the budget to the Municipal Council by the end
of September each year.

Participatory budgeting makes decision-making more transparent and has been found to lead to
high levels of participation, including the engagement of politically marginalised groups. This is
attributed to 'a strong incentive to participate in these assemblies since investment priorities and delegates and
councillors are chosen by direct voting and the number of delegates in each region (i.e district) is decided in relation
to the turnout at regional assemblies'. Finally, it leads to a transfer of resources to poorer areas of the city
(Smith, 2005:64-66).

- **Direct/Indirect Initiatives**

  Initiatives facilitate popular participation. They allow citizens
  to initiate a legislative measure or a constitutional amendment
  if they succeed in submitting a petition with the required

number of citizen signatures. Initiatives may be direct or indirect. Direct initiatives allow a proposal to go straight to the ballot box when the required number of citizen signatures is collected. Under indirect initiatives, the proposal initially goes to the legislature when the necessary number of citizen signatures is gathered. If legislature fails to approve the proposal, it can then be submitted to popular vote if a further number of citizen signatures are collected.

The Commission calls for the introduction of legislation to permit indirect initiatives in Ireland and Northern Ireland that do not contravene existing rights.

- **Establish an Independent Electoral Commission in Ireland**
  Typically, Electoral Commissions are independent regulatory agencies whose remit includes impartially assisting and supervising elections and referendums at both the local and national level. Other objectives of Electoral Commissions include enforcing electoral legislation, monitoring election spending, promoting public awareness and participation, facilitating voter participation and regulating political parties. A variety of organisations, including the Referendum Commission, the Standards of Public Office Commission, the Constituency Commission and the Department of the Environment, Heritage and Local Government, are currently responsible for some of these functions in Ireland. International practice certainly suggests that democracy in Ireland would be better served if one body had an overall role in relation to improving the functioning of the electoral system and increasing participation in elections.

  The idea of an Independent Irish Electoral Commission is not new. The Referendum Commission, for one, has called for such a body. Certainly in Ireland it would be of use in promoting public participation and facilitating voter registration.

An Irish Electoral Commission could, for example:
- Provide the research to help politicians, the media, academics, and policy makers understand the nature of political engagement among certain audiences and to develop strategies and

policies in response. In the first instance, it could examine the possibility of automatic registration through PPS number and work in collaboration with the Electoral Commission (NI) to investigate the possibility of automatic registration through national insurance number. Working with the Northern Ireland branch of the UK Electoral Commission, it could examine the feasibility support for Saturday polling, and extending the franchise to 16 year olds.

- Co-operate and collaborate with the Electoral Commission in Northern Ireland on issues of research, education, awareness campaigns etc.
- Provide outreach programmes and public awareness campaigns on the democratic process in Ireland and encourage people to get involved in elections.
- Support voter education programmes, particularly in disadvantaged areas, through targeted spending and resource materials.
- Ensure that everyone has equal opportunity to vote by monitoring the physical accessibility of voting sites and mechanisms to transcend communication barriers through the provision of accessible information and facilities such as Braille, large print, and sign language in all aspects of the electoral process.
- Recommend ways in which the gross disparities in the number of elected local representatives per voter could be addressed in the interest of better local democracy.
- Monitor women and non majority group representation in political institutions and public boards.

As in the UK, it could also:
- Regulate political donations and election and referendum campaign spending.
- Publish political parties' annual accounts.
- Handle national and regional referendums.
- Report on elections and referendums.
- Review electoral law and promote best practice.
- Provide grants to eligible political parties to support their policy development work.
- Advise on issues relating to political broadcasting.

The Independent Electoral Commission should have a statutory basis and have a proven and permanent source of funding. It should be accountable to the Oireachtas[4]. Appointments to it would need to be open and transparent and should follow the process outlined in the recommendation on the Standards in Public Office Commission in chapter four.

Commission Recommendations
The Commission recommends:

- Automatic Registration through Personal Public Service (PPS) / National Insurance Number.
- Reducing the candidacy age for elections to Dáil Eireann.
- Extending the postal voting option to all, including prisioners, on the electoral register.
- Introducing electronic voting for all elections in Ireland and Northern Ireland. The Commission believes that despite the bad experience Ireland had with the first attempts at E-Voting it is a system well worth introducing for the benefits it will bring. The new e-voting system should consider innovations that permit people to vote not only at polling stations but in supermarkets, post offices, public libraries or on their personal computers or mobile phones. All sites would have to be accessible for disabled people. It is imperative that such a system is introduced in a way that promotes confidence in the integrity of the system. In Ireland, it is also essential that the system staggers the counts, which are part of Irish political culture and play a role in generating interest in politics and elections, and preserves the information provided by them.

---

4   In the UK, for example, the Electoral Commissioners were recruited through open competition which broadly followed the guidance issued by the office of the Commissioner for Public Appointments. Ministers were not involved in the selection process and the recommended candidates had to be approved of by Parliament.

    The UK Electoral Commission does not answer to a Minister. It is accountable to the speaker's committee and through them to Parliament. The speaker's committee is chaired by the speaker of the House of Commons and has to have representatives from the Government front bench, the relevant House of Commons select committee as well as a number of back benchers.

- That all political parties should be conscious of the need to be seen to be active across all sectors of Irish society. It would be detrimental to Irish democracy if people living in socially disadvantaged areas believed that their political choices are limited.
- Introducing legislation which gives homeless people, travellers and others with a transitory lifestyle the right to register using an address near a place where they 'commonly spend' their time.
- Developing new participatory structures.
- Introducing legislation in Ireland and Northern Ireland that permits proposals, which do not contravene existing rights, to come before the legislature when the necessary number of citizen signatures is gathered (indirect initiative).
- Establishing an Independent Electoral Commission in Ireland.

References

Clancy, Paula, Ian Hughes, Teresa Brannick, 2005: 'Public Perspectives in Ireland'. Democratic Audit Ireland Project, Tasc.
http://www.tascnet.ie/upload/Democratic%20Audit%20Ireland%20Survey.pdf

CSO Third Quarter 2002: Quarterly National Household Survey, Voter Participation and Abstention. Cork: CSO.

The Electoral Commission (NI), 2004: The Northern Ireland Assembly Elections 2003. Belfast: The Electoral Commission NI.

The Electoral Commission UK, May 2005: Securing the Vote. London: The Electoral Commission.

International Institute for Democracy and Electoral Assistance (IDEA) www.idea.int

Kavanagh, Adrian P., 2005: 'Bin charges disputes, personality politics, Sinn Féin and increased local election turnout: a spatial analysis of the increased electoral participation in the 2004 local elections in the Republic of Ireland'. Paper presented at the PSA annual conference 2005. http://www.psa.ac.uk/2005/pps/Kavanagh.pdf

Lijphart, Arendt, 1997: 'Unequal participation: Democracy's unresolved dilemma'. American Political Science Review 91 No.1.

Local Elections 1999: Volumes 1 & 2, Department of the Environment, Heritage and Local Government.

Local Elections 2004: Department of the Environment, Heritage and Local Government.

National Youth Federation, National Youth Poll 2004, www.nyf.ie

Northern Ireland Young Life and Times Survey 2004 (http://www.ark.ac.uk/ylt/2004)

Smith, Graham, 2005: 'Power beyond the ballot 57 democratic innovations from around the world'. A report for the Power Inquiry UK.

3 Representation

D emocratic political institutions need to be reflective of the societies in which they operate. Yet around the world, governments and parliaments rarely mirror the composition of their society and Ireland and Northern Ireland are no exception. This issue was raised with the Commission in its consultations which highlighted:

- 'Theoretically we live in a democracy but not everyone has equal access to influence the system. How can this inequality continue?'
- 'Politicians are all the same, middle aged men in suits'.
- 'Young people find politics inaccessible'.
- 'There is a shortage of women in politics because the institutions are patriarchal'.
- 'Issues which interest women are low on the agenda, and active politics is a man's world with the hours and work structures making normal family life incredibly difficult for mothers'.
- 'Barriers around women's participation are the same today as they were ten years ago. Women are very participative at the local and community level but find it difficult to make the move to the political level. Legal changes (e.g. quotas) are required'.
- 'Representation is not a women's issue. It is a democratic issue. If not addressed, half of our population will continue to be underrepresented. Positive action must be taken to encourage the participation by women in politics at all levels'.

Recognising the under-representation of all those categories of the population covered by the nine grounds of the equality legislation in Irish political institutions, the Commission, as a consequence of its consultations, has focused on gender, age and socio-economic class.

Gender

Women account for approximately 50% of Irish society yet they are deeply disadvantaged politically. Of the 166 deputies elected to the 29th Dáil, 22 of them were women (13%). Furthermore, of the 157 people who held full Ministerial positions from 1922-2002, only 9.6% of them were women (Galligan, 2005:273).

In Northern Ireland the picture is no different. The assemblies elected in 1998 and 2003 were also overwhelmingly male: 18 women were elected in the second assembly election, a modest gain on the 15 outgoing female MLAs[5]. At the Northern Ireland local government elections in June 2005, 128 women were elected (Electoral Office Northern Ireland, 2005). This accounted for 21% of the 585 successful candidates and an increase of two percentage points on the 2001 results. At the 2005 Westminster election, three women were elected out of a total of 18 MPs (one each for the DUP, the UUP and SF) and one woman, Ms de Brún, was elected to the 2004 European Parliament, alongside two male candidates. The figures for the 2005 local and Westminster elections, though miserly, do represent historic highs for women's elected representation (Wilson and Wilford: forthcoming).

Of the 166 deputies elected to the 29th Dáil, only 22 of them were women

In the June 2004 local government elections in Ireland, 122 women were elected to county councils. This accounts for 16% of the county councillors elected and was only a small increase on the 1999 figure. (http://www.qub.ac.uk/cawp/election.html).

On an international scale, Ireland's performance in terms of gender representation is quite poor, ranking in joint 63rd position in the world classification of 183 countries listed by descending order of the percentage of women in the lower or single house, as of June 2004 (http://www.ipu.org/wmn-e/classif.htm). This puts Ireland lower than the European average (17%), lower than the average for the Americas (16%), lower than the Asian average (16%) and on a par with the average for sub-Saharan Africa (13%) (http://www.ipu.org/wmn-e/classif.htm).

---

5   At the second assembly election in November 2003, 18 female MLAs were elected out of a total of 108, though this was reduced to 17 when one of them, Mary Nelis (SF), resigned her seat and was replaced by a male nominee, Raymond Macartney. (There are no by-elections for the assembly: if for any reason a seat becomes vacant, through for instance ill-health, the party of the member concerned simply nominates a replacement. Bairbre de Brún, also SF, resigned her seat following her election to the European Parliament in June 2004, and was replaced by a former MLA, Sue Ramsey).

This gender gap reveals the limited influence women have in decision-making in Ireland and, more critically, raises fundamental questions about the state of representative democracy in Ireland. This disparity in gender representation is not solely confined to the political arena but is a feature of wider Irish society. Figures from the Irish Government's draft national plan for women reveal that in 1998 women accounted for only 3% of managing directors, only 9% of secretaries general in the civil service and only 7% of High Court judges (NWCI, 2002:13). In a recent survey of the top 1,000 companies, only 0.3% of the CEO/Directors were female.

Women are also underrepresented in the memberships of Vocational Education Committees (VECs), City and County Development Boards, City and County Enterprise Boards, Regional Authorities and Assemblies, Regional Tourism Authorities and State Boards and Bodies of Public Interest. However, recent research for the Democratic Audit Ireland project suggests that gender balance is being

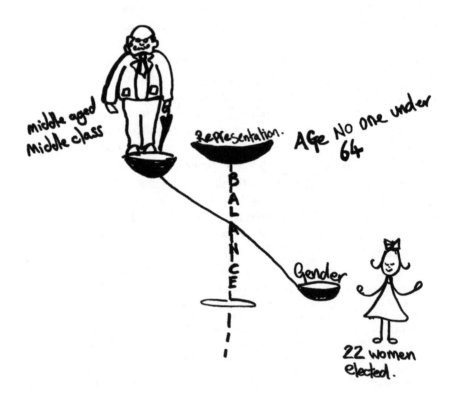

achieved on the boards of non departmental public bodies. The proportion of female to male chairs is somewhat less positive. An examination of a sample of bodies shows that 62% of them are chaired by men (Clancy and Murphy, 2005: 24). In Northern Ireland women make up just 27% of the chairs of these boards (Hinds, 2005:1).

Women in Northern Ireland fare better, proportionately, in appointments to the boards of public bodies rather than election. This is in no small measure due to the introduction of a competitive system of public appointments in the UK in the late 1990s which includes attention to gender balance. There are some 2,200 appointments to 135 public bodies, of which about 2,000 (covering 120 bodies) were the responsibility of the devolved administration (now the direct rulers), while the others remained the responsibility of the Northern Ireland Office (NIO). In the 2003 edition of *Public Bodies*, published by the Cabinet Office (2003), out of a total of 133 appointments made by the NIO, 51 were allocated to women, equivalent to 38.3 per cent and falling just below the UK government's 'national' target of 40 per cent. Before the suspension of devolution in 2002, the executive was considering a review of the arrangements for making appointments to public bodies, to ensure they were consistent with the expectations of the wider population and the needs of the devolved administration.

Within the EU, Ireland languishes at 19th place out of 25 in terms of the percentage of women in its national parliament

Measured against its fellow member states in the EU, Ireland languishes at 19th place out of 25 in terms of the percentage of women in its national parliament and compares woefully with the figures of 45%, 37% and 38%, in Sweden, Denmark and Finland respectively (www.ipu.org). Ireland also contrasts sharply with the figures of 39.5% and 50% for the devolved assemblies in Scotland and Wales (www.pol.ed.ac.uk/gcc). Crucially all of the above examples of relative success have involved the use of positive discrimination in the form of quotas or founding principles.

The Irish government has made commitments to change and improve the position of women in decision-making by signing up to the Beijing Platform for Action (1995) and the Convention on the Elimination of All Forms of Discrimination against Women (1979). Equality between women and men in all spheres is one of the fundamental principles of the EU, yet Ireland's record North and South shows evidence of deep and systematic inequality and challenges its democratic legitimacy.

The causes of this democratic deficit, in which half the population is represented by approximately one in ten TDs, are many and varied. Party selection procedures have been identified as the single most important obstacle to women's political participation (Galligan, 2005:285- 289). Other factors include:

- More limited opportunities for female candidates to build recognition and credibility.
- Family unfriendly working hours.
- Absence of childcare supports.

Party selection procedures have been identified as the single most important obstacle to women's political participation

A recent public attitude survey conducted by the Democratic Audit Ireland project in Ireland showed that 82% of respondents believe that female politicians are comparable or better than male politicians and that over 33% believe female politicians are better than men. This data reveals that the public views female politicians in a very positive light. When these figures are compared with data gathered on how women are treated as a group in Irish society, it is interesting to observe that only 2% of the respondents thought that they were treated unfairly. Twice as many respondents believed that young people were treated unfairly and five times as many people believed that the elderly received unfair treatment. Although the question was not referring explicitly to the political representation of these groups per se, the responses reflect a belief in Irish society that women are treated fairly.

The democratic deficit caused by the under-representation of women in legislatures has increasingly become a matter for attention among international bodies. Ireland has been criticised by the UN's Commission on the Status of Women for the low representation of women in elected office. The UN Commission urged the government to adopt temporary special measures such as quotas to rectify the situation. Despite this, the Irish government has firmly resisted implementing initiatives aimed at achieving substantive change (Galligan, 2005:293).

In the UK, for instance, the Sex Discrimination (Election of Candidates) Act 2000 allowed the political parties to achieve a better gender balance as it protects women-only shortlists for candidate selection in particular constituencies from potential discrimination claims. Other than the Northern Ireland Women's Coalition, whose candidates were all female (and none secured election in 2003), no party availed itself of this opportunity to promote women's representation at Stormont. Yet it was used with great effect in the Welsh assembly elections 2002, after which the Welsh assembly became the first legislative body in the world to be made up of equal numbers of men and women and to have a cabinet dominated by women. Prior to the Act, the Labour party in Scotland and Wales used the 'twinning' mechanism which paired two constituencies and asked party members to vote for one man and one women to bolster female representation.

Three strategies can be used to increase women's representation in modern democracies. These are equality rhetoric, equality promotion (positive action) and equality guarantees (positive discrimination). These strategies range from mentioning equality issues in party manifestos to the introduction of quotas. Quotas can include reserved seats in the legislature for women, legal quotas and quotas in party rules. Party quotas are the most common. Commentators note that 'women candidate quotas are now a global phenomenon' as more than 100 countries have had debates on the matter and more than 80 of them have adopted quotas of women candidates (Lovenduski, 2005:90).

women candidate quotas are now a global phenomenon

Party candidate quotas have been successful at addressing the gender gap in politics in the Scandinavian countries. Norway, Sweden, Finland and Denmark have boosted their number of female parliamentarians through quotas[6]. In Norway, by the end of the 1970s the Liberal, Socialist Left and Labour parties had adopted quotas which stipulated that at least 40% of candidates for election had to be women (NWCI, 2002:25). Similarly, in 1979 the five major political parties in Sweden introduced the 40:60 principle that is no fewer than 40% of candidates from one gender should be nominated for national, county and municipal elections. More recently, the French Government introduced a parity law to address the low levels of female political representation. In July 1999 the French Constitution was amended to include '*the law favours equal opportunities for women and men with regard to electoral mandates and electoral seats and political parties and groups shall contribute to the implementation of this principle according to the conditions determined by the law*'. A year later a law was promulgated '*with regard to equal opportunities for women and*

6   Quotas were ended in Denmark in 1996 following a significant improvement in the political representation of women (NWCI, 2002:23).

men for electoral mandates and electoral seats, commonly known as the parity law' (NWCI, 2002:23). The law requires that 50% of candidates be of each gender and covers municipal elections, regional elections, general elections, European elections, elections to the Corsican Assembly and senatorial elections. Furthermore, it penalises party lists which fail to respect the party requirement by refusing to register them and fines political parties or groups which do not select 50% of candidates of each sex for general elections (a 2% margin is allowed) (NIWC, 2002:24).

Parity law may have been effective in increasing the number of women councillors in France as the number of women councillors grew from 21.7% in 1995 to 47.5% in 2001. Yet as Lovenduski's research reveals, the parties 'followed the letter of the law' and placed women in the bottom three of the first six positions. This had an adverse impact on the number of female mayors and members of local cabinets who are selected according to the order in which they are elected. In 2001, only 6.7% of the mayors elected were female (Lovenduski, 2005:133). In the first general election to the French National Assembly after the introduction of the parity law, the number of female representatives increased to 12.3% from 10.2% in 1997. Political parties were prepared to forfeit a proportion of exchequer funding for not putting forward female candidates. Also 'women were concentrated in unwinnable constituencies' (Norris, 2004:196). As Lovenduski concludes, 'where the law provided strong sanctions it worked' (2005:133).

Arguments against candidate quotas suggest they are undemocratic as they chose candidates according to gender rather than merit. Also there are concerns they would undermine the credibility of elected female representatives.

Under representation may lead to voter apathy.

Age

The unrepresentative nature of politics may impact on voter apathy. This sentiment was echoed throughout our consultations, particularly amongst young people and their representatives who argued that young people might be disengaged from the traditional political process yet they still had a high level of interest in politics. It was also suggested that single issue politics rather than the traditional processes make it easier for youth engagement as they have a specific focus; tangible desired outcome; are not linked with political history;

are more emotive and clear cut; have a strong sense of justice/injustice; and are perceived to be more energetic and 'fun'.

Table 5. Age Profile of TDs per political party in 2002

Political Party	Number of TDs aged 44 and under	% of TDs	Number of TDs aged 30 and under	% of party's TDs
Fianna Fáil	23	28.4%	0	0
Fine Gael	8	25.6%	5	16.1%
Labour	0	0	0	0
Progressive Democrats	2	25%	0	0
Green Party	5	83.3%	0	0
Sinn Féin	1	20%	0	0
Independents	3	23%	1	7.69%

An examination of the age profile of Irish national political representatives shows that it is not representative of young people. According to the 2002 census, 21.2% of the Irish population is aged between 18 and 30, and 41.7% of the population is aged between 18 and 44. An analysis of the figures above reveals that all the parties are under-representative of these age categoies (interestingly the Green Party is over-representative of those aged between 31 and 44). The Labour Party is the least representative, not having a single TD aged 44 or under. Thirty year olds and under are, however, appallingly under-represented. Only six TDs aged 30 and under, five of whom are members of Fine Gael, were elected in 2002. This accounted for 3.6% of the total number of deputies in Dáil Éireann and reinforces young peoples' perceptions that politicians are 'old and grey'. Ironically, people aged 65 and over are also under represented in Dáil Éireann. Only five of the 166 deputies elected in the 2002 general election were aged 65 or over in the year of the election, even though this age group accounts for over 11% of the population (www.cso.ie).

The apparent lack of political will to redress the above imbalances in terms of internal party funding for measures promoting young people and women in political activity is worrying. An analysis of the amount of funding spent by each political party in these areas, as documented in the 2003 annual report of the Standards in Public Office Commission, reveals that the record of the Irish political parties in this arena is abysmal.

In 2003 neither of the two largest political parties spent any of their exchequer funding on the promotion of women in political activity. Of those parties that did allocate funding for the promotion of women in political activity, the Labour Party spent 6% of its total funding, while Sinn Féin and the Green Party spent 3.3% and 0.8% of theirs respectively. All of the main political parties, with the notable exception of the Progressive Democrats, allocated funding for the promotion of young people in political activity. The amounts spent ranged from 3.8% for Labour to 1.7% each for Fianna Fáil, Sinn Féin and the Greens.

Table 6. Spending by political parties of Exchequer funding under the Electoral Acts in 2002, as reported in 2003

Qualified Political Party	General Administration	Research, Education & Training	Policy Formulation	Co-ordination of the Activities of the Branches & Members	Promotion of Women in political activity	Promotion of Young People in political activity	Amount of total funding spent
	€	€	€	€	€	€	€
Fianna Fáil	1,124,672	3,695	60,000	709,758	Nil	(33,803)[1]	1,898,125
Fine Gael	556,275	2,997	Nil	317,634	Nil	29,399	906,305
The Labour Party	323,464	38,786	41,802	38,620	32,340	19,047	494,059
PDs	190,003	30,475	9,656	77,460	Nil	Nil	307,594
Green Party	142,288	3,604	7,032	24,907	1,443	3,101	182,375
Sinn Féin	193,416	30,676	31,300	74,753	11,445	6,074	347,664
Total[3]	2,530,118	110,233	149,790	1,243,132	45,228	57,6212 (91,424)	4,136,122

1. Figure included under "Co-ordination of the Activities of the Branches & Members".
2. Does not include the amount referred to at Note 1. Total deemed to have been incurred under this heading is €91,424.
3. Figures have been rounded to the nearest €.
(Table is taken from the 2003 Annual Report of the Standards in Public Office Commission, www.sipo.ie).

Socio-economic class

Not only are Irish politicians predominantly middle aged, they also tend to be largely middle class. Almost half (47%) of the TDs in the 29th Dáil come from the lower and higher professional classes. In Irish society as a whole, only 15% of the total population are lower and higher professionals (Galligan, 2005:287 and the 2002 census www.cso.ie). The same is true for local government in Ireland. Research conducted in 1999 revealed that the dominant occupation description of councillors was public representative as 118 Oireachtas members were elected or re-elected to their local council. 156 councillors were farmers, 66 listed their profession as teachers, 27 were Directors, 25 were publicans, 24 described themselves as housewives, 22 were managers, 14 were solicitors, five were factory workers and three were office workers (Kenny: 1999). The over repre-sentation of the higher and lower professional classes in Irish polit-ical institutions reinforces public perceptions that politics is the preserve of the educated and the wealthy. This is harmful to the health of Irish democracy as it excludes sections of Irish society from the decision-making process and reinforces perceptions within these areas/communities that politics is not for them.

Issues of representation, particularly under-representation amongst the disadvantaged and marginalised in society by virtue of disability, gender, sexual orientation, race, creed, class or age are essentially equality issues. Equality underpins democracy. Inequalities in political participation lead to inequalities in political representation which reinforces wider social inequalities and in turn deepens inequalities in political participation. (Baker, 2005:2).

Baker et al speak of equality of condition which aims to 'eliminate major inequalities altogether, or at least massively to reduce the current scale of inequality' (2004:33) and involves changing social structures. Equality of condition, they argue, is concerned with 'enabling and empowering people to exercise what might be called real choices among real options' (2004:34). This begs the question as to how this can be achieved and what can be done to level the playing field.

> *Almost half of Irish TDs come from the lower and higher professional classes.*

The Electoral System

No electoral system is perfect but some meet certain requirements better than others. In the course of its consultations the Commission found strong public support for political institutions in Ireland and Northern Ireland to be more representative of the society they serve. The Commission also noted that well publicised cases of clientelism and corruption in Irish politics had contributed to the political disillusionment of those with whom it engaged.

PR STV is the electoral system used in Ireland for general, local and European elections and in Northern Ireland for regional, local and European contests. It is not a widely used electoral system. Malta and Ireland are the only countries that use it to elect their lower houses of parliament. In contrast to the PR list systems, where voters chose between various party lists, under PR STV voters chose candidates not parties. It has been suggested that this approach fosters clientelism, means that votes tend to be cast on the basis of personality rather than political principle or ideology and can, in some cases, lead to a climate of political corruption.

> Malta and Ireland are the only countries that use PR STV to elect their lower houses of parliament.

The Commission notes that the additional member system (AMS) has emerged over the last couple of decades as the system of choice for electoral reformers internationally. Under this system, approximately one half of the seats in the legislature are allocated on a first past the post system to single seat constituencies and the rest are filled on the basis of a PR list. This produces two types of deputies, constituency deputies and deputies elected from party lists. Michael Laver's study found that if AMS was implemented in Ireland then Fianna Fáil would win most of the constituency seats and the other parties would win their seats from the PR list element of the election (1998:44). As a result, Fianna Fáil TDs would face a different set of electoral pressures to TDs of other parties. Laver concludes that 'there is no intrinsic reason why TDs from different Irish parties should not face different electoral pressures over candidate selection and constituency service. But, if a decision was made to introduce the AMS system in Ireland, it would be important for people to be aware that this is an important likely consequence' (1998:45).

This system commends itself to the Commission. Yet the Commission is aware that any move to reform the electoral system will require further research and public debate. The Commission believes that an independent electoral commission in Ireland, working in close co-operation with the Northern Ireland branch of the UK Electoral Commission, should assess the possible impact of the replacement of PR STV with AMS in both jurisdictions. In addition, the Commission suggests that any review of Ireland's electoral system should also consider the composition of the Seanad.

Commission Recommendations

The Commission calls for

- Increased spending to support the self-organisation of marginalised groups. This requires financial, training, and capacity-building supports. Targeted spending on community education programmes in disadvantaged areas would be one concrete step in developing the political capacity of marginalised groups who are limited by the inequalities that structure their lives and opportunities.
- Electoral Commission(s) to consider the replacement of PR STV with AMS for elections in Ireland and Northern Ireland.
- The introduction of obligatory gender quotas (50:50) for the candidates put forward by political parties to redress the gender imbalance in political institutions in Ireland and Northern Ireland[*].
- The introduction of family-friendly working hours in political institutions in Ireland and Northern Ireland. The Scottish parliament and the Welsh Assembly expressly adopted family friendly sitting hours. As a result, sessions rarely go beyond 6.00pm and follow school holidays.

References

Baker, John, Kathleen Lynch, Sara Cantillon and Judy Walsh, 2004: *Equality from Theory to Action*. Basingstoke: Palgrave MacMillan.

Baker John, 2005: '*Democratic strategies for reducing inequality*'. Presentation to the Democracy Commission.

Central Statistics Office. *Census 2002*, www.cso.ie

Centre for the Advancement of Women in Politics Database, Queen's University Belfast. http://www.qub.ac.uk/cawp/election.html

Clancy Paula & Murphy, Grainne, forthcoming: 'The State of Governance in Ireland: *Preliminary Analysis of Non-Departmental Public Bodies in Ireland – National Level*', work in progress, Democratic Audit Ireland Project, Tasc.

Clancy, Paula, Ian Hughes and Teresa Brannick, 2005: '*Public Perspectives on democracy in Ireland*', Democratic Audit Ireland Project, Tasc

---

[*] Within the Commission there was one dissenting member on the use of this method to redress the gender imbalance.

http://www.tascnet.ie/upload/Democratic%20Audit%20Ireland%20Survey.pdf

Electoral Office Northern Ireland (EONI), 2005: Local Government Election 5 May 2005 - Candidates Elected. Belfast: EONI

Farrell, David M., 2001: 'Electoral Systems a comparative introduction'. Hampshire: Palgrave.

Gallagher, Michael, Michael Marsh and Paul Mitchell, (eds), 2003: How Ireland Voted 2002. Basingstoke: Palgrave Macmillan.

Galligan, Yvonne, 2005: 'Women in politics' in Coakley, John and Michael Gallagher, (eds) Politics in the Republic of Ireland. Oxon: Routledge and PSAI Press.

Gender and Constitutional Change project, www.pol.ed.ac.uk/gcc

Hinds, Bronagh, 2005: 'Increasing female participation in public life' – paper presented at the RPA pathways to access and participation conference, Institute of Governance, Queen's University Belfast.

Inter Parliamentary Union database on women in politics, http://www.ipu.org/wmn-e/classif.htm.

Kenny, Liam (ed), 1999: From the ballot box to council chamber: a commentary on the local government elections. Dublin: Institute of Public Administration for the General Council of County Councils.

Lovenduski, Joni, 2005: Feminizing Politics. Cambridge: Polity Press.

McAllister, I and D.T.Studlar, 2002: 'Electoral Systems and Women's Representation: A Long-term Perspective'. Representation 39 (1).

National Women's Council of Ireland, 2002: Irish politics Jobs for the Boys! Recommendations on Increasing the Number of Women in Decision Making. Dublin: National Women's Council of Ireland.

Norris, Pippa, 2004: Electoral Engineering: voting rules and political behaviour. Cambridge: Cambridge University Press.

Reid, Liam, Female Councillor numbers continue to be low. Irish Times, 16/08/2004

Standards in public office commission, 2003. Annual report: www.sipo.ie

Wilson, Robin and Wilford, Rick, forthcoming: Democratic Audit of Northern Ireland – work in progress, Democratic Audit Ireland project. Dublin: Tasc.

Accountability and Transparency

4

I n various fora there were many issues raised about the current structures and practices of government in Ireland and a deep sense of concern with the suspension of the Assembly in Northern Ireland. The sentiments expressed to the Commission included the following:

- A belief that government in all its manifestations needs to be more accountable.
- Under-representation of significant sub-groups on public bodies is detrimental to Irish democracy. One of the complaints made to the Commission was that nominations to these bodies *are political prizes* and that they *need to be much more reflective of society*.
- *The collapse of the Northern Ireland Assembly has had a negative impact on commitment and interest in politics in Northern Ireland*.
- *Public bodies are used as a bulwark on ministerial responsibilities*.
- *there should be some form of open competition and transparency on appointment procedures*.
- *The absence of clarity in the division of roles of public bodies operating in the policy areas leads to inconsistency and a lack of transparency*.
- The Commission heard from groups who were deeply frustrated with *the power of public bodies to decide against the democratic wishes of the local authorities and the community at large*.
- A number of political representatives told the Commission that *the Dáil Committee system is useful but it is poorly understood outside the Dáil* and that *the party whip has a negative impact on government accountability*.
- *The Opposition should oblige government to discuss its plans not just its actions*.

- 'Public consultation seems to vary widely and consultations can be conducted on the whim of a civil servant or a government Minister. This is because there is no legal duty on the government to consult when preparing legislation'.
- 'There has been a dearth of green and white papers under the current government. Departments prefer to rely on consultancy studies and short consultations in order to frame legislation'.

Accountability is central to satisfying the basic democratic principle of popular control. A healthy democracy requires that governments are accountable to their citizens between elections as well as at them. It means that government and state officials are answerable to citizens, their political representatives, the media and "watch-dog" bodies/officials, for example the Comptroller and Auditor General or Ombudsman. It ensures that citizens are in a position to judge not only how well government has performed, but also its honesty, openness and effectiveness. In short, transparency and accountability are vital to democratic policy and decision-making.

In its consultations and investigations, the Commission has noted that accountability and transparency in Ireland have been weakened by:

> *A healthy democracy requires that governments are accountable to their citizens between elections as well as at them.*

1. The explosion in the number of non-departmental public bodies.
2. The increasing use of the private sector to provide essential services.
3. The absence of common boundaries in the geographical areas served by local and regional government and public bodies.
4. The growing role of the European Union.
5. Social Partnership.
6. Regulators.
7. The use of private legal firms to draft legislation.
8. The growth in the power of the executive.

1. Explosion in the number of non-departmental public bodies

The UK Nolan committee[7] defined non-departmental public bodies

---

7 Public Bodies are called Quangos (Quasi-governmental non-departmental agencies) in the UK.

as all bodies responsible for developing, managing or delivering public services or policies, or for performing public functions, under governing bodies with a plural membership of wholly or largely appointed or self-appointing persons (Hall & Weir, 1996:6).

A noticeable feature of the governmental system in Ireland has been the number of state-appointed bodies, commissions, autonomous public agencies, quasi government organisations or quasi non-government organisations, or boards (non departmental public bodies). The use of such bodies has been a feature of all governments during the 20th and 21st centuries. According to Collins and Quinlivan, the provision of state services in Ireland has traditionally been the responsibility of public bodies or agencies 'that *are neither government departments nor local authorities*' (2005:392). In 1927 Ireland had four such bodies. By 1990 this had increased to 100 (Coakley, 1999:29) and had reached 130 by the end of 1998 (Collins and Quinlivan, 2005: 392).

Research currently being conducted by the Democratic Audit Ireland project puts the number of non-departmental public bodies in Ireland at national level at approximately 500, with a further 400 operating at regional and local level. Ireland has a ratio of one public body to every 4,000 citizens in Ireland in comparison with 1: 10,000 in the United Kingdom (Clancy and Murphy, forthcoming).

More detailed data gathered suggests that up to half of those at national level and a majority of those at local level have come into existence in the past ten years. There are large variations across departments in their use of public bodies. The Department of Defence, for example, has just four non-departmental public bodies, while the Department of Education has 82. Four of the 15 Government Departments (Education and Science; Health and Children; Enterprise, Trade and Employment; and Justice, Equality and Law Reform) account for approximately 50% of all non-depart-mental public bodies (Clancy and Murphy, forthcoming).

Non-departmental public bodies are an efficient means of involving experts in specific work. They also provide an invaluable outlet for public-spirited experts in a given field to contribute to wider society. The democratic issue is how to balance the independence required by a public body to exercise its specialist expertise or make commercial decisions with the need for public accountability. As Shipan states, '*the fundamental conundrum of delegation to expert,*

In Ireland there is one public body to every 4,000 citizens. In the UK there is one public body to every 10,000 citizens.

independent agencies is that the very actions that allow for independence strike a blow to accountability, and more broadly to democratic theory, while the actions which would best guarantee accountability act to subvert independence and expertise' (2003:14).

Democratic Audit Ireland research indicates that they have been developed in an unplanned manner and in the absence of an overarching rationale or coherent system of accountability (Clancy and Murphy, forthcoming). This raises a number of issues in terms of transparency, accountability and freedom from political/elite patronage. Their sheer growth and number contributes to the degree to which modern government is opaque and impenetrable to the average citizen; to many advocacy and civil society groups; and in some cases to the officials and public servants which are charged with an oversight role. Developing a coherent and joined-up rationale for their establishment is essential.

The appointment procedures to the boards of these bodies are not always clear.

The white paper entitled Regulating Better, launched by the government in January 2004, goes some way towards achieving this. Accountability and transparency are two of the six key principles it sets out for better regulation. As part of its action programme it states that 'where new sectoral regulators are proposed, they will be established only if the requirement for a regulator can be clearly demonstrated and if the responsibility for the sector in question cannot be assigned to an existing regulator' (Regulating Better, 2004:44). It promises that the government will assess 'the possibilities for rationalisation of sectoral regulators including through the merger of existing regulators and/or through the sharing of common services' on an on-going basis. Following the white paper, a better regulation group was established and charged with reporting back to the Government regularly on the implementation of the action programme by Departments, Offices and Agencies (Regulating Better, 2004:44).

The appointment procedures to the boards of these bodies are not always clear and with appointed members it is often difficult to ascertain how citizens can render them to account. A recent example of how democratic accountability has been weakened in Ireland is the replacement of the ten regional health boards, which had a majority of public representatives as members, by the single Health Service Executive Authority whose members are all appointed by the Minister for Health and Children. The new Health Service Executive (HSE) is responsible for services that directly affect the lives of everyone in the country and which account for approximately one third of public expenditure yet the only formal line of democratic accountability is to the Dáil, a legislature which is among the weakest in any western democracy in its capacity to hold the executive to account. New legislation provides for four regional fora to facilitate exchanges of information between public representatives and officials of the HSE. However, it is not intended that these fora will be a substitute for democratic accountability.

Currently, ministers are responsible for appointing the majority of members to non-departmental public bodies. There is no clearly defined mechanism to ensure that appointments are free from undue political or other influence, or that there is an independent element in the appointments' process[8]. Although those appointed are typically of high credentials and integrity, there are, nonetheless, public perceptions and concerns that appointments to these bodies are subject to cronyism on the part of government ministers and their political parties.

In Ireland, there is little evidence that these bodies are adequately accountable to the Oireachtas.

In Ireland, there is little evidence that non-departmental public bodies are adequately accountable to the Dáil or Seanad. The absence of any formal involvement of the Oireachtas in approving appointments by Government to the boards of state agencies, an involvement that in other countries is a guarantee that the tendency of governments' patronage is balanced by the public interest is a serious shortcoming of the current system. Some of the Irish politicians who met with the Commission voiced their frustration with the growth of non-departmental public bodies and their inability to hold them to account.

The UK Democratic Audit project developed the following criteria to measure the openness and transparency of non-departmental public bodies:

- Subject to State codes of practice and ethics legislation.
- Requirements to produce annual accounts.
- Requirements to publish an annual report.

---

8   In many situations members are nominated by representative or specialist
    bodies; in others the Ministerial appointment is constrained by written
    criteria. For example, the chair of An Bord Uchtala according to section 80
    of the 1952 Adoption Act must be or have been a Judge of the Supreme
    Court, the High Court or Circuit Court, a Justice of the District Court, or is
    a barrister or solicitor of at least ten years standing.

- Disclosure of interests of appointed members of boards as well as employees.
- Subject to public right to attend Board or committee meetings
- Requirement to release reports of meetings.
- Subject to a public right to inspect agendas and minutes of meetings.
- Requirement to hold public meetings.
- Requirement to make publicly accessible a register of members interest .

(Hall and Weir, 1996:8)

The measures introduced to provide for a more effective governance of these bodies have not been sufficient.

Since the early 1990s, successive Irish governments have introduced a number of measures to provide for a more effective governance of non departmental public bodies in Ireland. These measures include Comptroller and Auditor General Act, 1993, Ethics in Public Office Act, 1995, Freedom of Information Act, 1997 and 2003, Ombudsman for Children Act, 2002 and the Code of Practice for the Governance of State Bodies 2002.

The enactment of this legislation has done much to improve the ways in which the working of non-departmental public bodies is transparent and subject to good governance practices. Yet they have not been sufficient in a democracy.

The Ethics in Public Office Act 1995 provides for the disclosure of interests of holders of certain public offices and designated directors of and persons employed in certain positions in certain of these bodies. Preliminary analysis by Clancy and Murphy suggests that just 40% of bodies were subject to this Act. In addition, their study found that the number of public bodies to which the Code of Practice for the governance of state bodies applies is unclear (forthcoming).

Another source of concern is the number of bodies which fall outside the scope of the Freedom of Information (FOI) Act and the office of the Comptroller and Auditor General. The lack of clarity around this issue, documented by the Democratic Audit Ireland research, is even more worrying. For example, only 24 agencies listed under the Department of Health are subject to FOI. Yet the Department of Health states that the Act applies to more than 70 non-departmental public bodies in the health sector. This is but one example of the confusion surrounding the application of the FOI Act. Only 32% of the public bodies assessed came under the remit of the

Comptroller and Auditor General. Other bodies may be covered by the office of the Comptroller and Auditor General if 50% or more of their budget is provided through the parent Department (Clancy and Murphy, forthcoming). That a list of the bodies subject to the FOI Act and the remit of the Comptroller and Auditor General is not readily available to the public is unacceptable.

Similarly, research to identify which non-departmental public bodies are covered by the Act revealed uncertainty and lack of clarity within the Central Unit of the Department of Finance, which is responsible for determining which agencies have FOI status, and within the FOI office itself. Often it is only when an information request is received that an agency is identified as having FOI status (Clancy and Murphy, forthcoming).

2. The increasing use of the private sector to provide essential services

The increasing use, without an agreed policy context, of the private sector to provide essential services such as hospital and nursing home care, in the absence of adequate systems of regulation and protection of vulnerable patients, raises strong concerns regarding accountability.

One example is the announcement that sites of public hospitals will be offered to private hospital developers to provide beds which will predominantly benefit those with health insurance and the professionals who treat them.

3. The absence of common boundaries in the geographical areas served by local and regional government and public bodies.

In Northern Ireland, for example, there are four health boards but five education and library boards, with different boundaries. Neither share boundaries with the 26 district councils (Wilson and Wilford, forthcoming). Attempts by the current review of public administration in Northern Ireland to achieve common boundaries risk making local government more remote by reducing the number of councils.

In Ireland, there are two regional assemblies, eight regional planning authorities, seven regional tourism boards and ten regional drugs task forces, and many other regional configurations of government services each serving different geographical areas. Each government agency uses different boundaries for the planning, organisation and delivery of services at the regional level. A county such as Roscommon can be in a number of different regions, depending more on arbitrary decisions than on the overall development of the county. The confusion of boundaries impacts negatively on accountability and transparency.

4. The growing role of the European Union.

On joining the European Economic Community (EEC) in 1973 following a referendum that hugely endorsed this move, the Oireachtas lost the 'sole and exclusive power of making laws' bestowed on it by Article 15.2.1 of the Constitution. As the Community deepened and widened, an increasing number of policy and legislative decisions were made at that level, often bypassing the Oireachtas as well as parliaments in other member states. It is worth noting that this practice was facilitated by successive governments in Ireland. The European Communities Act 1972, for example, permitted the amendment of Acts of the Oireachtas by ministerial statutory instruments. It took almost 25 years for this practice to be found unconstitutional.

Following the defeat of the first referendum to ratify the Nice Treaty, the government 'looked to enhanced parliamentary scrutiny as a means of legitimating a second referendum' (Laffan & Tonra, 2005:455). This led to the passing of legislation to establish a select committee for European Affairs.

Also after the first referendum on the Nice Treaty, the National Forum On Europe was established by the government and charged with promoting public debate on the EU, its enlargement, its future and Ireland's place in it. Its purpose is to provide a politically neutral public space within which political views of all shades on the EU and on Ireland in the EU can be put forward. Membership is limited to members of the Oireachtas. MEPs, from North and South, have the right of attendance and participation, within agreed procedures. The

Forum also has a Special Observer Pillar which includes representatives of the trade union movement and employers' and farmers' organisations, as well as voluntary and community organisations.

5. Social Partnership

Since 1987 Ireland's economic and social policy has been conducted by means of social partnership between the state and major economic and social interests. As a form of participative democracy, it enables the social partners - employers, trade unions, farmers and the community and voluntary sector - to enter discussion with government on a range of issues and to reach a consensus on policy. It is widely accepted that social partnership has played a crucial part in Ireland's recent economic and social development.

Social Partnership is a refinement of the Social Dialogue model widely used in Europe and enshrined in the Draft EU Constitution. It can be argued that the Irish model has taken the social dialogue process further than in Europe generally by including farming representative organisations and community and voluntary organisations as well as employers and unions.

It is important to realise that social partnership occupies only that space ceded to it by the government of the day. The current agreement 'Sustaining Progress', for example, had to stay within the parameters of the Fianna Fail/PD Programme for Government. Nonetheless concerns have been expressed about the process's transparency and democratic accountability. It is criticised because the social partners are not asked to debate in a public forum and, perhaps more strongly, for by passing the Oireachtas. In its consultations, the Commission heard differing views on the social partnership process. These included:

Social partnership occupies only that space ceded to it by the government of the day.

- 'Real power lies with the executive and the social partners, not with Leinster House'.
- Criticism from members of the opposition parties and government backbenchers that 'social partnership has sidelined democratically elected representatives'.
- 'The community and voluntary sector's views are not important under social partnership'.

Accountability by Shadowing

- 'The [social partnership] process has increased the community and voluntary sector's access to the institutions and included the sector's issues on agendas'.

The Commission supports the continuation of Social Partnership as a form of participatory democracy but considers that its long term sustainability requires it to be more formally connected to the political process. It acknowledges some difficulty in achieving this without compromising the right and duty of the opposition of the day to oppose government policy. Nevertheless, greater transparency and accountability of Social Partnership to the Oireachtas is desirable and would, in the view of the Commission, actually strengthen Social Partnership.

6. Regulators

In Ireland, due to the Government's privatisation policy and changes in EU law, many largely state-owned companies, in the energy and transport sectors have witnessed the transfer of regulatory responsibility from the relevant minister to independent regulators. Regulators are appointed by Government but are required to be independent of it. They are granted strong powers to regulate their industry and can perform a valuable policing function within it. They often come under criticism for lacking accountability.

By law, regulators are charged with explaining their activities each year in an annual report; have accounts audited by the State's Comptroller and Auditor General; and may be asked to appear before Dáil committees (O'Brien, 1 March 2002). In terms of the complexity of the markets in which they work, it can often be difficult to effectively hold a regulator to account as Dáil committees would need to be equipped with experts to properly scrutinise regulatory activities.

As part of its action programme the white paper *Regulating Better* states that the '*question of the capacity of the Houses of the Oireachtas and its committees to review new regulatory structures will be examined in the context of resources*' (2004:42). This paper was part of the government's response to the OECD review of regulatory reform in Ireland which recommended that the Irish government '*strengthen the accountability of sectoral regulators by building capacities for appropriate overview by Parliamentary committees, and clarify the roles of sectoral regulators and the Competition Authority to ensure a uniform competition policy in the regulated sectors*' (OECD, 2001:12).

7. The use of private legal firms to draft legislation

The government's tendency to use private legal firms to draft legislation, for example the Airports Bill, threatens transparency and democratic accountability. This practice not only directs money from the public purse into the private sector without any apparent criteria and rationale, but can also lead to conflicts of interest that could prove detrimental to Irish democracy.

8. The growth in the power of the executive

The increased power of the executive over parliament during the course of the 20th century is a feature of most established parliamentary democracies. Academics and political representatives have noted the decline in assemblies and contribute it to disciplined political parties; big government; lack of parliamentary leadership; and increase in interest group power (Heywood, 1997:311).

Comparative studies of parliamentary democracies worldwide have rated the Irish parliament as among the least powerful of legislatures (Gallagher, 2000:2). In democratic theory, parliament plays an important role making government accountable for its actions. In practice, however, the Irish parliament has little control over government and little power to defeat legislation. The dominant role of political parties and the strength of the party whip in Irish politics are the main reason for this. In a keynote speech to launch the Democratic Audit Ireland project, former Ombudsman, Kevin Murphy, noted that 'the Oireachtas has neither the capacity nor the willingness to hold the Government responsible to it as provided for in article 28.4.1 of the Constitution' (2005:3). He attributed this in the most part to TDs greater loyalty to their party than to the Dáil. This is facilitated by the strength of the party whip system and the extent of fusion between government and parliament.

> the Irish parliament has been rated as among the least powerful of legislatures.

In the Dáil, it is the norm that every TD votes in accordance with the party line. Votes against the party whip are rare and those who choose this action face expulsion from the parliamentary party. Tight party discipline is effective in providing stable government. Yet its inflexibility weakens parliamentary accountability.

Unlike other parliamentary systems, where there are some ministers who are not also MPs, all government ministers are TDs in Ireland. When compared with other parliamentary democracies, Ireland has 'complete fusion' of executive (Government) and legislature (parliament) in contrast to the 'moderate to high fusion' found in Germany and the UK, 'moderate separation' in France and Sweden and 'high separation' in the USA (Gallagher, 2000). Only two of the approximately 150 ministers since 1922 in Ireland have never been TDs, compared with an average European figure of 25% (Gallagher, 2005:237).

Consequently, there is little psychological separation between the executive and the legislature in Ireland, particularly in the minds of government backbenchers, and few TDs enter Dáil Éireann with the intention of developing a parliamentary career. Most want to be in government, not the scrutinisers of government. This is in direct contrast with countries where '*a significant number of ministers are drawn from outside parliament and where many MPs know they will never be a minister, it is inherently more likely that MPs will seek to maximise the power of "parliament" as a non-party body*' (Gallagher, 2000:6).

It would be wrong to describe Dáil Éireann as powerless. Although the initiative of making policy lies with the Government, which can by virtue of its majority and the strength of the whip system ensure all its proposals are passed, the Dáil's provisions for the scrutinising of government behaviour have improved in recent times. The Dáil has three mechanisms through which it can check the Government - debates; parliamentary questions; and committees. Of these three, the committee system, particularly since the 1997 reforms, has been described as the most effective in bringing the government to account.

The powers of the Oireachtas have been curtailed by the courts which '*in broad terms, impose powerful constraints on what political actors can do*' (Gallagher, 2000:11). In November 2001, a High Court ruling found that the '*Oireachtas did not have the power to set up enquiries that are likely to lead to findings of fact or expression of opinion adverse to the good name of individuals not belonging to the Dáil*' (Gallagher, 2005:232).

One suggestion for increasing the powers of the Dáil vis-à-vis the Government is to strengthen the committee system and to permit the committees to discuss legislation before it goes to the full parliament rather than after, as currently happens (Gallagher, 2005:238). However, it would seem that there is little political will for this as the value placed on strong government is high within Irish political culture. This was reflected in the 1996 report of the Irish Constitutional Review Group which stressed that '*concern to ensure .... checks on Government action should not fetter the ability of Government to decide and act in the public interest and should if possible, enhance that capacity, subject to full democratic check*' (Gallagher, 2000:26).

The recent controversy surrounding the illegal charging of elderly people in long-stay nursing homes highlights the weakness of the Dáil in holding the government to account and raises the issue of ministerial responsibility. Officials with the Department of Health had been aware since 1976 that there were, at the very least, difficulties with the imposition of nursing home charges. The Government did not act on the issue until 2004. It was the Dáil which eventually brought the Government to account when the matter was raised by the opposition. Following this, the Minister for Health and Children, Mary Harney, requested legal advice from the Attorney General.

The report by John Travers into the management and administration of charges for people in public long stay places exonerated all previous ministers, stating that '*no documentation was made available to demonstrate or to indicate that the minister had been fully and adequately briefed by the department on the serious nature of the issues*' (Travers, 2005: 4.66) and '*it may be considered that there have been shortcomings over the entire period since 1976 at political level on the part of ministers in not probing more strongly and assiduously the issues*' (Travers, 2005: 5.37). More worryingly, in terms of the Oireachtas's ability to hold the executive to account, the Joint Oireachtas Committee on Health and Children found that there was an '*urgent need to clarify the responsibilities of Ministers and the extent to which they can reasonably be held accountable for the actions of the Department and agencies under their charge*' (Joint Committee Report June 2005).

The need for stronger accountability mechanisms was one of the issues at the centre of the recent review of the Belfast Agreement in Northern Ireland. The ten statutory committees of the Northern Ireland assembly, created by the Agreement to shadow the Executive Departments, enjoyed significant powers to initiate primary legislation and scrutinise the expenditure, administration and policy of the Department they 'shadowed'. Each committee report was debated on the floor of the chamber. Research on their performance and on the effectiveness of the standing public accounts committee and the committee of the centre that monitored the Office of the First Minister and Deputy First Minister (OFMDFM) suggests that '*the committees found an effective role in relation to the legislative and policy activities of the executive*'. Members of the Legislative Assembly (MLAs) also made extensive use of written and oral questions to hold ministers to account but were constrained by the views of the Secretary of State on reserved matters. If the Secretary of State wished to seek members' opinions on legislative changes, he could decide to do so by referring any such proposals to the assembly by way of an ad hoc committee (Wilson and Wilford, forthcoming).

The committees were also constrained by the structure of the executive committee which took the form of a grand coalition containing members from the four main political parties. This was in keeping with nature of the Belfast Agreement which endorsed a consensual as opposed to adversarial approach to politics. Consequently, the assembly lacked a formal opposition. Concerns about accountability were expressed during the review of the Belfast Agreement and were reflected in the document published by An Taoiseach and the British Prime Minister on 8 December last which failed to win the consent of any party to its content (Wilson and Wilford, forthcoming).

Devolution provided specific mechanisms for regionally elected representatives to hold the regional executive to account. Under direct rule, regional accountability is significantly reduced. At present, law, policy and the allocation of expenditure are effectively determined by the direct rule Ministers in the Northern Ireland Office who answer directly to Westminster. Wilson and Wilford argue that 'the procedures at Westminster to deal with Northern Ireland matters are woefully inadequate' (forthcoming).

Commission Recommendations

- To make appointment procedures to the boards of non-departmental public bodies more transparent and accountable the Commission recommends the extension of the Standards in Public Office Commission's remit[*]. The Standards in Public Office Commission should be given powers to draft guidelines for appointments to the boards of non departmental public bodies. The parent Department would then be responsible for advertising positions and recruiting through open competition, while recognising the need for balance. This process should be subject to the scrutiny of the Oireachtas. Similarly the appointment of the chair of each commercial state body and of the larger non-commercial bodies should be subject to ratification by the Seanad or relevant Oireachtas committee. The Commission calls for:

- Immediate clarification of the bodies to which the Freedom of

---

[*]   One member of the Commission disagreed with this recommendation.

Information Act and the powers of the office of the Comptroller and Auditor General applies.

- Extension of the provisions of the FOI Act and the remit of the Comptroller and Auditor General to all non-departmental public bodies.

- Legislation giving the Oireachtas power to set up enquiries (at the time of writing this is in progress).

- Sufficient resources to be made available to members of Oireachtas committees to help them use, to the full extent, their powers of oversight.

- the parties and interested civic actors in Northern Ireland to get around a table, in advance of further rounds of political negotiation, to discuss 'the establishment over time of a normal, civic society, in which all individuals are considered as equals, where differences are resolved through dialogue in the public sphere and where all people are treated impartially', as outlined in the recent policy document A Shared Future by the Northern Ireland Office. This forum should be convened by a neutral broker and could ease public concerns that MLAs continue to be paid in the absence of the assembly, as well as lending a sense of direction amid the current worrying drift. Ideally, as a consequence of this forum the parties would then themselves be able to present to the Governments a position over which they had ownership, and which commanded civic endorsement, as to the way in which democratic structures in Northern Ireland can be stably re-established.

- The Government to establish common boundaries in the geographical areas served by local and regional government and public bodies in Ireland.

- Legislation to increase the scrutiny powers of the Seanad. The Commission believes that in EU affairs, Senators, working alongside the select committee for European Affairs, could be responsible for reviewing draft EU legislation of major national policy; analysing legislative and other proposals going before EU councils; and developing a medium term policy framework dealing with the opportunities and challenges facing Ireland in Europe. The Commission also endorses the Seanad sub-committee's recommendation that the Seanad, as part of the social partnership process, should:

- Analyse and review the reports (and ideally debate them with the Directors and Chairpersons of the following bodies) produced by the National Economic and Social Council (NESC), the National Economic and Social Forum (NESF), and the National Centre for Partnership and Performance (NCPP).
- Debate with the social partners, prior to negotiations, the principles that might inform the new agreement and what was achieved and outstanding from the previous agreement.
- Debate the quarterly reports on the implementation of the social partnership agreements.

• Public discussion on the diversion of money from the public purse into the private sector and the strong implications this has for accountability.

• Political parties to consider permitting more free votes.

References

Clancy, Paula & Murphy, Grainne forthcoming: 'The State of Governance in Ireland: Preliminary Analysis of Non-Departmental Public Bodies in Ireland – National Level', work in progress, Democratic Audit Ireland Project, Tasc.

Coakley, John, 1999: 'The foundations of statehood' in John Coakley and Michael Gallagher (eds), Politics in the Republic of Ireland. London: Taylor Francis.

Collins, Neil and Aodh Quinlivan, 2005: 'Multi-level governance' in John Coakley and Michael Gallagher (eds), Politics in the Republic of Ireland. London: Routledge.

Department of An Taoiseach, 2004: Regulating Better, a government white paper. Dublin: Stationery office

Gallagher, Michael, 2000: 'Parliamentary control of the executive in Ireland: non-party, inter-party, cross-party and intra-party'. Paper presented at the joint sessions of the European Consortium of Political Research in Copenhagen, April 2000.

Gallagher, Michael, 2005: 'Parliament' in John Coakley and Michael Gallagher (eds), Politics in the Republic of Ireland. London: Routledge.

Hall, Wendy and Stuart Weir, 1996: 'The untouchables. Power and Accountability in the quango state'. London: The Scarman Trust.

Heywood, Andrew, 1997: Politics. Basingstoke: MacMillan.

Joint Committee on Health and Children, June 2005: 'Report on the Report on certain issues of management and administration in the Department of Health and Children associated with the practice of charges for persons in long stay care in health board institutions and related matters'.

Laffan, Brigid and Ben Tonra, 2005: 'Europe and the international dimension' in John Coakley and Michael Gallagher (eds), Politics in the Republic of Ireland. London: Routledge.

Murphy, Kevin, 2005: 'Democracy in Ireland'. Keynote address at the launch of the Democratic Audit Ireland project.

O'Brien, Carl, 'Market Regulators have a subversive job to do'. Irish Examiner, 3 January 2002.

OECD reviews of regulatory reform 2001: 'Regulatory Reform in Ireland'. Paris: OECD.

Travers Report, March 2005: 'Report on certain issues of management and administration in the Department of Health and Children associated with the practice of charges for persons in long stay care in health board institutions and related matters'.

Seanad Éireann sub committee on Seanad Reform, 2004: 'Report on Seanad Reform'.

Shipan, Charles R, 2003: 'Independence and the Irish Environmental Protection Agency: a comparative assessment'. Dublin: Policy Institute TCD.

Wall, Martin, Mark Hennessy and John Downes, 'Report to focus on Leas Cross mortality rate'. Irish Times, 22 June 2005.

Wilson, Robin and Wilford, Rick, forthcoming: Democratic Audit of Northern Ireland – work in progress, Democratic Audit Ireland project. Dublin: Tasc.

Local Democracy

5

ocal democracy allows local citizens themselves or through their directly elected representatives to settle local affairs and permits local communities to control local services, as well as participate in the processes and responsibilities of government. It is the level of government most accessible to citizens and provides the most opportunities for participating in public affairs. For most citizens and their political representatives, local government is often their first experience of democratic institutions and systems. In this regard, local government is an important arena for the political education of citizens and their representatives.

"healthy local democracy underpins a healthy state democracy"

A variety of divergent views on local government in Ireland were shared with the Commission in its consultations. These included:

- *'Local government should have more autonomy'.*
- *'The centralisation of decision-making and the increasing powers of city and county managers undermine local democracy'.*
- *'We don't have local government in Ireland, we just have local administration'.*
- *'Local government should be protected against corruption and given proper self financing powers'.*
- *'Central management is required to take the controversial decisions and prevent clientelism'.*
- From a councillor elected in the June 2004 local elections the Commission heard that *'new councillors often face open and subtle contempt from managers and officials'.*
- *'Ireland is too small to warrant strong local government'.*

- *'We have never worked out what should be at the national, regional and local level'.*
- Submissions made to Commission highlighted petty restrictions on public access to Council meetings and lack of advance knowledge of agendas.

With these statements in mind, the Commission decided to examine local democracy and government in Ireland and Northern Ireland against models of good practice in local government elsewhere in the European Union.

Local Democracy in Ireland

Local government in Ireland consists of five elected city councils; 29 elected county councils; 75 elected town councils and five elected borough councils of which the city and county councils have been described as the 'primary units' of local government and are the providers of services (Collins & Quinlivan, 2005:387). The functions of local Government in Ireland have been classified into the eight programme groups summarised in Table 7.

Table 7. Summary of Local Government functions in Ireland

Programme Group	Title	Summary of activities/ services
1.	Housing and building	Provision of social housing, assessment of housing needs, housing strategies, dealing with homelessness, housing loans and grants, accommodation for the traveller ethnic group, voluntary housing.
2.	Roads and transportation	Road construction and maintenance, traffic management, public lighting, collection of motor taxes, taxi licensing.
3.	Water and Sewage	Water supply, waste water treatment, group water schemes.
4.	Planning and development	Adoption of development plan for area, granting or refusing planning permissions, undertaking urban or village renewal works and plans.
5.	Environmental protection	Waste collection and disposal, waste management and planning, litter prevention, the fire service and fire prevention, civil defence, pollution control, burial grounds, building safety.
6.	Recreation and amenity	Public libraries, parks and open spaces, swimming pools, recreation centres, the arts, culture, museums, galleries and other amenities.
7.	Agriculture, education, health and welfare	Making nominations to Vocational Education Committees, processing higher education grants, veterinary services.
8.	Miscellaneous services	Maintaining the register of electors for elections, financial management, rate collection, provision of animal pounds.

Source (Callanan, 2004:68)

*local government
in Ireland is
dependent on
central government
for a substantial
proportion of its
funding.*

Local government in Ireland is funded through rates on commercial properties; the local government fund[9]; central government grants; and charges for specific services e.g. bin charges. In 2000, 47% of the current expenditure of local authorities came from central government, rates accounted for 25%, and charges for services 28% (CLRAE, 2001:8).

Since the abolition of the domestic rates tax system in 1978 and agricultural rates in 1982, local government in Ireland has been dependent on central government for a substantial proportion of its funding. The loss of rates revenue significantly reduced local government's ability to generate revenue independently of central government and the decision in 1997 to abolish domestic water charges further undermined the independence of local authorities. This was reversed somewhat with the introduction of pay by weight bin charges on 1 January 2005.

Funding is not the only way in which central government exerts control over the local authorities. Other controls are administrative in the form of regulations and prescriptions or institutional/infrastructural in terms of local government access to central government decision-making processes. In 2004, the Institute of Public Administration (IPA) noted that 'instructions from central government can be so prescriptive that there is often little discretion for local implementation' (IPA, 2004: pp24-25). This mirrors the report from the Council of Europe's Congress of Local and Regional Authorities of Europe (CLRAE) in 2001 which found that 'local government is still much submitted to central government's, and in particular the Minister for the Environment and Local Government's, detailed regulations.... it is desirable that the system of detailed central government regulations be systematically reconsidered. In appropriate cases it could either be abolished or replaced by statue law' (CLRAE, 2001:15).

In summary, the relationship between central government and local government in Ireland can be described as principal and agent rather than partnership.

---

9   The Local Government fund, which consists of government grants and motor tax receipts, was established by the Local Government Act, 1998. It is financed by motor taxation and an exchequer contribution which is index linked. Most of this money can be spent on any programme, with the discretion of the council. Nonetheless, some of the funding from central government is for specific programmes (e.g. higher education grants) and can only be used for these alone.

Role of the City/County Manager

In its consultations, the Commission heard contrasting views on the role of the county/city manager in local government in Ireland. Some of those who consulted with the Commission felt that managers were given too much power at the expense of directly elected local representatives while others pointed to the role managers played in taking the difficult decisions avoided by the councillors.

Managers, appointed through the Local Appointments Commission for a seven year term, are given responsibility for executive functions (the non-reserved functions). Any local authority function that is not specifically described in law as a reserved function (responsibility of the councillor) is deemed to be an executive function (responsibility of the manager).

The powers of the councillors can be categorised as finance; legislation; political affairs; policy decisions and the control of the executive branch. Councillors can, for example, refuse to adopt the manager's estimates. The council can also overturn a manager's decision, using a Section 4 motion[10] to allow general planning permission to an individual where general criteria would indicate a refusal. Councillors also play a general supervisory role which they exercise by resolution of the elected council. Finally, a three quarters majority of the city/county council can suspend a manager and he/she can be removed from office with the consent of the Minister.

In Ireland the city/county manager's role in decision-making has removed political responsibility from councillors. This is particularly true where controversial decisions are concerned. In recent times a tendency on the part of central government to give powers to managers over certain functions, particularly those that have been locally contentious, has emerged. This is evident in the Housing (Traveller Accommodation) Act, 1998, which states that if the councillors should fail to adopt a local traveller accommodation plan then 'the manager shall by order adopt the draft accommodation programme'. Similarly, following some councils' difficulties in adopting waste management plans, the Waste Management (Amendment) Act 2001 was passed. It states that 'the duties of a local authority under this section with respect to the making of a waste management plan shall be carried out by the manager of the authority and, accordingly, the making of such a plan shall be an executive function'.

---

10   (Section 4 of the County Management Act 1955)

Although city/county managers are the only senior public servants who must account on a monthly basis for their actions and although they have a reputation for 'honesty and diligence', they are, nonetheless, unelected (Collins & Cradden, 2001:64). The absence of a professional political executive, to the extent that there is neither political leadership nor direct supervision of sectors of the local administration, means the council appears to lack influence. This has led to a democratic deficit at the local level of democracy in Ireland.

The Commission believes that this deficit can be tackled by the direct election of Mayors in Ireland. The Local Government Act 2001 provided for the direct election of county and city council mayors from 2004. This provision was repealed under the Local Government (No.2) Act 2003, in response to fears amongst TDs that party members would lose to protest candidates or local characters. A directly elected mayor with executive powers would strengthen the elected members' political and policy-making role and their involvement in local affairs. He/she through his/her leadership would also increase interest in local government and provide a strong counter balance to the manager.

There is a democratic deficit at the local level of democracy in Ireland.

Recent developments in local democracy in Ireland

There have been a number of changes to local government in Ireland since the early 1990s, some of which have endeavoured to address this deficit. The Local Government Act 1991 established eight regional authorities on which nominees from the relevant local authorities sat to monitor the implementation of EU structural fund spending and to coordinate public service policies at the regional level. The 1991 Act gave local authorities general powers of competence and abolished the *ultra vires* doctrine, which stated that a local authority had to be able to adduce precise legal authority for its action. Prior to this, Irish local authorities could only act if they had explicit legal authority to do so.

In 1997, Ireland signed the European Charter of Local Self-Government and following a successful referendum on the matter in 1999 a specific provision for local government (article 28A) was included in the Irish Constitution for the first time. The constitutional provision not only recognises the major political role of local government as part of the democratic structure of the Irish state, it also stipulates that local authorities should be directly elected and that local elections are held at least every five years. Prior to this provision, Irish local authorities had no constitutional standing. Central government also had the power to limit the functioning and financing of local authorities and to defer local elections by an Act of the Oireachtas. It frequently used its powers to postpone local elections.

Much of the legislation on local government was consolidated under the Local Government Act 2001. Yet the act fell short of prior expectations in that it 'recognised but did not increase (and in cases failed to define) the powers of local authorities'. It also failed to abolish the dual mandate which allowed politicians hold seats at both national and local levels of government (Quinn, 2003: 453). Two years, however, later the dual mandate was removed under the Local Government (No.2) Act 2003.

Recent changes in local government structures, such as those outlined in the Department of the Environment, Heritage and Local Government's 'Better Local Government' policy document, have been influenced by Ireland's experience of social partnership and have involved moves to involve civil society in local decision-making processes. In city and county councils, trade unions, and local community and voluntary sector organisations, to name but a few, have been invited to join strategic policy committees (SPCs). SPCs were set up to give councillors a more meaningful role in policy review and development and are required to draw not less than one third of membership from relevant sectoral interest groups. The full elected council remains the decision maker. When created, it was envisaged that the SPCs would enhance local democracy in a representative and participative sense by strengthening the powers of councillors and provide an opportunity for broader local participation. Research shows that on average each SPC has 12 members and that all local authorities have met the requirement that at least one third of members are drawn from sectoral interest groups with the community, voluntary and disadvantaged sector having the highest level of representation (Boyle et al, 2003:27). Since their inception it has been found that their effectiveness differs significantly across and within authorities. Two issues in particular have arisen with regard to SPCs - the range and supply of policy issues and the engagement and legitimacy of sectoral representatives.

It has been suggested that SPCs should be given the power to consider issues which have a local dimension but are outside their

"Nobody is an expert in the big policy issues. One of the arguments for democracy is that it pulls the expertise in and goes beyond it."

current brief (educational and food safety issues). In this regard, SPCs could play an important role in the process of identifying local needs in these areas and determining how the local authority could address them. The economic, social and cultural development strategies drawn up by city/county development boards, which contain representatives from local government, local development agencies, state agencies and social partnership, would be a good starting point for SPC involvement in the identification of local needs outside their current remit (Boyle et al, 2003:36).

Concerns have been expressed about the engagement and legitimacy of the sectoral representatives (Boyle et al, 2003:xi). It is argued that the process of appointment should endeavour to ensure that they are as representative as practicable and that there should be regular feedback between them and their sector. One method of increasing the participative nature of local government would be the election of delegates from popular assemblies to SPCs as in the Porto Alegre model. Public meetings could be held in each of county/city council areas at which the previous development and investment plans are reviewed. After this initial county/city wide meeting, smaller neighbourhood assemblies (these could take place in local electoral areas) could come together and draw up lists of development priorities for their locality. These could then be formally presented at the second county/city meeting. At this second meeting, delegates (members of the general public) are elected to SPCs (the number of delegates elected being proportional to the number of citizens attending the first county/city meeting), where they would work to translate neighbourhood priority lists into an overall list of development and investment priorities for the region. This would make local decision-making more transparent, participative and representative.

The chairs (elected councillors) of the SPCs, together with the chairpersons of the Council, make up the Corporate Policy Group (CPG). The CPG is intended to act as a sort of cabinet to deal with financial issues and provide a forum for discussion of policy positions affecting the council, to be agreed for submission to full council. They also co-ordinate the politics of a local authority. The CPGs should be given a more executive role in managing local affairs. This would increase the role of elected representatives with regard to local management.

Local authorities have extensive powers under the Planning and

> *Local authorities should have a statutory mandate to plan the economic, social, cultural and physical development of their areas in an integrated way.*

Development Acts to address the physical development of the areas and communities for which they are responsible. These powers include an obligation to consult extensively and provide a framework for the adoption of development plans. By contrast, the legal powers of local authorities to plan the economic, social and cultural development of their areas are weak or non-existent. The Commission believes that local authorities should have a statutory mandate to plan the economic, social, cultural and physical development of their areas and communities in an integrated way. There should be widespread consultation and all public bodies operating in the area of the local authority should be obliged to engage in the process of planning.

Local Democracy in Northern Ireland

Local authorities in Northern Ireland have weaker powers than their counterparts in Ireland. This is of particular democratic concern when the regional institutions are suspended and Northern Ireland is ruled directly from Westminster. Local Government in Northern Ireland consists of 26 district councils which are responsible for environmental services (e.g. refuse collection and disposal), regulatory services (e.g. building control) and leisure services. Local government in Northern Ireland is weaker than in the rest of the United Kingdom. Key local government functions elsewhere in the United Kingdom, such as housing, education and social services, are performed by appointed area boards in Northern Ireland.

The funding of local government in Northern Ireland also differs somewhat from the rest of the United Kingdom. In the rest of the United Kingdom, local government is funded from a central government grant and from local fees and taxes. In Northern Ireland, local government is financed by government grants, fees, charges and district rates rather than council tax.

Local government structures and functions are currently being examined as part of Northern Ireland's Review of Public Administration. The Review was set up by the Northern Ireland executive in 2002 and is charged with developing proposals to transform the way in which public services are developed, organised and delivered with a view to enhancing both political and financial accountability as well as improving efficiency and cost effectiveness.

In addition to a series of commissioned papers, the review team published a document for consultation setting out a range of options (Wilson and Wilford, forthcoming).

This paper set out five options, ranging from the most centralised to that offering most scope for local government. The 'strong local government' option quickly became the focus (Wilson and Wilford, forthcoming).This option involved giving the councils significantly greater powers, perhaps even a power of general competence, and reducing the number of public bodies delivering services accordingly. These reforms were suggested with a view to achieving common geographical boundaries as far as possible in terms of those public bodies that remained. At present in Northern Ireland, there are four health boards but five education and library boards with different boundaries. Neither share geographical boundaries with the 26 district councils (Wilson and Wilford, forthcoming).

the work of the Review of Public Administration in Northern Ireland should reflect the principles of subsidiarity and power sharing.

The number of authorities has inevitably become the largest issue in this debate. In its most recent consultation document the review has proposed three options around configurations of seven, 11 and 15 councils. The Commission supports the work of the Review of Public Administration in Northern Ireland and calls for its recommendations to reflect the principles of subsidiarity and power sharing. As far as possible the Review's recommendations should be compatible with local government structures in Ireland in order to maximise cross border co-operation.

International Good Practice

In comparison with other EU states, local government in the Ireland and Northern Ireland has a high level of control from central government, weak financial independence, a narrow range of powers and few locally elected representatives. Although they are more powerful than their Northern Irish counterparts, Irish local authorities play minor roles in health, education, public transport, and electricity and gas distribution, and have no statutory input into policing matters.

Local governments in France, Austria, Belgium and Italy have security and policing powers while personal health, family welfare services, and primary and secondary education competencies are allocated to the local, and in some instances, regional levels of government in Germany, Denmark, France, the Netherlands and Austria, to name but a few (Local Government Reorganisation and Reform, Government of Ireland, 1991).

Table 8 outlines the tier(s) of government involved in seven policy areas across 15 West European states. In Denmark, for example, local governments have extensive responsibilities in the education and health sectors. They manage school facilities and hospitals, as well as pay teaching staff and private sector health practitioners. Swedish local governments have similar responsibilities in the health and education sectors. In Finland, these education services are provided by the municipalities who also manage hospitals and care centres. Danish municipalities care for the elderly, the needy, kindergartens and most social welfare services such as the payment of old age pensions and family allowances (Dexia, 2004: 28). Interestingly, in all three countries, local governments can set the tax rate for local personal income tax. However, in Denmark and Sweden, the government can cap the tax rate when it believes that taxpayers are being excessively taxed (Dexia, 2004:37).

Table 8. Selected functions by tier of government in Western Europe

	Education (prim, sec.)	Housing	Health/ Hospitals	Welfare	Refuse	Leisure	Fire
Belgium	PM	RM	PM	MP	M	RMP	M
Denmark	C	CM	C	CM	M	SCM	M
Finland	M	M	M	SM	M	M	SRM
France	N (DM)	M	S	MD	M	SDM	M
Greece	N	N	N	NM	M	NM	N
Germany	SM	SM	C	SM	M	SM	M
Ireland	N	CB	N	N	CM	M	CM
Italy	P	PM	R	RPM	PM	RPM	M
Netherlands	M	PM	PM	M	M	PM	M
Norway	CM	M	C	M	M	M	M
Portugal	N	N	N	N	NM	NM	NM
Spain	PM	M	SRM	RM	PM	NRPM	NRM
Sweden	M	M	C	M	M	MC	M
Switzerland	CAM	M	CAM	M	M	CAM	CA
UK	(CM)	M	N	NC	CM	CM	CM

Key: C=county; M=municipal; N=national; S=state; R=regions; P = provincial; D = department; CA = canton; ( ) indicates local control but highly centralised.

Source: (John, 2001:36)

Analysing this table, it can be deduced that responsibility for the education (primary and secondary) sector is allocated at the sub-national level, be it provincial, municipal, state, regional or county in 11 of the 15 countries listed. The same is true for both the health/hospital and welfare sectors. If a league table were drawn from this, it would show that Ireland comes third, behind Greece and Portugal in terms of the power of central government in these seven sectors across 15 countries.

Having assessed Irish local government's powers from a comparative West European perspective, the Commission wishes to start a debate on the future development of local government in Ireland by asking what is the optimum level of government for given competencies. This will involve an analysis of good international practice in the division of powers among various levels of government and a rational consideration of what activities are best carried out at which levels of authority (the real meaning of subsidiarity). In this regard the Commission echoes a question posed in the Barrington report, '.. *does the current distribution of functions as between local government and other central public agencies give the best use of public resources and level of service, taking account of cost, social and other relevant factors?*' (1991:13).

what is the optimum level of government for given competencies?

In terms of good international practice, there is a growing movement to define local self-governance as a *universal right*. International organizations and multilateral groups such as the EU, the Council of Europe, International Union of Local Authorities (IULA) and the UN Centre for Human Settlements (Habitat) have adopted standards for national governments 'to *devolve decision-making to the level closest to the people as a means of giving meaning to democratic principles*' (IDEA, 2001: 21-26).

One such standard is the Council of Europe's European Charter of Local Self Government (1985) which Ireland signed in October 1997 and ratified in May 2002. Article 3 of the Charter states that '*local self-government denotes the right and the ability of local authorities, within the limits of the law, to regulate and manage a substantial share of public affairs under their own responsibility and in the interests of the local population*'.

Although it does not specify what it means by a 'substantial share' of public affairs, the Charter does recognise the importance of the subsidiarity, as reflected in Article 4 which states that as '*public responsibilities shall generally be exercised, in preference, by those authorities which are closest to the citizen. Allocation of responsibility to another authority should weigh up the extent and nature of the task and requirements of efficiency and economy*'.

The principle of subsidiarity, that public services should be devolved to the lowest practicable level at which they can be discharged efficiently and effectively, is one of the cornerstones of EU governance and should be the general rule of thumb for the allocation of powers across levels of government.

This begs the question as to how the principle of subsidiarity can be best applied in Ireland, North and South. Certainly from our analysis it can be concluded that what we have at present is at best a minimal interpretation of the principle.

Our consideration of the good practice in the allocation of powers across levels of government also refers to Anwar Shah's framework for the assignment of expenditure responsibilities across the various levels of government in terms of policy, standards and oversight; provision/administration; and production distribution. According to Shah's analysis, local government should have policy standards and oversight; provision/administration; and production/distribution powers in the following sectors: environment; education, health and social welfare; highways; parks and recreation; police; and water, sewer, refuse and fire protection.

Table 9. Representative Assignment of Expenditure Responsibilities

Function	Policy, Standards & oversight	Provision/ Administration	Production/ Distribution	Comments
Interregional & international conflicts resolution	U	U	N, P	Benefits and costs international in scope
External trade	U	U,N,S	P	Benefits and costs international in scope
Telecommunications	U,N	P	P	National regulation not feasible
Financial Transactions	U,N	P	P	National regulation not feasible
Environment	U,N,S,L	U,N,S,L	N,S,L,P	Externalities of global, national, state and local scope
Foreign Direct Investment	N,L	L	P	Local infrastructure is critical
Defence	N	N	N, P	Benefits & costs national in scope
Foreign Affairs	N	N	N	Benefits & costs national in scope

continued overleaf

Monetary policy, currency, banking	U, ICB	ICB	ICB, P	Independence from all levels essential. Some international role for common discipline
Interstate commerce	Constitution, N	N	P	Constitutional safeguards important for factors and goods mobility
Immigration	U, N	N	N	U due to forced exit
Transfer payments	N	N	N	Redistribution
Criminal & civil law	N	N	N	Rule of law, a national concern
Industrial policy	N	N	P	To avoid beggar thy neighbour policies
Regulation	N	N,S,L	N,S,L,P	Internal common market
Fiscal policy	N	N,S,L	N,S,L,P	Coordination is possible
Natural resources	N	N,S, L	N,S,L,P	Promotes regional e quity and internal common market
Education, Health & Social welfare	N,S,L	S,L	S,L,P	Transfers in kind
Highways	N,S,L	N,S,L	S,L,P	Benefits and costs of various roads vary in scope
Parks & Recreation	N,S,L	N,S,L	N,S,L,P	Benefits and costs may vary in scope
Police	S,L	S,L	S,L	Primarily local benefits
Water, sewer, refuse, fire protection	L	L	L,P	Primarily local benefits

Note: U is supranational responsibility, ICB is independent central bank, N is national government, S is state/provincial government, L is local government and P is non-government sectors/civil society. Source: Shah 2004

Lessons for local democracy in Ireland and Northern Ireland?

The Commission favours devolving powers from the centre in these policy areas and calls for debate and research into what is the most appropriate level for revenue raising and for the delivery of services. Certain powers could be devolved to regional rather than local authorities. In Ireland, the creation of a regional level of government has been in response to the distribution of EU structural funds. At present, members of the regional authorities and the two regional assemblies – Border Midland Western and Southern and Eastern, are not directly elected but are nominated from the constituent local authorities. In terms of their functions, regional authorities are limited to monitoring the implementation of EU structural fund spending in their area and co-ordinating public service policies at the regional level. They have little or no statutory powers. In this regard, regional government in Ireland is out of line with the rest of Europe.

Many government activities take place at regional level. As pointed out in a previous section, there are no agreed regional boundaries for government activities. Ireland is almost unique in western Europe in not developing a coherent, integrated and democratically controlled level of government at regional level. The argument that Ireland is too small for tiers of government does not hold up in the face of the existence of activities of so many bodies at regional level. What is lacking is an effective means of integrating these activities and making them subject to democratic accountability. The role of regional government is to integrate government activities that are 'too big' for local authorities but 'too small' for national government. The greater Dublin area is an obvious example where there is a need to integrate policies at regional level to provide solutions to problems of transport, waste management, urban sprawl, crime and health service provision. The same case can be made for the other regions of the country. Each region should have a directly elected assembly of people elected with a mandate to address regional issues – indirect election of local authority representatives is a form of dual mandate that does not necessarily work in the interests of regional government. Regional authorities should have shared revenue raising powers with central and local government, without necessarily raising the overall level of taxation.

Within the subsidiarity principle, as outlined in the Charter on Local Self-Government, emphasis is laid on efficiency and economy. The Commission agrees with the Congress on Local and Regional Authorities in Europe that the devolution of greater powers to Irish and Northern Irish local authorities needs to be 'realistic' and 'gradual'. While there have been significant reforms in local government in the last decade or two, we have not witnessed a devolution of powers or any great increase in local democracy.

The Commission stresses that devolution of powers to the local or regional levels of government must be done in tandem with decentralization of revenue raising powers. Devolution of power can

The role of regional government is to integrate government activities that are 'too big' for local authorities but 'too small' for national government.

only be effective if it is accompanied by some measure of devolution of tax-raising functions to the same local level. A link between spending and raising money is required to promote responsibility and accountability. Currently there is a disconnection in the public mind between the receipt/use of public services and the payment for them. Coupling the devolution of powers with the decentralisation of revenue raising would also increase transparency by making the link between taxation and spending clear. A progressive local tax regime, which would not pose additional burdens on the disadvantaged, could be used to fund local services. A local property tax would be a possible option. Equalisation across areas that are disadvantaged due to their peripheral status etc. would be necessary. The Commission notes that the Irish Government's review of local government financing has been asked to 'consider the potential for rationalisation of expenditure and propose options for revised arrangements for the funding of local authorities and carry out an in depth examination of these funding options' and awaits its recommendations. It recognises, however, that the review's remit does not extend to examining the appropriate locality for revenue raising and for the delivery of services.

Devolution of power needs to be accompanied by decentralisation of revenue raising

Successive Irish governments may have signed up to the subsidiarity principle in EU treaties and the European Charter on Local Self-Government yet no mention was made of it in the Local Government Act 2001. This questions the willingness of Irish Governments to apply the principle in practice. In this light, it is interesting to repeat Garret FitzGerald's thoughts on this, 'my own experience has led me to believe that, contrary to popular belief, our failure to address seriously the need to devolve authority to local bodies lies as much in successive governments' still-remembered unhappy experiences of past local authority misconduct as in an active desire by central government to retain power for its own sake' (FitzGerald, 2003: 71).

One of the arguments forwarded by those with whom the Commission consulted for maintaining strong central government at the expense of local democracy is that Ireland is, by European standards, one of the less densely populated countries. It has a population density of 55 persons per square kilometre, the EU average is 117 (www.cso.ie). In addition, Irish towns and cities tend to be smaller and more widely separated than elsewhere in Europe. Approximately 60% of the Irish population live in urban areas. These factors mean that the cost of providing and operating a satisfactory infrastructure can be great.

Yet there are West European countries with lower population densities that successfully apply the subsidiarity principle, particularly in their health and education sectors. In Finland, for example, there are 17 persons per square kilometre and 63% of the population live in urban areas (www.ktl.fi). Sweden also has a low population density, 22 persons per square kilometre, but a higher urbanization figure as 83% of Swedes live in cities/towns. Finally, Norway is the most sparsely populated of the Scandinavian countries with a population density of 14 people per square kilometre but has 74% of this population concentrated in urban areas.

Not only do local authorities in Ireland and Northern Ireland have less power than their West European neighbours, they also have fewer representatives. In Ireland there are 42,000 constituents per council while in Northern Ireland this figure is much higher at 60,510. These figures are in marked contrast to many of our fellow EU member states. For instance, in France there are 1,580 constituents per council, while in Germany there are 4,925. In Denmark, a country of similar population size to Ireland, this figure is 18,760 (Carmichael, 2002:11). Northern Ireland and Ireland's high number of constituents per council can impact negatively on experiences of local democracy to the extent that it makes local government 'remote from the people and is among the factors reducing the likelihood of participation' (Quinn, 2003:451).

Table 10.

Country	Population per council
France	1,580
Iceland	1,330
Germany	4,925
Italy	7,130
Norway	9,000
Spain	4,930
Sweden	30,040
Belgium	16,960
Denmark	18,760
Portugal	32,300
Ireland	42,000
UK	118,400
- England	119,850
- Scotland	156,205
- Wales	127,812
- Northern Ireland	60,510

Source: Carmichael, 2002:11

Furthermore, in Ireland there is no consistency in the number of electors to councillor across the county and city councils. For example, there are 1,117 electors per councillor in Leitrim county council compared with 5, 784 electors per councillor in Cork county council. The situation is no different for city councils. Dublin city council has 6,717 electors per councillor while in Galway city council the ratio is 2,955 electors to one councillor. Inequality in the value of an elector's vote in elections to Dáil Éireann is expressly forbidden by the Irish Constitution which in Article 16.2.3 states ' *the ratio between the number of members to be elected at any time for each constituency, as ascertained at the last preceding census, shall so far as it is practicable, be the same throughout the country*'. This provision does not apply directly to local elections. However, the disparities in the ratio of electorate to councillor across constituencies are clearly contrary to the spirit of the Constitution which asserts that '*all citizens shall as human persons be held equal before the law*'. In contradicting the principle of political equality these disparities are, in every respect, undemocratic and need to be addressed immediately.

Commission Recommendations

The Commission wishes to restate the case for strong local government and the role of democratically elected councillors within it. To this end it calls for:

- Research and public debate into the most appropriate level for revenue raising and for the planning, organisation and delivery of public services.
- Central government to devolve more powers from the centre to local government. The Commission stresses that this must be done in tandem with decentralization of revenue raising powers. Coupling the devolution of powers with the decentralisation of revenue raising would also increase transparency by making the link between taxation and spending clear. A progressive local tax regime, which would not pose additional burdens on the disadvantaged, could be used to fund local services[*]. Equalisation across areas that are disadvantaged due to their peripheral status etc. would be necessary.

---

[*]   One member of the Commission disagreed with this recommendation.

- The election of delegates from popular assemblies to SPCs to enhance the participatory structures of local democracy in Ireland.
- Local authorities should have a statutory role for the overall development of their areas. They should, for example, be given powers to engage in a consultation process to formulate a development plan that covers the economic, social and cultural development of their areas and communities, similar to the powers they play in relation to physical planning. SPCs should play a key role in developing such integrated plans.
- CPGs to be provided with a more executive role in managing local affairs.
- The direct election of Mayors to local authorities in Ireland.
- The Review of Public Administration in Northern Ireland to reflect the principles of subsidiarity and power sharing in its recommendations. As far as possible the Review's recommendations should be compatible with local government structures in Ireland in order to maximise cross border co-operation.
- The introduction of legislation to place a cap on the spending of candidates in local elections. The Electoral Act of 1997 introduced a new system for controlling and limiting election expenditure by political parties and candidates in Ireland for elections to Dáil Éireann, the European Parliament and to the office of President. No provisions were made for local elections. Under the Local Elections (Disclosure and Expenditure) Act 1999, all candidates have to provide local authorities with details of expenditure incurred in the time between the Government issuing the polling day order and the actual polling day, covering a period of about four weeks. They also have to make returns on donations received. In their analysis of spending by candidates in the 1999 local elections, Michael Marsh and Kenneth Benoit discovered that spending matters, as the candidates who spent a larger share in their districts won a larger share of the district vote (2002:17). This is undemocratic as it favours political parties and/or individuals with or with access to large amounts of money.
- Central Government to charge the Constituency Commission with revising the boundaries at the local authority level to ensure greater balance in the number of electors to councillor across the county and city councils.

References

Advisory Expert Committee, 1991: *Local Government Reorganisation and Reform*. Dublin: Government publications.

Boyle, Richard, Peter C. Humphreys, Orla O'Donnell, Joanna O'Riordan and Timonen Virpi Timonen, 2003: *Changing local government: a review of the local government modernisation programme*. Dublin: Institute of Public Administration.

Callanan, Mark, 2004: 'Local and Regional government in transition' in Neil Collins and Terry Cradden (eds), *Political Issues in Ireland Today*. Manchester: Manchester University Press.

Carmichael, Paul, 2002: *Review of Local Administration briefing paper on multi-level governance* http://www.rpani.gov.uk/multilevel.pdf.

Central Statistics Office www.cso.ie

Collins, Neil and Terry Cradden, 2001: *Irish Politics Today*. Manchester: Manchester University Press.

Collins, Neil and Aodh Quinlivan, 2005: 'Multi-level governance' in John Coakley and Michael Gallagher (eds), *Politics in the Republic of Ireland*. London: Routledge.

Congress of Local and Regional Authorities of Europe, 2001: *Report on Local Democracy in Ireland*. Strasbourg: Council of Europe.

Dexia, 2004: *Local Finance in the twenty-five countries of the European Union*. Paris: Dexia editions.

FitzGerald, Garret, 2003: *Reflections on the Irish State*. Dublin: Irish Academic Press.

Housing (Traveller Accommodation) Act 1998

IPA (Institute of Public Administration), 2004: *Review of the Operation of Strategic Policy Committees*. Dublin: Institute of Public Administration.

John, Peter, 2001: *Local Governance in Western Europe*. London: Sage Publications.

Local Government Act 2001

Marsh, Michael and Ken Benoit, 2002: 'Campaign spending in the local government elections of 1999'. Paper presented at the annual conference of the PSAI.

Muintir na Tire/Institute of Public Administration, Towards a New Democracy? – Implications of Local Government Reform 1985

National Public Health Institute of Finland www.ktl.fi

Quinn, Brid, 2003: 'Irish Local Government in a comparative context' in 'Reform in Irish local Government' in Callanan, Mark and Justin F. Keogan, (eds), *Local Government in Ireland Inside Out*. Dublin: Institute of Public Administration.

Shah, Anwar, 2004: *Fiscal Decentralization in Developing and Transition Economies*. Washington: World Bank.

Sisk, Timothy D. (ed), 2001: *Democracy at the local level. International IDEAs handbook on participation, representation, conflict management and governance*. Sweden: IDEA.

Waste Management (amendment) Act 2001

Wilson, Robin and Wilford, Rick, forthcoming: Democratic Audit of Northern Ireland – work in progress, Democratic Audit Ireland project. Dublin: Tasc.

Media

6

The central role of the media in safeguarding Irish democracy was highlighted in recent Democratic Audit Ireland survey results where respondents placed the media in third position after the 'people at election times' and 'opposition parties/ independent TDs' in holding government to account (Clancy et al: 2005). Moreover, across all age groups the media were listed as the group which made the most impact on people's everyday lives (Clancy et al: 2005).

A free, diverse and vibrant media lie at the heart of a healthy democracy.

In its consultations, the Commission heard:
- *'The lack of diversity of ownership in the print media in Ireland is a threat to Irish democracy'.*
- *'No government has the guts to take on the concentration of media ownership in Ireland'.*
- *'Public service broadcasting is under threat'.*
- *'Media in Ireland are not always impartial'.*
- From politicians that *'media fail to give good coverage to Dáil debates and the activities of Dáil committees'* and that there is a tendency in the media to *'focus on personalities rather than policies'.*

A free, diverse and vibrant media lie at the heart of a healthy democratic society. By disseminating information on the actions of Government into the public domain, the media not only report on matters of public interest but act as a watchdog over Government.

The media in Ireland have been constrained in their ability to act as watchdog by out-dated libel laws and recent amendments to the Freedom of Information Act.

The National Newspapers of Ireland (NNI), for one, argue that Irish defamation laws are more restrictive than the laws pertaining in many other developed democracies. These are currently under review in a draft Bill proposed by the Minister for Justice Equality and Law Reform Michael McDowell, which also proposes to set up a statutory but independently appointed press council and ombudsman. Concerns were expressed at cabinet level that amendments to defamation law were not being accompanied by the introduction of privacy legislation. At the time of writing it is not clear whether the publication and the passage of this Bill through the Oireachtas will be delayed to consider the need for privacy legislation.

The introduction of Freedom of Information legislation in 1997 gave Irish citizens a legal right to access information held by government departments and public bodies and was extremely important to journalists. Yet in April 2003 an amendment to it limited public access to public records[11]. Government papers (the definition of which was extended under the second act) cannot be accessed before it is ten years old (instead of five, previously) and the authorities are allowed to deny or not confirm, the existence of confidential documents. One of the effects of the 2003 amendment to the Freedom of Information act was to roll back on the ease with which journalists could access such information. Kinsella argues that the amendments 'led to a collapse in journalistic requests for public records', which fell from almost 2,400 in 2003 to fewer than 900 in 2004 (Kinsella, 2005:13).

Following information gathered from written submissions and public consultations, the Commission identified the following as the challenges that need to be addressed:

- Lack of diversity in media ownership.
- The role of the public service broadcaster, RTE.
- Media and politics.
- Absence of press regulation.

---

11   An individual now has to pay 15 euros to seek permission to look at government and court documents, including minutes and internal departmental communications deemed to be of public interest. An appeal against refusal costs 75 euros, whatever the result of the appeal.

Concentration of Media Ownership

Diversity of information and perspectives is necessary within a healthy democracy to inform citizens of the choices available to them across policy areas and political parties. Diversity requires 'competition between ideas, competition between versions of reality, and between media enterprises and products' (Kinsella, 2005:4).

As noted above, concerns have been expressed in Ireland in recent years that this diversity of views has been undermined by the concentration of media ownership.

The press in Ireland consists of four national dailies and two national evening newspapers, five national Sunday newspapers, around 50 regional and 12 local newspapers. Roughly 600,000 national newspapers and 650,000 regional newspapers are sold in Ireland each day and week respectively (www.ejc.nl/jr/emland/ireland.html). Following a long period of stagnation which lasted well into the 1980s, rationalisation and acquisition in the Irish regional newspaper market is now a clear trend. In 1993, there were 53 different companies controlling 87% of regional newspapers, since then there has been huge rationalisation (Horgan, 2001a:174).

Independent News and Media PLC is the dominant actor in the Irish newspaper industry; around 80% of Irish newspapers sold in Ireland in 2001 were sold by companies which are fully or partially owned by Independent newspapers. The group publishes five leading national newspapers, 12 regional papers and owns the Belfast Telegraph group, the largest newspaper publisher in Northern Ireland (Oliver, Irish Times: 24 June 2005).

Thomas Crosbie Holdings, another heavy hitter in the Irish newspaper industry, has two national titles, eight regional titles and shareholdings in two radio stations (Oliver, Irish Times: 24 June 2005).

More recently Johnston press, the fourth largest publisher of local and regional newspapers in the UK, bought out Scottish Radio Holdings. Johnston Press now owns six regional titles in the Irish market.

Finally, other players in the print media market in Ireland include the Leinster Leader Group, Dunfermline Press, the Alpha Newspaper Group and the 3i Group plc which own seven, three, five and three regional titles respectively (Oliver, Irish Times: 24 June 2005).

Table 11. Summary of title ownership in Ireland

Group	National titles	Regional titles	Local radio
Independent News and Media plc	Irish Independent The Star (daily and Sunday version) The Evening Herald The Sunday Independent The Sunday World 29.9% of the Sunday Tribune	The Kerryman The Corkman The Wexford People The Wicklow People The Bray People The Enniscorthy Guardian The Carlow People The Gorey Guardian The New Ross Standard The Fingal Independent The Drogheda Independent he Dundalk Argus	
Thomas Crosbie Holdings	The Irish Examiner The Sunday Business Post	The Evening Echo Waterford News and Star The Western Post The Sligo Weekender The Kingdom The Newry and Down Democrat The Nationalist and Leinster Times The Roscommon Herald	Midwest Radio (shareholding) Red FM Cork (shareholding)
Johnston Press	The Kilkenny People The Longford Leader The Leitrim Observer The Tipperary Star Leinster Leader		
The Limerick Leader	The Leinster Leader The Leinster Express The Offaly Express The Dundalk Democrat The Limerick Chronicle The Tallaght Echo		
Dunfermline Press	The Meath Chronicle The Anglo-Celt Cavan The Westmeath Examiner Group		
Alpha Newspaper Group	The Midland Tribune The Roscommon Champion The Longford News The Tullamore Tribune The Athlone Voice		
3i group plc	The Derry & Donegal News The Donegal Democrat The Belfast Newsletter		

Source: (Oliver, Irish Times, 24 June 2005) and (Browne, Village, 24-30 June 2005)

The Irish Government and the Irish Competition Authority have conducted reviews into the concentration of press ownership. The Commission on the Newspaper Industry, established in 1995 by the then Minister for Enterprise and Employment Richard Bruton after the collapse of the Irish Press, reported that ' *the Commission is satisfied that there is in the industry generally a sufficient plurality of ownership and of title to maintain adequate diversity of editorial viewpoint and of cultural content*' (1996:30).

Despite this conclusion, fundamental concerns remain. Horgan, summing up the position, says, '*the print media in Ireland, in which one organisation at present has an overweening role, is (partly because of this fact) subject to forces which limit its agenda, impoverish it culturally and render it more vulnerable to external forces, both commercial and ideological*' (2001b:54). This raises legitimate concerns about impartiality of Irish media in their examination of Government and big business. According to Horgan all of these factors have an '*inevitable effect, not only on the choice of topics deemed suitable for treatment, but often on the treatment of these topics as well* (2001b:52). The way in which the news is reported and commented on by individual journalists cannot be divorced from the political or commercial interests of the newspaper for which they write.

The Commission on the Newspaper Industry also noted that it 'would be concerned that any further reduction of titles or increase in concentration of ownership in the indigenous industry could severely curtail the diversity requisite to maintain a vigorous democracy' (1996:34).

When it presented its report in 1996 Independent Newspapers plc owned five Irish national titles (Irish Independent, Sunday Independent, Evening Herald, Sunday World and had a 50/50 joint venture with United Newspapers for The Star) and ten Irish local weekly newspaper titles.

Ireland has 54 radio stations licensed by the Broadcasting Commission of Ireland (BCI). It has five national stations, four operated by the public service broadcaster RTE (Radio 1, 2FM, Lyric FM and Raidío na Gaeltachta) and one commercial station (Today FM). Local/regional radio is strong in Ireland. Listenership figures for January to December 2004 show that 55% of the population listened to any local/regional station compared with figures of 27% for RTE Radio 1 and 24% for 2FM (http://www.bci.ie/listen_figures).

The main players in the local/regional radio market are Emap Plc; Denis O'Brien's Communicorp Ltd; UTV; and Thomas Crosbie Holdings.

Table 12. Summary of Private ownership of Radio Stations

Emap Plc	Communicorp Ltd	UTV	Thomas Crosbie Holdings
Highland Radio	98FM	LM FM Dundalk	Midwest Radio (shareholding)
Today FM	Spin 103	Q102 FM	Red FM (shareholding)
FM104 Dublin	Newstalk (majority shareholding)	Limerick Live 95FM	
	East Coast FM (shareholding)	Cork 96 and 103 FM	

(Oliver, Irish Times: 24 June 2005)

"Unlike the no holds barred world of regional and local newspapers, the Government (via its main regulator) appears a little squeamish about any one company building up an unhealthy presence in the radio sector" (Oliver, Irish Times, 24 June 2005). Earlier in 2005 the BCI imposed a cap on ownership and control of the radio sector. Consequently, no one company can own and control more than 17.9% of the sector. The BCI is also in the process of reviewing its whole policy in this area.

Public Service Broadcasting

It is widely agreed that an impartial, informative and accessible public broadcasting service is imperative in a democratic society. Lord John Reith, the BBC's first director general, described public service broadcasting as *'the voice of the nation'* with a duty to *'educate, inform and entertain'* (Halligan, 2002:60). Joe Lee states that public service broadcasting *'ought to be to provide a forum conducive to fostering a tradition of vigorous, open, pluralistic debate'* (1997:10-11). The challenge is how to harness the potential of the media, particularly the public service broadcaster, to enhance democracy.

According to Ursula Halligan, public service broadcasting contains a loose set of principles which are:

- to be funded either entirely or via some element of public finance;
- to reach everyone;
- to fortify democracy by informing and educating citizens and by providing programmes for minorities;
- to promote national identity;
- to be independent from vested interests including the government of the day;
- to make programmes that appeal to a wide range of tastes;
- to be accountable to public and not to market forces (2002:60-61).

RTE, the Irish public service broadcaster, is financed from licence fees and commercial advertising and has a public service remit to *'provide a comprehensive range of programmes in the Irish and English languages that reflect the cultural diversity of the whole island of Ireland and include, both on television and radio, programmes that entertain, inform and educate, provide coverage of sporting, religious and cultural activities and cater for the expectations of the community generally as well as members of the community with special or minority interests and which, in every case, respect human dignity'* (Broadcasting Act 2001).

In a paper prepared for the Commission, Patrick Kinsella argues that the greatest challenge faced by Ireland's public service broadcaster at present is the manner in which private interests are attempting to redefine it as a certain type of programming rather than as a service (2005:7). This narrow view advocates putting public money into a fund from which any broadcaster could apply for a

The challenge is how to harness the potential of the media, particularly the public service broadcaster, to enhance democracy.

subsidy which via open competition would allow independent producers 'provide a superior product or more cost effective use of public resources' (Kinsella: 2005:8). This is what has occurred with the creation of the Broadcasting Commission of Ireland which has been charged by statutory provision with developing a scheme for the distribution of 5% of the TV licence revenue to assist the production of TV and radio programmes under a number of headings. This has not been a positive move for public service broadcasting in Ireland. The Commission agrees with Patrick Kinsella that Ireland's public service broadcaster needs to be independent and financially strong. If RTE was weakened, we could face erosion of public space where public affairs would be moved elsewhere in the schedule or removed altogether. The Commission contends that the exclusively public service broadcasting role for RTE should be reinforced and protected against any political interference by the government of the day.

Media and politics

The commonly held perspective on the role of the media in politics is that it should facilitate individual participation in collective self-government. It should do this through widespread provision of information which allows for better decision making. Yet this does not seem to be the case. After the 2001 UK general election, a study of television coverage found that:

- there was too much coverage of the election;
- the overall coverage was predominantly negative in tone and content;
- there was too much focus on the leaders and their personalities and the campaign process (Electoral Commission, 2002:55).

Analysis of media coverage of the 2001 UK general election by the Loughborough University Communication Research Centre discovered that 62% of the election items in the first week of the campaign focused on the electoral process itself rather than policies (Golding et al, The Guardian: May 2001). By the end of the campaign, 37% of news items concentrated on the election process. This meant that the campaign received almost four times more coverage than the most mentioned issue, Europe, at 9.5% (Golding et al, The Guardian: June 2001).

Ireland is no different in this regard. After the 2002 general election, Paul Cullen, critical of his profession's behaviour during the campaign, scathingly commented that 'journalists, who should be setting the agenda on behalf of the people, ended up running around helplessly after the politicians, falling for their cheap publicity stunts and failing to ask the hard questions' (Cullen, Irish Times: 23 May 2002).

Primary research made available to the Commission on the role of the media in the Northern Ireland assembly election 2003 by Democratic Dialogue and the 2004 European Parliament elections in Ireland by Tasc support Paul Cullen's critique.

A content analysis of the coverage of the 2004 European Parliament election in the three daily Irish broadsheets and the three Irish Sunday broadsheets, as well as the Sunday World, in the three week period from 23 May to 11 June (election day) 2004, showed that:

- 11% of the articles had as primary content a reference to an issue of direct relevance in either a European, national or local context;
- fewer than 6% of the articles focused primarily on a European issue;
- slightly more than one third (34.7%) of the articles dealt in the first instance with either party and/or candidate canvassing or campaigning;
- almost one quarter (23.3%) of the articles were primarily concerned with some aspect of inter-party or candidate rivalry or criticism;
- a quarter of the articles focused on the election process itself e.g. poll findings, expected voter turnout, analysis of vote management strategies, voting information.

During the election campaign little attention was paid to policy issues. In particular the leading articles in the Sunday papers addressed the election solely in terms of a contest between parties and candidates. Instead of informing the reader of a candidate's political position on policy issues, coverage of individual candidates frequently focused on features of their personality and other aspects of their personal and professional lives. (Clancy et al: 2004)

Interestingly this research showed that 'compared with the perform-ance of the media coverage, the political parties and the candidates on the whole made a much more creditable/serious effort to address issues'. Three fifths of

Coverage of candidates frequently focused on features of their personality and other aspects of their personal and professional lives.

the information presented in the 156 press releases analysed addressed either a European or a national issue while a further 4.5% dealt with a local issue. 16% of them focused on some aspect of inter-party rivalry or political critique.

In their analysis of media coverage of the 2003 Northern Ireland assembly elections, Robin Wilson and Liz Fawcett concluded that:

- *'There was virtually no explanation, until the last minute, of what voters were voting for.'*
- In so far as the prospective review was addressed it was portrayed in the media as negotiations.
- The election was framed in the media - regionally, in Dublin, London (and to an extent) internationally - as a *'masculinist, communalist battle between two tribes and confined to four parties'*. This meant that particular emphasis was placed on who would emerge as 'top dog' in the nationalist and unionist communities thereby leaving little space for the discussion of the 'bread and butter' issues.

(Wilson & Fawcett: 2004)

Press Regulation

Openness, transparency, and accountability should not only apply to politics but also to the media. *'Every democratic society should interrogate itself continuously. The media is central to that ethos of interrogation. But the media itself is a central constituent component of society. It too requires interrogation'* (Lee, 1997:17). Brandenburg and Hayden argue that the Irish media do engage in some self-reflection not only about the way in which the political system manipulates and manages the media relationship but also about the media's own handling of spin (2003:192-194). The Commission agrees with Kinsella that the right amount of media regulation is the minimum amount consistent with public accountability (2005:17).

At present Ireland does not have a press council. The Legal Advisory Group on Defamation set up by the Minister for Justice, Equality and Law Reform in 2002 controversially proposed the establishment of a statutory, government-appointed press council that would prepare a press code of conduct and investigate complaints concerning alleged breaches. Its proposed council contradicts practices elsewhere and was rejected by the NUJ, NNI and ICCL to name but a few. According to the Alliance of Independent Press Councils Europe (AIPCE), this system 'would not only go against the trend in Europe and throughout much of the world - where independent rather than State-controlled press regulation is the norm - it would also diminish press freedom and undermine the independence of Irish newspapers' (www.pcc.org.uk). More recently, the Minister Michael McDowell reiterated his own preference for 'an independent rather than State-appointed body, composed of persons representative of civic society, with minority representation from media interests and journalists only', and which would have statutory recognition (McDowell, 2005). The establishment of an independently appointed press council and ombudsman are being considered in a draft Bill proposed by Minister McDowell, which would also include a review of defamation law.

The Commission believes that it is crucial that any future press council should be independent, a tool neither of the industry nor the Government but of the public's right to and need for a free and responsible press and should have statutory protection. The Commission does not believe in a state appointed regulatory body but supports the establishment of an independent press ombudsman and a press council recognised in law. The press council should be established by the press industry but should have an independent chair and take the majority of its members from civil society. One of its preliminary tasks should be to draft a code of editorial ethics. The Commission believes that the council should be recognised in law and its deliberations legally privileged. This will strengthen freedom of expression by making it possible to cite compliance with the Press Council's standards as proof of "reasonable publication" in libel actions. It will also provide quicker and more effective redress for people who feel that they have been misrepresented. The Commission does not support the recommendation from the Legal Advisory Group that people who use the press council's machinery be legally debarred from pursuing a libel action in the courts. Recourse to the courts should still be available to citizens.

Commission Recommendations

- The Commission supports the establishment of an independent press ombudsman and press council recognised by law.
- The Commission believes that the draft bill on establishing a

press council needs to be amended to address the lack of diversity of media ownership in Ireland. The concerns expressed by the Commission on the Newspaper Industry in 1996 have been realised and need to be addressed. Immediate action is required to:

- guarantee plurality of ownership in the newspaper industry to maintain the diversity of editorial viewpoints necessary for a vigorous democracy and to promote cultural diversity in the industry;

- address the concentration of ownership in the media generally, on a media-wide basis as well as on a single media basis.

- The Commission calls for recent amendments to Freedom of Information Act to be reversed[*].

- The Commission contends that the exclusively public service broadcasting role for RTE should be reinforced and supports a definition of public service broadcasting that focuses on the service rather than on a type of programming.

- Suggests televising tribunals.

References

Brandenburg, Heinz and Jacqueline Hayden, 2003: 'The media and the campaign' in Gallagher, Michael, Michael Marsh and Paul Mitchell (eds), How Ireland Voted 2002. London: Palgrave.

Broadcasting Act 2001.

Broadcasting Commission of Ireland www.bci.ie

Browne, Emma, 'Who controls the media?' Village, 24-30 June 2005.

Clancy, Paula, Teresa Brannick with Angela Flanagan, 2004: 'What the papers said. Analysis of the media coverage of the 2004 European elections'. Dublin:Tasc http://www.tascnet.ie/upload/Feb05%20media%20analysis.pdf

Clancy, Paula, Ian Hughes, Teresa Brannick, 2005: 'Public Perspectives on democracy in Ireland'. Democratic Audit Ireland Project: Tasc
http://www.tascnet.ie/upload/Democratic%20Audit%20Ireland%20Survey.pdf

Cullen, Paul, 2002: 'How media settled for bit part in farce of campaign'. The Irish Times, 23 May 2002.

Dooley, Seamus, 2005: Presentation to the Democracy Commission

Electoral Commission (UK), 2002: General Election 2001. London

European Journalism Centre www.ejc.nl

Golding, P and D. Deacon, 2001: 'An election that many watched but few enjoyed'. The Guardian, 12 June 2001.

Halligan, Ursula, 2002: 'Are you being served? Commercial Versus Public Broadcasting', in

---

[*]   One member of the Commission disagreed with this recommendation.

Damien Kiberd (ed), 'Media in Ireland, issues in broadcasting'. Dublin: Open Air.

Horgan, John, 2001a: Irish Media, a critical History since 1922. London: Routledge

Horgan, John, 2001b: 'Newspaper ownership in Ireland and its effects on media diversity: the Commission on the Newspaper industry re-visited' in Eoin Cassidy and Andrew McGrady (eds), Media and the marketplace: ethical perspectives. Dublin:IPA

Kinsella, Patrick, 2005: 'Democracy and the media'. Presentation to the Democracy Commission.

Lee, Joe, 1997: 'Democracy and public service broadcasting' in Damien Kiberd (ed), 'Media in Ireland the search for diversity'. Dublin: Open Air.

McDowell, Michael, 2005: 'Minister's statements on privacy and defamation'. Seanad Éireann, 9 February 2005. www.justice.ie

O'Neill, Onora, 2003: 'Rethinking freedom of the press'. Dublin: Royal Irish Academy

Oliver, Emmet, 'Takeovers spell good news for regional media organisations'. Irish Times, 24 June 2005.

Press Complaints Commission UK www.pcc.org.uk

Report of the Commission on the Newspaper Industry, 1996. Dublin: Government Stationery Office.

Wilson, Robin and Liz Fawcett, 2004: 'The Media Election: Coverage of the 2003 Northern Ireland Assembly poll'. Democratic Dialogue:
http://cain.ulst.ac.uk/dd/papers/dd04mediaelect.pdf

Conclusion

D emocracy has been described as critical and contestable. It is critical to the extent that is not perfect in practice and contestable because it is open to reflection, reform and renewal. Accepting the former, the Commission has endeavoured through its consultation process and the recommendations outlined in this report to achieve the latter.

At the outset it quickly became clear that people, although disillusioned and disenchanted, were not disengaged. This raised a number of concerns. Firstly there was the concern that if the disillusionment and disenchantment were not addressed then people would become disengaged. Secondly the Commission was aware that there were many who were already disengaged by virtue of a lack of information, a lack of experience, a lack of opportunity to participate in issues that affected them and so forth. Thirdly the Commission had heard from those who tried to engage but faced obstacles in doing so. Finally in its discussions with those at the helm of Irish democracy, the political representatives, the Commission realised that they too were often disillusioned and disenchanted.

The recommendations highlighted within this report are made with a view to addressing these concerns and to engaging citizens through, to name but a few:

- Democratic citizenship education at all levels from primary school to adult and community programmes.
- Increased and enhanced opportunities for participation, particularly in local democracy.

- Attempts to redress the under-representation of women and those living in socially disadvantaged areas in political institutions.
- The removal of procedural obstacles to electoral participation for all entitled to vote.
- Improved transparency and accountability to assist public understanding and scrutiny of political decisions.
- Openness and transparency in appointments to the boards of public bodies.
- Strengthened powers for the legislature.
- The guarantee of a diverse and vibrant media.

The Commission hopes that these recommendations will not only facilitate and mobilise citizens but assist those whose job it is to strengthen democracy in Ireland and Northern Ireland on a day to day basis.

Time will tell if the Commission has succeeded in this task. It hopes that through the public reflection it stimulated and the reforms it recommended that it has helped to renew and revitalise democracy on the island of Ireland.

Bibliography

Advisory Expert Committee, 1991: *Local Government Reorganisation and Reform*. Dublin: Government publications.

Aontas, 2004: Community Education 2004. Aontas:Dublin

Arlow, Michael, 2001: 'The Challenges of Social Inclusion in Northern Ireland: Citizenship and Life Skills'. http://www.ibe.unesco.org/Regional/baltic_sea/Balticpdf/vilnius6e.pdf

Baker, John, Kathleen Lynch, Sara Cantillon and Judy Walsh, 2004: *Equality from Theory to Action*. Basingstoke: Palgrave MacMillan.

Baker, John, 2005: 'Democratic strategies for reducing inequality'. Presentation to the Democracy Commission.

Boyle, Richard, Peter C. Humphreys, Orla O'Donnell, Joanna O'Riordan and Timonen Virpi, 2003: *Changing local government: a review of the local government modernisation programme*. Dublin: Institute of Public Administration.

Brandenburg, Heinz and Hayden, Jacqueline, 2003: 'The media and the campaign' in Gallagher, Michael, Marsh, Michael and Mitchell, Paul (eds), *How Ireland Voted 2002*. London: Palgrave

British Advisory Group on Citizenship, 1998: 'Education for Citizenship and the teaching of democracy in schools'. London: Qualifications and Curriculum Authority.

Broadcasting Act 2001.

Broadcasting Commission of Ireland www.bci.ie

Browne, Emma, 'Who controls the media?' Village, 24-30 June 2005.

Callanan, Mark, 2004: 'Local and Regional government in transition' in Collins, Neil and Cradden, Terry (eds), *Political Issues in Ireland Today*. Manchester: Manchester University Press.

Callanan, Mark and Keogan, Justin F. (eds) 2003: *Local Government in*

Ireland Inside Out. Dublin: Institute of Public Administration.

Carmichael, Paul, 2002: *Review of Local Administration briefing paper on multi-level governance*. http://www.rpani.gov.uk/multilevel.pdf

Central Statistics Office. *Census 2002*, www.cso.ie.

Centre for the Advancement of Women in Politics Database, Queen's University Belfast. http://www.qub.ac.uk/cawp/election.html

Clancy, Paula, Brannick, Teresa, Flanagan, Angela, 2004: 'What the papers said. Analysis of the media coverage of the 2004 European elections'. Tasc: http://www.tascnet.ie/upload/Feb05%20media%20analysis.pdf

Clancy, Paula, Hughes, Ian and Brannick, Teresa, 2005: 'Public Perspectives in Ireland'. Democratic Audit Ireland Project, Tasc. http://www.tascnet.ie/upload/Democratic%20Audit%20Ireland%20Survey.pdf

Clancy Paula & Murphy, Grainne, forthcoming: 'The State of Governance in Ireland: Preliminary Analysis of Non-Departmental Public Bodies in Ireland – National Level', work in progress, Democratic Audit Ireland Project, Tasc.

Coakley, John, 1999: 'The foundations of statehood' in Coakley, John and Gallagher, Michael (eds), *Politics in the Republic of Ireland*. London: Taylor Francis

Coleman, Eileen, Gray, Eileen and Harrison, Conor, 2004: Submission of the Civic Social and Political Education (CSPE) Support Team of the Second Level Support Service to the Democracy Commission.

Collins, Neil and Cradden, Terry, 2001: *Irish Politics Today*. Manchester: Manchester University Press.

Collins, Neil and Quinlivan, Aodh, 2005: 'Multi-level governance' in Coakley, John and Gallagher, Michael (eds), *Politics in the Republic of Ireland*. London: Routledge.

Congress of Local and Regional Authorities of Europe, 2001: *Report on Local Democracy in Ireland*. Strasbourg: Council of Europe.

Connolly, Brid, 2003: 'Community Education: Listening to the voices', *Adult Learner*. Dublin: Aontas.

CSO, 2003: *Quarterly National Household Survey, Voter Participation and Abstention*. Cork: CSO

CSPE Junior Certificate Syllabus.

Cullen, Paul, 2002: 'How media settled for bit part in farce of campaign'. The Irish Times 23/05/2002.

Democratic Audit Ireland Project – work in progress. Dublin: Tasc

Department of An Taoiseach, 2004: Regulating Better, a government white paper. Dublin: Stationery Office.

Dexia, 2004: *Local Finance in the twenty-five countries of the European Union*. Paris: Dexia editions.

Dollard, Gerard, 2003: 'Local Government Finance: The policy context' in Callanan, Mark and Keogan, Justin F. (eds), *Local Government in Ireland Inside Out*. Dublin: Institute of Public Administration.

Dooley, Seamus, 2005: Presentation to the Democracy Commission

Duffy, Joe, 2002: '*The poor only come out at Christmas? The media and social exclusion*' in Kiberd Damien (ed), '*Media in Ireland, issues in broadcasting*'. Dublin: Open Air.

The Electoral Commission (UK), 2002: *General Election 2001*. London

The Electoral Commission (NI), 2004: *The Northern Ireland Assembly elections 2003*. Belfast: The Electoral Commission NI.

The Electoral Commission UK, May 2005: *Securing the vote*. London: the Electoral Commission.

The Electoral Commission UK, April 2004: *Age of electoral majority report and recommendations*. London: the Electoral Commission

Electoral Office Northern Ireland (EONI), 2005: Local Government Election 5 May 2005 - Candidates Elected. Belfast: EONI.

European Journalism Centre www.ejc.nl

Farrell, David M., 2001: '*Electoral Systems a comparative introduction*'. Hampshire: Palgrave.

Faulks, Keith, 2005: '*Rethinking citizenship education in England: some lessons from contemporary social and political theory*'. Paper presented at Citizenship Education and Social Justice seminar in Queen's University Belfast, 2005. http://www.qub.ac.uk/edu/seminar/seminar_paper_faulks2.doc.

FitzGerald, Garret, 2003: *Reflections on the Irish State*. Dublin: Irish Academic Press.

Gallagher, Michael, 2000: '*Parliamentary control of the executive in Ireland: non-party, inter-party, cross-party and intra-party*'. Paper presented at the joint sessions of the European Consortium of Political Research in Copenhagen, April 2000.

Gallagher, Michael, 2005: '*Parliament*' in Coakley, John and Gallagher, Michael (eds), *Politics in the Republic of Ireland*. London: Routledge.

Gallagher, Michael, Marsh, Michael and Mitchell, Paul (eds), 2003:

How Ireland Voted 2002. Basingstoke: Palgrave Macmillan.

Galligan, Yvonne, 2005: 'Women in politics' in Coakley, John and Gallagher, Michael (eds), *Politics in the Republic of Ireland*. Oxon: Routledge and PSAI Press.

Gender and Constitutional Change project, www.pol.ed.ac.uk/gcc

Gleeson, Jim and Munnelly, Jarlath, 2004: 'Developments in citizenship education in Ireland: context, rhetoric and reality'. http://civiced. indiana.edu/papers/2003/1053010537.pdf.

Golding, P and Deacon, D. 2001: 'An election that many watched but few enjoyed'. The Guardian, 12 June 2001.

Hall, Wendy and Weir, Stuart, 1996: 'The untouchables. Power and Accountability in the quango state'. London: The Scarman Trust.

Halligan, Ursula, 2002: 'Are you being served? Commercial Versus Public Broadcasting', in Kiberd Damien (ed), 'Media in Ireland, issues in broadcasting'. Dublin: Open Air.

Hammond, John. 2002: 'Why Social and Political Education at Senior Cycle' in 'Charting the Future Social and Political Education in the Senior Cycle of Post-Primary Schools'. Dublin: CDVEC CDU and Combat Poverty Agency.

Harris, Clodagh, 2005: 'Democratic Citizenship Education in Ireland', *Adult Learner*. Dublin: Aontas.

Heywood, Andrew, 1997: *Politics*. Basingstoke: MacMillan

Hinds, Bronagh, 2005: 'Increasing female participation in public life' – paper presented at the RPA pathways to access and participation conference, Institute of Governance, Queen's University Belfast.

Honohan, Iseult, 2005: *Active Citizenship in contemporary Democracy*. Presentation made to the Democracy Commission.

Horgan, John, 2001: *Irish Media a critical History since 1922*. London: Routledge

Horgan, John, 2001: 'Newspaper ownership in Ireland and its effects on media diversity: the Commission on the Newspaper industry re-visited' in Cassidy, Eoin and McGrady, Andrew (eds), *Media and the market-place: ethical perspectives*. Dublin: IPA.

Housing (Traveller Accommodation) Act 1998.

International Institute for Democracy and Electoral Assistance (IDEA) www.idea.int

Inter Parliamentary Union database on women in politics. http://www.ipu.org/wmn-e/classif.htm.

IPA (Institute of Public Administration), 2004: *Review of the Operation* of Strategic Policy Committees. Dublin: Institute of Public Administration.

John, Peter, 2001: Local Governance in Western Europe. London: Sage Publications

Johnson, Catherine and Marhsall, Ben, June 2004: Political Engagement among young people: an update. London: The Electoral Commission.

Joint Committee on Health and Children, June 2005: 'Report on the Report on certain issues of management and administration in the Department of Health and Children associated with the practice of charges for persons in long stay care in health board institutions and related matters'.

Kavanagh, Adrian, 2002: Unequal Participation unequal influence – voter participation and voter education in Dublin's South West Inner City. Dublin: South West Inner City Network.

Kavanagh, Adrian, Mills, Gerald and Sinnott, Richard, 2004: 'The geography of Irish voter turnout: a case study of the 2002 General Election'. Irish Geography, Volume 37(2).

Kavanagh, Adrian P, 2005: 'Bin charges disputes, personality politics, Sinn Fein and increased local election turnout: a spatial analysis of the increased electoral participation in the 2004 local elections in the Republic of Ireland'. Paper presented at the PSA annual conference, 2005. http://www.psa.ac.uk/2005/pps/Kavanagh.pdf

Kenny, Liam (ed) 1999: From the ballot box to council chamber: a commentary on the local government elections. Dublin: Institute of Public Administration for the General Council of County Councils.

Keogan, Justin F., 2003: 'Reform in Irish local Government' in Callanan, Mark and Keogan, Justin F. (eds), Local Government in Ireland Inside Out. Dublin: Institute of Public Administration.

Keogh, Helen, 2003: 'Learning for Citizenship in Ireland: the Role of Adult Education' in Medel-Anonuevo, Carolyn and Mitchell, Gordon (eds) Citizenship, Democracy, and Lifelong Learning. Philippines: UNESCO.

Kinsella, Patrick, 2005: 'Democracy and the media'. Presentation to the Democracy Commission.

Kymlicka, Will, 1999: 'Education for Citizenship' in J.M. Halstead and T.H. McLaughlin (eds), Education and Morality. London: Routledge

Laffan, Brigid and Tonra, Ben, 2005: 'Europe and the international *dimension'* in John Coakley and Michael Gallagher (eds), *Politics in the Republic of Ireland*. London: Routledge.

Lee, Joe, 1997: *'Democracy and public service broadcasting'* in Damien Kiberd (ed), *'Media in Ireland the search for diversity'*. Dublin: Open Air.

Lijphart, Arendt, 1997: *'Unequal participation: Democracy's unresolved dilemma'*. American Political Science Review 91 No.1.

Lloyd, John, 2004: *What the Media are doing to our politics*. London: Constable.

Local Elections 1999 Volumes 1 & 2, Department of the Environment, Heritage and Local Government.

Local Elections 2004, Department of the Environment, Heritage and Local Government.

Local Government Act 2001

Lovenduski, Joni, 2005: *Feminizing Politics*. Cambridge: Polity Press.

Mackay, Fiona, 2001: *Developing the equality agenda in Scotland and Wales*. Presentation made at the Equality Commission of Northern Ireland, the Equality Conference 2001: Mapping the Equality Agenda. www.pol.ed.ac.uk/gcc/print/printmackayspeech.html.

Marsh, Michael and Benoit, Ken, 2002: *'Campaign spending in the local government elections of 1999'*. Paper presented at the Annual conference of the PSAI.

McAllister, I. and Studlar, D.T., 2002: *'Electoral Systems and Women's Representation: A Long-term Perspective'*. Representation 39 (1).

McDowell, Michael, 2005: 'Minister's statements on privacy and defamation'. Seanad Éireann, 9 February 2005. www.justice.ie

Meehan, Elizabeth, 2002: *Gender and Constitutional Change*. Presentation at a conference of the ESRC Research programme on devolution and constitutional change, London 2002. www.pol.ed.ac.uk/gcc/print/printmeehan.html

Muintir na Tire/Institute of Public Administration, Towards a New Democracy? – Implications of Local Government Reform 1985

Murphy, Kevin, 2005: *'Democracy in Ireland'*. Keynote address at the launch of the Democratic Audit Ireland project.

National Public Health Institute of Finland www.ktl.fi

National Women's Council of Ireland, 2002: *Irish politics Jobs for the Boys! Recommendations on Increasing the Number of Women in Decision Making*. Dublin: National Women's Council of Ireland.

National Youth Council of Ireland, 2004: Submission to the Democracy Commission

National Youth Federation, National Youth Poll 2004, www.nyf.ie

NCCA, 2004: *Proposals for the future of Senior Cycle Education in Ireland*

NCCRI, 2005: *Submission to the Democracy Commission.*

NCO, 2000: *National Children's strategy*

Norris, Pippa, 2004: *Electoral Engineering: voting rules and political behaviour.* Cambridge: Cambridge University Press.

Northern Ireland Young Life and Times Survey 2004 (http://www.ark.ac.uk/ylt/2004)

O'Brien, Carl, 'Market Regulators have a subversive job to do'. Irish Examiner, 3 January 2002.

OECD reviews of regulatory reform, 2001: 'Regulatory Reform in Ireland'. Paris: OECD.

O'Neill, Onora, 2003: 'Rethinking freedom of the press'. Dublin: Royal Irish Academy.

Oliver, Emmet, 'Takeovers spell good news for regional media organisations'. *Irish Times*, 24 June 2005.

Press Complaints Commission UK www.pcc.org.uk

Quinn, Brid, 2003: 'Irish Local Government in a comparative context' in 'Reform in Irish local Government' in Callanan, Mark and Keogan, Justin F. (eds), *Local Government in Ireland Inside Out.* Dublin: Institute of Public Administration.

Reid, Liam, *Female Councillor numbers continue to be low. Irish Times,* 16 August 2004.

Report of the Commission on the Newspaper Industry, 1996. Dublin: Government Stationery Office.

'Report on certain issues of management and administration in the Department of Health and Children associated with the practice of charges for persons in long stay care in health board institutions and related matters'. Travers Report, March 2005.

Roche, Desmond, 1982: *Local Government in Ireland.* Dublin: Institute of Public Administration.

Seanad Éireann sub committee on Seanad Reform, 'Report on Seanad Reform' 2004.

Shah, Anwar, 2004: *Fiscal Decentralization in Developing and Transition Economies.* Washington: World Bank

Sheehy, Edward, 2003: 'City and County Management' in 'Reform in Irish local Government' in Mark Callanan and Keogan, Justin F.

(eds), *Local Government in Ireland Inside Out*. Dublin: Institute of Public Administration.

Shipan, Charles R., 2003: '*Independence and the Irish Environmental Protection Agency: a comparative assessment*'. Dublin: Policy Institute TCD

Sisk, Timothy D. (ed), 2001: *Democracy at the local level. International IDEAs handbook on participation, representation, conflict management and governance*. Sweden: IDEA.

Smith, Graham, 2005: '*Power beyond the ballot 57 democratic innovations from around the world*'. A report for the Power Inquiry UK.

Standards in public office commission, 2003: *Annual report*: www.sipo.ie

Wall, Martin, Hennessy, Mark and Downes, John, *Report to focus on Leas Cross mortality rate*'. Irish Times, 22 June 2005.

Ward, Eilis, 2002: '*Citizenship Studies*'. A curricular proposal for Social and Political Education in the Leaving Certificate (Established). Dublin: CDVEC CDU

Waste Management (amendment) Act 2001.

Watt, Philip, 2005: *Approaches to Cultural and Ethnic Diversity and the role of citizenship in promoting a more inclusive intercultural society in Ireland*. Paper presented to the Democracy Commission.

Wilson, Robin and Fawcett, Liz, 2004: '*The Media Election: Coverage of the 2003 Northern Ireland Assembly poll*'. Democratic Dialogue: http://cain.ulst.ac.uk/dd/papers/dd04mediaelect.pdf

Wilson, Robin and Wilford, Rick, forthcoming: Democratic Audit of Northern Ireland – work in progress, Democratic Audit Ireland project. Dublin: Tasc.

Appendix 1

Diary of Activities

1 July 2005
The Democracy Commission held a National Consultative Conference at the NICVA Offices in Belfast.

29 June 2005
The Democracy Commission held a National Consultative Conference in Liberty Hall in Dublin.

27 May 2005
Clodagh Harris made a presentation on Citizenship Education in Ireland to the EU Learning Partnership on Active Citizenship.

17 May 2005
The Democracy Commission held a Media Seminar at which the Commission invited the following to make presentations:

     Mr. Seamus Dooley, Irish Secretary of the NUJ;
     Mr. Patrick Kinsella, School of Communications, DCU;
     Ms. Geraldine Kennedy, Editor, *Irish Times*;
     Mr. Gerard Colleran, Editor, *The Star*.

28 April 2005
Clodagh Harris met with a group of students from UNESCO Centre, University of Ulster, Coleraine.

20 December 2004
The Democracy Commission attended a Citizenship Education Network meeting.

9 December 2004
The Democracy Commission met with elected members of Fianna
Fáil.

3 December 2004
Clodagh Harris addressed a meeting of the National Women's
Council of Ireland.

26 November 2004
The Democracy Commission hosted a one-day public event at Liberty
Hall, Dublin.

22 October 2004
The Democracy Commission hosted a think-in day at which the
following were invited to make presentations:
> Dr John Baker, Equality Studies Centre, UCD;
> Professor Iseult Honohan, Politics Department, UCD;
> Dr. Garret FitzGerald.

15 October 2004
Clodagh Harris presented research paper 'Election 2004, spoiled ballots
- the silent issue', at the Political Studies Association of Ireland annual
conference in Limerick.

9 October 2004
The Democracy Commission hosted a workshop at the Irish Social
Forum.

6 October 2004
The Democracy Commission met with elected members of the SDLP,
UUP and DUP in Belfast.

9 August 2004
The Democracy Commission met with the NI Equality Authority and
the Electoral Commission NI.

16 July 2004
The Democracy Commission met with the Director of the General
Council of County Councillors.

2 July 2004

The Democracy Commission met with the National Council for Curriculum Assessment.

10 June 2004

The Democracy Commission met with the Citizen Education Network.

31 May 2004

Launch of the Democracy Commission's progress report in the Mansion House, Dublin.

22 – 23 May 2004

Clodagh Harris attended the annual assembly of the National Youth Federation in Letterkenny, Donegal.

18 May 2004

The Democracy Commission held a public meeting in Jury's Hotel, Western Road, Cork hosted by the Cork Centre for the Unemployed.

17 May 2004

Clodagh Harris met with student union representatives in CIT and UCC.

13 May 2004

The Democracy Commission met with FEASTA (Foundation for the Economic of Sustainability).

4 May 2004

The Democracy Commission met with members of the Community and Voluntary Pillar, the Community Platform and the CV 12 group. This meeting was facilitated by Community Action Network.

30 April 2004

The Democracy Commission met with the Canals Community Platform representing the areas of Inchicore, Bluebell and Rialto.

31 March 2004

The Democracy Commission held a Public Meeting in Derry, hosted by Disability Action.

23 March 2004
Commissioner Bernadette McMahon made a presentation at a seminar on "*Citizenship and disadvantaged women*", held in the Croke Park Conference Centre. The event was hosted by the Larkin Centre.

23 March 2004
Commissioner Nora Owen spoke at the public meeting on "*Democracy, Diversity and Dissent*", organised by the Irish Council for Civil Liberties.

18 March 2004
Democracy Commission met with a group of Community Activists from the Blanchardstown / Blakestown area.

4 March 2004
The Democracy Commission met with Independent Senators.

25 February 2004
The Democracy Commission met with Independent TDs.

18 February 2004
The Democracy Commission met with elected members of Sinn Féin.

16 February 2004
The Democracy Commission met with elected members of the Labour Party.

20 January 2004
The Democracy Commission met with elected members of the Progressive Democrats.

13 January 2004
The Democracy Commission met with elected members of the Green Party.

12 January 2004
The Democracy Commission held a public meeting in Belfast at the invitation of NICVA, WEA and NCIF.

12 January 2004

The Democracy Commission met with the de Borda Institute in Belfast.

18 December 2003

The Democracy Commission met with elected members of Fine Gael.

5 December 2003

The Democracy Commission held a public meeting in Thurles.

18 October 2003

The Democracy Commission hosted a workshop at the Irish Social Forum.

Written Submissions received by post and e-mail

1.	Simon Nugent	26.	Bernard Leddy
2.	Roy Johnston	27.	Damien Nee
3.	Proinnsias Breathnach	28.	Mary Ryan
4.	The de Borda Institute	29.	John Weir
5.	E-Ireland forum	30.	Jack MacDonald
6.	C. Dennis Kelly	31.	Vincent Salfia
7.	Brendan McSherry	32.	Gearoid O'Sullivan
8.	Patrick McDonnell	33.	Rose Ferguson
9.	Cathal Horan	34.	Parents for Justice Group
10.	Patrick Leo Curran	35.	Desmond Graham
11.	Michael K. Ewing	36.	Michael Dunne
12.	Patrick Mangan	37.	Thomas Sweeney
13.	NICVA	38.	Anna Kavanagh
14.	Young Citizens in Action	39.	Volunteer Development Agency
15.	Civic Social and Political Education Support Service	40.	Larry Dunne
		41.	Mamie Bowen
16.	Hans Zomer	42.	Rosie Cargin
17.	Zero Waste Alliance Ireland	43.	Maurice Aherne
18.	Bantry Integrated Development Group	44.	James Fleury
19.	John Colgan	45.	CDU CDVEC
20.	Jim Frawley	46.	Ann Kirwan
21.	Renee Murtagh	47.	Oliver Ward
22.	Eadestown and District Community Council	48.	Paul O'Grady
		49.	National Association for Youth Drama
23.	Brendan Kelly	50.	Gerard Barnard
24.	Finbarr Townsend	51.	Edward Redding
25.	Norman Campbell	52.	Thomas Scannell

53. Timothy Murphy
54. NCCRI
55. Age Action Ireland
56. National Disability Authority
57. Power Partnership
58. Helen Keogh
59. Jenny Boylan
60. Trust
61. Claire Pickell
62. Sue Targett
63. South West Inner City Network
64. Tallaght Partnership
65. John Slattery
66. William Finnerty
67. Clare Environment Alliance
68. Maura Harrington
69. John Moriarty
70. The Wheel
71. Irish Citizens for Trustworthy E-voting
72. Daragh O'Murchu
73. Mary Kinane, Dun Laoighaire-Rathdown County Council
74. James Cotter
75. Bottlehill Environmental Alliance
76. Catherine Ansboro
77. CHASE
78. Natasha Harty
79. Declan Moley
80. John Lambe
81. Karen Devine
82. Young Fine Gael
83. Irish Social Forum
84. Muiris Mac Carthaigh
85. John F. Higgins
86. Roger Garland
87. Richard Barrett
88. Irish Refugee Council
89. Darach Murphy
90. Crispin Welby
91. National Youth Council
92. ICCL
93. Daryl D'Art and Thomas Turner
94. Daniel Dunne
95. Educate Together
96. Gavin Crowley
97. John Fitzgibbon
98. St. Patrick's Day Converging Voices Symposium
99. The Graduate online youth quiz
100. Dublin Community TV

Organisations invited to make submissions

1. ICCL
2. European Movement
3. Centre for Cross-Border Studies
4. Afri
5. The National Federation of Voluntary Bodies
6. Common Purpose Ireland
7. Irish Traveller Movement
8. GLEN
9. Dóchas
10. Simon Community
11. Focus Ireland
12. NALA
13. The Wheel
14. Women's Aid
15. NYCI
16. NWCI
17. Comhlamh
18. INOU
19. EAPN (Ireland)
20. An Taisce
21. Combat Poverty Agency
22. Debt and Development Coalition Ireland
23. Trocaire (Trust)
24. Threshold
25. Society of St. Vincent de Paul
26. Comhairle
27. Age & Opportunity
28. Centre for Independent Living
29. ICA
30. People with Disabilities in Ireland Ltd
31. Senior Citizens Parliament in Ireland
32. Community Action Network
33. Clann Credo
34. AHEAD
35. Age Action Ireland Ltd
36. Let in the Light
37. Rape Crisis Centre
38. CORI
39. Amnesty International
40. Aontas
41. Community Workers Co-operative
42. Macra na Feírme
43. Business in the Community
44. Co-operation Ireland
45. Pavee Point
46. Create
47. Union of Students in Ireland
48. Alone
49. Area Development Management Ltd
50. Children's Rights Alliance
51. Cluid Housing Association
52. Concern
53. Consumers Association of Ireland

54. Dublin Employment Pact
55. Dublin Inner City Partnership
56. EarthWatch
57. FLAC (Free Legal Advice Centres)
58. GOAL
59. Gorta
60. The Green Party
61. The Heritage Council
62. Homeless Agency
63. Homeless Girls Society Ltd
64. The Housing Institute of Ireland
65. Irish Centre for Human Rights
66. Human Rights Commission
67. ICTU
68. IFA
69. IFPA
70. Irish Association of Social Workers
71. Irish Commission for Justice and Peace
72. Irish Commission for Prisoners Overseas
73. Irish Council for Social Housing
74. Irish Council of Churches
75. Irish Social Policy Association
76. National Association of Widows in Ireland
77. National Association of Tenants' Organisations
78. National Consultative Committee on Racism and Interculturalism (NCCRI)
79. Oxfam Ireland
80. Parents Association for Vocational Schools and Community Colleges
81. Parents Council for Post Primary
82. Parents for Justice Ltd
83. Peace and Neutrality Alliance
84. Penal Reform Trust Ltd
85. Psychological Society of Ireland
86. Irish Refugee Council
87. Simon Communities of Ireland
88. Sociological Association of Ireland
89. Trust
90. Women in Technology and Science
91. Women in the Home
92. Women Managers' Network
93. Women's Committee (ICTU)
94. Youth Council for Northern Ireland
95. Youth Council of Ireland

Appendix 4

Commissioner Biographies

David Begg, Chair of the Commission.
Mr. David Begg is General Secretary of the Irish Congress of Trade Unions which represents over 700,000 workers on the island of Ireland. He was formerly chief executive of Concern World Wide. He is a director of the Irish Central Bank and chairperson of the bank's internal audit committee.

Ivana Bacik
Professor Ivana Bacik is Reid Professor of Criminal Law, Criminology and Penology at Trinity College Dublin. A practising barrister, she teaches criminal law, criminology and penology, and feminist theory of law. She is also a feminist campaigner and political activist and has stood for election to the European Parliament as a member of the Labour Party. She is the editor of the *Irish Criminal Law Journal*.

Ruth Barrington
Dr Ruth Barrington is the Chief Executive of the Health Research Board, a post she has held since September 1998. She is the author of Health, Medicine and Politics in Ireland, 1900-1970 (1987) which analyses the forces that have shaped the Irish health services. She has published a number of articles on health and research policy, the most recent being 'Terrible Beauty or Celtic Mouse - the Research Agenda in Ireland' in *New Hibernia Review*, Autumn 2002.

John Hanafin
Mr. John Hanafin is a Senator and former deputy Lord Mayor of North Tipperary. He was recently appointed national corporate fundraiser for Fianna Fáil.

Tony Kennedy
Mr Tony Kennedy has been Chief Executive of Co-operation Ireland since August 1992. Previously he has held the positions of Chief Housing Officer, Wakefield MDC, Regional Director (North West), N.I. Housing

Executive and Area Housing Manager, Belfast, N.I. Housing Executive. Mr Kennedy was awarded an OBE in the 2004 New Year's honours list.

Bernadette MacMahon

Sr. Bernadette MacMahon (DC) is co-ordinator of the Vincentian Partnership for Social Justice, which works for social and economic change, tackling poverty and exclusion. The partnership runs voter education programmes and is currently engaged in building a national Active Citizenship Network.

Elizabeth Meehan

Professor Elizabeth Meehan is Director of the Institute of Governance, Public Policy and Social Research at Queen's University Belfast. She was brought up in Scotland and attended Sussex and Oxford Universities. Her research interests are: women and politics; citizenship and participation; and British-Irish relations in the context of the EU.

Mark Mortell

Mr. Mark Mortell joined Fleishman-Hillard, International Communications Consultants in August 2002. He is Head of FH consulting. He served as a member of both Bray UDC and Wicklow County Council in the 1980s and has served on a number of State committees.

Nora Owen

Mrs. Nora Owen is a former Minister for Justice and deputy leader of Fine Gael. She represented Dublin North from 1981 to 2002. She has been involved in parliamentary training in Africa and Eastern Europe.

Donal Toolan

Mr. Donal Toolan is a disability rights activist, actor and award-winning journalist. He was co-ordinator of the Forum of People with Disabilities, a rights-based organisation that furthers strategies to ensure the participation of people with disabilities. He is a member of the executive of the Irish Council for Civil Liberties.

Caroline Wilson

Ms. Caroline Wilson is currently working as Good Relations Officer with Belfast City Council. Prior to this post, she worked with the Student Movement in Northern Ireland and a number of other youth organisations. She has led groups of young leaders to South Africa, Croatia, Serbia and Cyprus to compare and contrast communities emerging from violent political conflict and building democracy.

Papers

presented to the

Democracy Commission

Democratic strategies for reducing inequality

By **Dr. John Baker,** Equality Studies Centre, UCD

Your request: "The Commission would be grateful if you could address the issue of democratic processes/mechanisms as tools to deepen equality particularly among young people and those living in socially disadvantaged areas in a 20 minute presentation."

I am honoured to be invited to talk with you about this and thank you for the opportunity to do so. At the same time I am very conscious of the limits of my knowledge and understanding of the field and I would be horrified to be thought of as an 'expert' who can give you the answers to your questions. But then isn't this part of the point of democracy? None of us are truly experts in the major policy questions that confront our society, and one of the central arguments for democracy is that it is only by putting together our diverse understandings, experiences and perspectives that we can hope to construct adequate answers to the problems of the day.

In what I have to say today I will be drawing very heavily on the book I wrote with Kathleen Lynch, Sara Cantillon and Judy Walsh called Equality: From Theory to Action, especially Chapters 2 and 6. I know that at least some of you have read the book so what I'll say may be all too familiar.

If I had lots of time I would fill in the background to what I have to say by discussing the relation of democracy to equality. All I will say by way of preliminaries is that although you have asked me to address inequalities to do with socially disadvantaged areas and young people, I think there are several other important inequalities that can be addressed in similar terms and I don't propose to limit myself to the two you have specified.

In all of these cases, the *fundamental* problem is that the groups in question are marginalized and disadvantaged in Irish society, that these inequalities generate inequalities in political participation, and that those political inequalities in turn reinforce wider social inequalities. You should not labour under the illusion that we can somehow bring about substantial equality in democratic participation without reducing inequalities throughout society: there is no 'internal settlement' in the political system, any more than in the educational or any other system. All of this creates a serious 'chicken-and-egg' problem to which I will return at the end.

Abstracting from these issues for a moment, the specific question you have asked me is what can be done in the design of the political system itself to promote greater equality, which I take to be, first, a question about increasing the participation of disadvantaged groups and, secondly, of countering the oppressive tendencies of majority rule. Here are six headings that are worth exploring.

1. Supporting the self-organisation of marginalized groups

If there were one activity that is worth prioritising above all the rest, in my view it would be supporting the self-organization of marginalized groups. I emphasize the idea of 'self-organization': if we want real change for Travellers, disabled people, working class people, women, gays and lesbians, immigrants, young people, etc., it is not enough to rely on members of other groups, speaking on their behalf. They need to be resourced to participate themselves, through their own organizations.

There are at least two aspects of the kind of support that is necessary here.

Material support

First of all, there is straightforward material support. To organize effectively for change, people need meeting rooms, offices, computers, telephones, photocopiers, libraries, travel expenses, office staff, paid organizers and lobbyists. Well-resourced groups like IBEC can pay for all this out of their membership fees, but where is this material support to come from for poorly-resourced groups? In a small number of cases, the collective support of large numbers of individuals can succeed in supporting self-organization. The best example of this is the trade union movement. But for most organizations, it is hard even to survive, much less to thrive, on funding from one's own members. There is no need to remind the people in this room of the limited sources of support from funding institutions in Ireland, which in any case are vulnerable to changes in funders' priorities. So the main prospect for serious, long-term, core funding for the self-organization of marginalized groups is state funding. This funding should be secure, core funding with very few strings attached. It is appropriate enough for it to be conditional on proper auditing of accounts and on maintaining certain basic standards of democratic procedure in relation to membership, election to office and decision-making mechanisms. But it has to be protected against being withdrawn for essentially political reasons, as occurred with the Citizen Traveller campaign. The whole point of this kind of funding is to enable marginal groups to develop their own perspectives and political strategies, however critical they might be of the state.

Training and capacity-building

The second kind of support is training and capacity-building. People do not develop the competence to participate in democratic organizations by instinct: they need to learn how to do it through practice, reflection on that practice, and acquiring relevant knowledge. One part of this training, is education for citizenship in the formal educational system. Another, which I return to below, is the experience of democratic participation in a wide variety of settings. But a third must be explicit training and capacity-building programmes for members of organizations themselves. A good example of this in the US is Midwest Academy, which has been training activists for 30 years. Here in Ireland, I think an excellent resource is the Combat Poverty Agency publication *Working for Change: A Guide to Influencing Policy in Ireland*. In the examples of participatory governance in India and Brazil that I will mention in a minute, part of the process has been intensive training of the participants. More generally, any of the other initiatives I am about to mention need to be supplemented by appropriate training.

Anti-democratic?

Is it legitimate for a liberal democratic state to finance the explicitly political activities of marginalized groups in these ways? I would argue that it is, because the object of the exercise is to level the playing field in the political sphere between these groups and their privileged counterparts. The relevant political principle is simply the aim of giving every citizen an equal opportunity to influence collective decisions. It is not about the state favouring one set of political objectives over others, but about helping all its citizens to pursue their own political objectives with roughly similar effectiveness.

2. Strengthened local participatory structures

A second type of strategy for promoting democratic equality is to develop strengthened local structures for participating in decision-making. People living in socially disadvantaged areas face a range of policy problems, some of which are similar to those in advantaged areas and some of which are distinctive in quality or scale. In addition, they are much less well resourced than people in advantaged areas for dealing directly with the formal political system through lobbying, direct contact with public representatives, the use of informal social networks and so on. Developing means by which they can become more directly involved in policy-making and prioritising is therefore another way of helping to level the playing field.

Porto Alegre

One of the most widely cited examples of local democratic empowerment is the Participatory Budgeting process developed in Porto Alegre in Brazil and currently being extended to more than 100 other Brazilian cities with Workers' Party governments. In this case, which I know of only through published accounts, there is a highly developed system through which local communities participate in decision making relating to the allocation of the municipal budget for services including road improvements, water, drainage and other public services. The process is thoroughly described in a number of sources so I will only mention a few of its prominent features. It takes place in parallel with the formal political system: the adoption of the Participatory Budget, which covers only that part of the municipal budget directly concerned with certain public services, is formally within the power of the city council, but this does not seem to lead to serious conflict. The process is supported by skilled facilitators and by intensive training for participants so that ordinary citizens are empowered to understand, challenge and reconstruct budgetary proposals. Among the most promising aspects of the process is the fact that, in contrast to most other contexts, there is very little evidence of unequal participation by class or gender. The Participatory Budget shows that such democratic involvement is perfectly feasible even in a relatively poor country.

Kerala

Another very interesting example I have read about is the Campaign for Decentralized Planning in the Indian state of Kerala. In this case, as well, the process involves providing structures through which ordinary citizens can have a serious influence on planning the delivery and priorities of local services. As in Porto Alegre, it involves the use of skilled facilitators and an intensive training programme for participants. Another similarity is that participation by women and members of disadvantaged groups (in this case, Scheduled Castes and Scheduled Tribes) has been disproportionately high.

Ireland?

Although I have read up some of the written reports on these cases, I cannot claim to have detailed knowledge of them or to be in a position to compare them to some of the attempts to engage local communities here in Ireland in processes of local planning. I think that would be an interesting area for the Commission to look into.

3. Separate representation for marginalized groups

A third strategy for using democracy to support equality is to construct and develop ways for directly representing the interests and perspectives of marginalized groups.

Electoral

There has been some attention to this strategy at national and local electoral level in some countries. The clearest example I have come across is the system in New Zealand / Aotearea for the representation of Maoris through a separate electoral roll that Maoris can opt onto and that has its own constituency boundaries. The electors on this roll currently elect seven of the 120 members of the New Zealand Parliament. It is not clear to me that there are any feasible applications of this model to Ireland at the level of electoral politics although it could be interesting to hear whether the Travelling community would consider it a positive proposal to have their own TD elected from a national roll of Travellers (assuming that such a roll would have approximately 1/166th of the country's adult population).

Partnership

Where the idea of separate representation really comes into its own in an Irish context is in connection to partnership bodies at both local and national level. We already have something like this in national partnerships through the role of the Community and Voluntary Sector in the NESF, the NESC and national partnership agreements. What is different there, and deserves more attention, is the difference between the genuine representation of marginalized groups through representatives of their own choosing and the more attenuated sense in which these groups are represented by organizations that aim to act on their behalf but have no lines of accountability to the groups themselves. I know that there is work being done at the level of local partnership, in particular, to try to ensure that the representatives of local communities, of disabled people, of Travellers, of gays and lesbians, of older people, and so on, are chosen by and accountable to organizations composed of members of these groups rather than simply being people chosen from the top as likely advocates of their views. But I cannot speak with any authority on those initiatives.

As with the issue of resources, it cannot be right for organizations to be included or excluded in partnership processes on the basis of political decisions about their policy positions. So long as they are prepared to engage in the process, they should have a right to a seat at the table, and with that right comes the right to accept or reject proposed agreements. It seems extraordinary to me that the groups that rejected *Sustaining Progress* have been excluded from partnership at all levels of national consultation. That kind of reaction simply reinforces their vulnerable status.

Anti-democratic?

There is resistance in some quarters to the idea that forms of governance based on the direct representation of marginalized groups is truly democratic, based on the assumption that true democracy only occurs through elections in which everyone participates. I think this is a mistaken criticism. The point of ensuring that marginalized groups have their own representatives is, as before, to try to level the playing field between these groups and other, more advantaged groups, not to give them more than their share of influence. In a political system where a Traveller is *never* elected; where a disabled person is only elected once in a blue moon, and virtually never on account of an agenda specifically dealing with disability issues; where if a gay man or lesbian is elected, the first issue is whether or not even to disclose the fact and the next is usually to reassure voters that one's sexual orientation has nothing whatever to do with one's policies - in such a system, the idea of ensuring that the voices of these groups are actually heard is a way of enhancing political equality, not of subverting democracy.

4. Quotas for members of marginalized groups

A more familiar mechanism for promoting equality is the use of quotas. Here again we can distinguish between quotas within formal electoral systems and quotas in other structures of governance.

Electoral

Within electoral systems, there is quite a lot of international experience now with gender quotas, which typically operate through the nominating procedures of political parties and sometimes through a direct requirement that some minimum number of women has to be elected to a particular body (my impression is that the number is usually one). I hesitate to say much on this because I think some of you probably already know more about this than I do. Such a system is much easier to operate in proportional representation systems using party lists than in first-past-the-post systems or in the PRSTV system we use in Ireland but it is not impossible. What is harder is to extend it to marginalized groups other than women because the groups are much more indeterminate and fluid.

Quangos

But here again there are other structures of governance where the use of quotas is more feasible. Many quasi-governmental organizations have appointed boards, and there are no serious problems in stipulating that these organizations should be gender-balanced or in stipulating that they should contain specified numbers of members of other marginalized groups. The fact that these bodies are not elected does not mean that they are outside the bounds of the idea of democracy, since they still play an important role in democratic government. If the members of these bodies are also nominated by appropriate organizations of marginalized groups, there is a convergence of the ideas of separate representation and quotas.

Anti-democratic?

The use of quotas has its critics, and some of the problems they've raised are worthy of attention. The main one is that in the absence of any form of accountability to the group, it is hard to ensure that the group member acts in any plausibly representative capacity. Just because a representative is a woman, or gay, or disabled, does not mean that she or he has a perspective that is representative of even a significant proportion of women or gays or disabled people. But even in the absence of mechanisms of accountability, it is often possible to see over time whether the people filling quotas are acting in line with or contrary to the perspectives they are chosen to reflect, particularly if there are well-resourced and articulate organizations of the groups in question.

What in my view is *not* a serious objection to quotas is the claim that they subvert democracy by restricting the choices of voters. They surely *do* restrict the choices of voters but they do so precisely because the choices of voters lead to the disproportionate power of dominant social groups. If the aim of a democracy is to try to give everyone an equal say in decision making, then its systematic bias in favour of dominant groups needs to be corrected, and quotas are one way of doing that.

5. Non-majoritarian decision-making

This last point connects nicely with the issue I raised earlier about the tendency of majoritarian decision-making procedures to ignore the interests and perspectives of minorities. For minorities to be constantly out-voted is another way democratic procedures can depart from the democratic ideal of an equal say for all.

We review in our book some of the key forms of non-majoritarian decision making and I will only summarize some points here.

Deliberative consensus

One line of thought that has a lot of currency in contemporary democratic theory is that decision making should be more deliberative in character, aiming to achieve a consensus based on good reasons rather than a result reflecting the power plays of interested participants, and various experiments have been carried out in this vein. It is not that easy to institutionalise deliberative democracy, though, because when the chips are down it is hard to find institutional mechanisms to stop people using their power to pursue their interests.

Non-majoritarian voting procedures

A second promising direction to look in is the use of non-majoritarian voting procedures. I know that you have already had a submission from Peter Emerson of the de Borda Institute on this question, an Institute with which I also have an association, and all I would say is that although I am less inclined than Peter to think that majoritarianism is the root of nearly all evils, I think it is worth looking at the value of non-majoritarian systems as procedures for reflecting the views of significant marginalized minorities.

Inter-group agreement

A third alternative to majoritarianism is inter-group agreement, that is, that instead of deciding issues by following the wishes of the majority, you decide them by finding policies that all the relevant groups can agree to. This is in fact the model of a negotiated settlement in industrial relations and of partnership in decision making more generally, and it is a key dimension of the Belfast Agreement in Northern Ireland. A weaker version is a commitment to 'consult' with all interested parties: that's the form it tends to take when dealing with groups like Travellers or disabled people.

Anti-democratic?

All of these ideas are likely to be objected to by people who identify democracy with majority rule, but that is a simple mistake. The real problem with all of them is not that they give minorities too much power but that they give them too little, since all three processes are still likely to lead to decisions that are weighted disproportionately towards the interests of the majority.

6. Extension of democratic participation to different spheres

The final proposal I think it is worth mentioning today for promoting equality is the extension of democracy to areas of collective decision-making outside the formal sphere of government. If we are interested in empowering marginalized groups as a way of reducing inequality, then we have to recognise that many of the key decisions that disempower these groups take place outside the sphere of the state: in families, schools, religious congregations, housing estates, welfare offices, workplaces and boardrooms. So democratising these institutions would play a direct role in reducing inequality. In addition, as I said at the start, all of these settings are schools of citizenship. If they are organized in an authoritarian way, it should come as no surprise that people find it difficult to participate democratically in the formal political system. This theme of extending democracy throughout social relations is obviously a big one and way too far-ranging to pursue today, but I think it would be a pity if it weren't on the Commission's agenda.

Chicken and egg

Those, then, are some ideas about how democracies can be designed to reduce inequalities. But there remains the chicken-and-egg problem I mentioned early on, namely that existing levels of inequality in society generate inequalities of participation, which in turn reduce the likelihood of policies being adopted that will counteract these tendencies. The political capacity of marginalized groups is limited by the inequalities that structure their lives and opportunities. But how far will members of privileged groups go towards levelling the playing field when the field is clearly tipped in their favour?

I do not think that there is any easy answer to this problem, and it is not particularly my brief today to suggest one. But I do think that yet another item that should not fall off your agenda is the question of developing a strategy through which whatever recommendations you make can be implemented. I would suggest that such a strategy would include a serious dialogue with and mobilization of the marginalized groups I have mentioned.

Presentation made at The Democracy Commission's Media Seminar

by **Mr. Gerard Colleran,** Editor of the *Irish Star*, May 17 2005

LET ME start with a confession: I don't have a very pronounced or self-conscious sense of my role in democracy as editor of *The Star*.

Truth to tell I'm too busy just surviving in the piranha tank that is the Irish newspaper industry to contemplate such lofty notions too very often.

One of my daily mantras is borrowed from that of another far more celebrated journalist, the American, Ambrose Bierce, who liked to intone: "Grant us Oh Lord the Grace this day <u>NOT</u> to be found out!"

I have never been comfortable with the notion that the media in general, and newspapers in particular, should have a central role in the education of public opinion.

That's not to say that newspapers should not carry matters of opinion as part of its stock 'n trade. Rather my concern centres on our supposed role as educators.

It sounds all too proper for me, to be supervisory of public attitudes and beliefs, much too involved as a player with a desired outcome in civic society.

There are two great schools of thought when it comes to what we in the newspaper business are doing.

- A newspaper is merely a product, like all other products available in a free, democratic, market-driven society.

And:

- A newspaper is a central player in the great democratic debate, with a heavy weight of responsibility to actively participate, to argue, to inform.

There is no one-best-way to understanding the role of newspapers and the media in a modern, 21st Century First World democracy.

A newspaper is both a product as far as consumers are concerned and a player in the great democratic, civic society debate. To confine us to one role or the other is to fail to understand the function and reality of newspapers.

At one level we are a product like all other products – like a Snickers bar for instance.

- Both products must have attractive and acceptable packaging.
- The taste must be just right so as to maintain current consumer support and hold out the prospect of attracting even more.
- Both products must have the required 'bite', enjoyment, lingering quality and after-taste.
- They must both satisfy key consumer demands on price, points of sale and must have the required promotion if they are to have any longevity in the market.

Product ingredients vary from time to time but in The Star we have a contract with our customers to provide a daily supply of news (hard, soft and human interest and opinion), showbiz, celebrity, sport - and not necessarily in that order.

The people who hand over their hard-earned cash for our product expect certain ingredients. Like Snickers consumers who would notice the absence of peanuts, our supporters would equally be outraged if there were no Britneys, no Damien Duffs, no Colin Farrells, no Mad Mullahs and so on.

Therefore, the key role of the modern newspaper is to satisfy consumer demands. The interpretation of those demands – not an easy task in a fast-moving, pick-and-choose, consumerist society – defines the success or failure of our newspaper enterprise.

The one way that we can ensure success into the future is to keep close to our consumers, our readers. We must know what they want – and then we must supply it.

Supplying what readers want requires the deployment of skilled journalistic resources. Good journalism provides the material that will satisfy consumer demands.

Good journalism is the start-point of a virtuous circle. Good journalism is good business.

There is no doubt then that newspapers are products like other fast-moving, highly-perishable products.

However, it's also clear that newspaper products have a quality attached to them which makes them key players in civic and public debate – in the context of Ireland and the Western World, the press has an influence beyond the reality of its 'product' status.

That's why, for instance, Colin Powell said: "The most effective means of ensuring the government's accountability to the people is an aggressive, free, challenging, untrusting press."

Newspaper readers in Ireland are, I believe, increasingly demanding a more accountable government. This kind of journalism forms part of the product-mix of a successful newspaper and discharges Colin Powell's injunction quoted earlier.

One has to concede that while at one level a newspaper is no more than a Snickers bar, the implications for newspapers not doing their job – by failing to provide for example the necessary untrusting challenge to government and other power centres – as compared to Snickers manufacturers supplying below-standard nuts, are vastly different.

Newspapers have a bounden duty to supply the product-mix expected of them. Failure to challenge government will, without any doubt whatsoever, lead directly to self-serving administrations, waste of resources, politicians who consider themselves masters rather than servants, lying and cheating by the political elite.

Sounds familiar, doesn't it.

We in the newspaper industry have not been as challenging as we could or should have been. We have failed to take full account of Thomas Jefferson's (1787) stricture:

> "The two enemies of the people are criminals and government, so let us tie the second down with the chains of the Constitution so the second will not become the legalised version of the first."

We in the newspaper and media business generally have been too willing to believe, much too compliant, much too forgiving of our political servants.

Mark Twain said: "The Government is merely a servant – merely a temporary servant: it cannot be its prerogative to determine what is right and what is wrong, and decide who is a patriot and who isn't. Its function is to obey orders, not originate them..."

In all honesty, can we really, hand on heart, say that journalism in Ireland has been strong enough, aggressive enough, disbelieving enough, and angry enough when it comes to our political servants who would be our lords and masters.

Because of history and reasons of convenience, our political elites have availed of a largely compliant media to maintain an effectively closed, shutdown system of administration. As other nations were opening up, our political servants were emasculating the Freedom of Information Act – and largely got away with it.

These two fingers to the sovereign people of Ireland came in the context of manifest lies that helped win the last election for the current administration. Promises on medical cards, social housing, gardai and much more were promptly abandoned after the 2002 election on the grounds of cost.

Before that election a senior member of Cabinet privately admitted that spending had been allowed to get out of control in order to boost jobs – in order to create feel-good conditions in the run-up to voting. We'd simply have to pay later!

Within six months of the last election we branded this administration as a bunch on cheats. 'Screwed by Liars' was our splash headline the following November, with the announcement of the budget.

In due course, the people of this country endorsed our views by delivering a pretty savage kicking to Fianna Fáil in last year's European and local elections.

Our accusing posture towards the government within a short period of the 2002 election is now the norm. What we said then is now orthodoxy.

Sickened to their back teeth by a relentless campaign in The Star, echoed, though not given full throttle, in other newspapers, the Government tricked around with the notion of bringing the press under State control.

They already have RTE in their grip – and the so-called independent broadcasting sector is similarly forced into line through legislation.

But what about the press – the only media sector truly

independent of government control? Well, now the Government would attempt the Triple Crown!

The Mohan Commission report was scary – it recommended a nine-member Press Commission, with the members appointed by the Government. Even the current administration, including Justice and Law Reform Minister Michael McDowell, couldn't argue for that!

Eventually, this has been watered down to a self-regulatory system, which may be recognised in statute. A Press Complaints Commission would be appointed, with representatives drawn from the general public and from the press.

As a kind of quid pro quo, the Government will reform the libel laws – something that should have been done decades ago on the recommendations of many, including the Law Reform Commission.

When it comes to delivering this reform of our outdated libel laws, I won't hold my breath. I doubt we'll have anything worth writing home about until at least after the next general election. After that it's anybody's guess.

Thankfully, the public mood as far as libel cases are concerned has altered in favour of the press over the past number of years. The hands-down, no-questions-asked win we at *The Star* had over Government spin doctor Mandy Johnston early last year was clear evidence of a shift in public mood.

However, as one threat, that of libel, seems to recede, another emerges over the European horizon.

Now we have privacy! Hanover and Naomi are now held out as a means of softening the press's cough.

And the tendency to push back press freedoms is significant. At a recent seminar, I heard a solicitor denounce newspapers for referring to the vicious teenage rapists of a woman in County Clare as animals. *The Star* was one of those newspapers.

She, however, considered it a gross invasion of these rapists' privacy to be named and described in this way.

I now have the sense that privacy will now take up from where defamation has, hopefully, left off - and the burden imposed will deliver a weaker style of journalism and a lighter bottom line for media businesses.

In the main, media generally and newspapers in particular, come under sustained attack as a result of its coverage of tragic, highly-charged and sensitive matters such as murder, rape and other kinds of sexual crimes, suicides, terror outrages and so on. Also there is often criticism of media coverage of funerals.

Newspaper articles and photographs of celebrities, the children of celebrities, politicians or people well known to the public also tend to draw fire – particularly where this coverage deals with their private lives.

In my experience the most strident criticism comes from people who are not directly linked to the tragic events being covered or to the victims, or indeed to the deceased.

In my entire career in journalism I've never received a complaint from a bereaved family about the use of pictures of the deceased or the sad funerals that followed.

On the contrary, my experience professionally and personally has been that families treasure press reports of loved ones lost to them. It's confirmation for them that their loss has been recorded, that their son or daughter didn't pass through life unnoticed and unrecorded.

Nevertheless there is sustained criticism of media coverage of disasters, no matter what size.

It confirms for me that there is a strengthening voice out there, grounded on political correctness, which is determined to remove from our sight any true images of the real world.

They want us to live in a kind of Matrix. There is no pain, no awfulness, no tragedy, no suffering.

We live our lives in a cloud of pretence – things are good. Lives are always lived to the full, rewarding and fulfilled.

Newspaper journalists and media generally have a responsibility to present the world as it really is - in all its disparate manifestations. When I fell to thinking about this topic the first thing that struck me was that surviving in this piranha tank has some additional spin-off benefits which enhance democracy.

One obvious, but often-overlooked fact, is that survival in business sustains jobs. We have over 100 mainly young people dependent on our two publications for their weekly wage. One hundred regular and decent wage packets go a long way towards sustaining democracy.

Furthermore, it is my firm belief that journalism is best sustained by the free market. True democracy depends on choice - if you are not producing a popular product you fail.

People can occasionally be fooled. But in the longer term they are not fools. If your product is not decent and true, you fail. It is for the people to decide.

Another celebrated American journalist, Joseph Pulitzer, he who endowed the world famous Pulitzer Prizes for literature and journalism, was an ardent believer in the need for journalism to be commercially viable and pay its own way.

Like Pulitzer, I think this is not just guided by the realities of day-to-day commercial life. Solvency, commercial success and the building up of some wealth are the keys to freedom. Previous generations of Irish people paid dearly to learn that simple lesson: You only have freedom of action if you have a few quid in your pocket.

Pulitzer summed all this up rather pithily: "If a newspaper is to be of real service to the public, it must have a big circulation . . . because circulation means advertising, and advertising means money, and money means independence."

Newspapers must never be ashamed of commercial success. Our highest ethic must be to stay in business, stay strong through satisfying the demands of our readers.

By staying strong we pay our bills, we pay our wages – and out of our wages, mortgages are paid, roofs are put over the heads of families, bread put on the table.

So, the role of the press in democracy? That's a big idea, not one on which I dwell.

And, if the truth be told, I always tend to wonder about people who do dwell on that matter. It's rather like Liam Lawlor referring to Liam Lawlor.

Such self-important self-awareness, such a self-conscious search for a role by some people involved in media is, quite honestly, located somewhere between frightening and laughable.

I always fear, also, that if the press facilitates a definition of its role in a democracy, it falls into the arms of those who would bind it hand and foot.

Understanding the role of the press comes first – next comes control.

We in the media should sidestep this bear trap. We should not help them define us. Instead, our mission should be to simply exist.

By existing, by doing what we do best, we live up to the higher calling of giants on whose shoulders we now stand.

We should just exist. That's good enough for me.

By existing we pose the greatest threat to those who despise freedom, choice, democracy.

> "Why should freedom of speech and freedom of press be allowed? Why should a government which is doing what it believes to be right allow itself to be criticized? It would not allow opposition by lethal weapons. Ideas are much more fatal things than guns. Why should any man be allowed to buy a printing press and disseminate pernicious opinions calculated to embarrass the government?"

The words of VI Lenin.

Presentation made at The Democracy Commission's Media Seminar

by **Mr. Séamus Dooley,** Irish Secretary, NUJ, 17 May 2005

When commercial television was introduced to Britain Sir Robert Fraser, in welcoming the triumph over those who favoured only public service models of broadcasting, declared, "The old system of monopoly in Britain was carried away by a wave of democratic thought and feeling"[12].

I think that phrase "a wave of democratic thought and feeling" reflects the contempt with which at least some of those involved in the media - publishers, editors and even journalists - hold for those who would question the role and function of the media.

Fraser's irritation at the intrusion of questions about democratic values and responsibilities into a debate about making money reflects a normally unspoken view of many media owners – that citizens should accept without question or quibble the diet offered to them.

Debate is tolerated within the context of current controversy – through letters pages, phone-ins and occasional publication of "right of reply" style columns.

In Ireland we have not had an informed debate on the role and function of the media in democracy and opportunities for public discourse have been squandered.

That is why I warmly welcome this forum and the context in which it takes place.

Those who challenge the media establishment in the public arena frequently find themselves vilified by an army of usual

---

12   Quoted in Communications by Raymond Williams. (Penguin, 1977)

suspects, the victim of unfriendly fire from a variety of pulpits.

Admission of the remote possibility that journalistic standards have slipped is met with sound and fury – and if journalists raise that possibility, the offending critic is likely to be accused of betrayal of the worst type, of selling out to those who would undermine the right to freedom of expression. Thus I risk a broadside for even suggesting that we have failed to use recent opportunities for self-examination.

The application by RTE for a licence fee increase could have provided the context for a meaningful debate on public service broadcasting but instead became media frenzy about the wages of Pat Kenny and Gay Byrne.

Of course there was a public interest in, as well as a public curiosity about, the level of earnings of stars who spent so much time in our sitting rooms and offices and I welcome the publication of information that should always have been in the public domain.

What would have been more useful, however, was a debate on the very concept of public service broadcasting, on the role and function of television and radio in democracy and, more crucially, an examination of the responsibilities of those not bound by the public service remit which defined RTE.

The virulent attacks on RTE in some cases had their basis in commercial rather than editorial or philosophical considerations. In the same way the publication of the Mohan Report[13] could have provided a context for a wider debate on the nature of contemporary Irish journalism. Instead the Mohan Report forced the newspaper industry players, including the NUJ, to form a coalition aimed at stalling the creation of a State-appointed Press Council.

Newspaper commentary has, perhaps understandably, focussed on media resistance to the concept of a State-controlled Press Council. The NUJ is opposed to a Press Council appointed by or controlled by the State and so many of the concerns echoed by commentators would find an echo in NUJ policy.

We have long believed that there should be a Press Council funded by the newspaper industry and representative of the industry, including editors and journalists, but also reflective of civic society. The threat of a State-appointed council forced a reluctant partnership between NNI, RNAI, magazine publishers, the NUJ and even the

---

13   Report of the Legal Advisory Group on Defamation 2003 (Department of Justice, Equality and Law Reform)

UK press in Ireland, whose commitment to the project has yet to be proven.

What has been most illuminating about the media reaction to the Mohan report has been the knee-jerk reaction to sections of the media to the call for greater newspaper accountability. I bow to no one in my commitment to the concept of freedom of expression. The NUJ strongly believes that it is in the interest of the media - and more importantly, in the public interest - that the newspaper industry should take responsibility for media regulation.

But I cannot accept the shrill tone of some media critics who have represented proposals to establish a Press Council and Media Ombudsman as an attack on media freedom, a conspiracy by the State, aided and abetted by the NNI, the NUJ and the RNAI, to undermine the very fabric of democracy.

That reaction is not confined to one sector of the media. The Star, the Sunday Times and the Sunday Independent are very different editorial creatures but they have been united in their use of high profile commentators to attack the concept of an accountable media. And much of the commentary has been based on misinformation and a misinterpretation, some of it deliberate, of what exactly is involved in the process of media accountability.

Ethical journalism has nothing to fear from independent systems of regulation and accountability. Those who claim that the market place is the ultimate press council adopt a simplistic approach to the central role of the media in shaping public opinion.

Without the promise of libel reform, newspaper owners would not have accepted the principle of a press council. The carrot and stick approach of the Minister for Justice, Equality and Law Reform, Michael McDowell has resulted in an internal debate on a code of practice and on the most effective model for an Irish Press Council. What is regrettable is that the debate has taken place in private and that to date there has not been the opportunity for public discourse. With the forthcoming publication of a draft bill I hope civic interest groups will come forward with their thoughts and ideas.

I hope that there will be a broad welcome for the Press Industry Steering Committee proposals, which I believe are broadly acceptably and have much to recommend them. There will be a role for civic society and the Press Council will operate independently of the industry.

There have been understandable concerns about the erosion of standards in Irish journalism and the NUJ shares that concern. The majority of Irish editors and journalists are ethical, conscientious men and women with integrity and in the context of a discussion on standards, I think it is important that we should avoid applying the same measure of tar to all editors and journalists.

Newspapers are commercial products and the desire to maximise market share at all costs has had a negative impact on journalism. The dominance of marketing values has led to a diversion of resource from editorial budgets into free magazines and CDs.

Thus inadequate provision is made for news coverage, with an increased dependence on syndication and agency copy.

Reduction in editorial expenditure is reflected in dwindling staff numbers in newsrooms. In the drive to drag down costs journalists and photographs are increasingly tied to base, resulting in a Dublin-centric focus in the vast majority of Irish newspapers.

The absence of investigative journalism in the Irish print media is frequently attributed to our repressive libel regime but little is said of the refusal of media organisations to invest time and resources in this vital area of journalism.

As a trade union, we have seen a growth in anti-union companies and are constantly battling against media organisations where the pay and conditions are significantly worse than in unionised companies. In the media sector, there is a direct correlation between poor pay and employment conditions and low journalistic standards.

In my experience most newspapers that show contempt for workers have no difficulty in showing contempt for their readers.

There is a direct relationship between pay and conditions, journalistic standards and press freedom. High standards can only be sustained if journalists enjoy good wages and conditions. The casualisation of the industry and the pressure on journalists to accept inappropriate contracts of employment act as a disincentive to educated, enthusiastic young men and women to enter the profession.

In the context of this forum perhaps the most significant issue for democracy in Ireland is the dominance of a small group of companies. Predictably the issue of concentration of ownership is one that has not provoked significant debate within the media, while politicians have run scared of tacking the problem.

The Commission on the Newspaper Industry in Ireland failed to deal with the issue of concentration of ownership and cross owner-ship in a meaningful way, noting that there was not "any grounds at present for intervention by the State on the basis of undue concentration of media-wide ownership in Ireland." [14]

The Commission was established in 1996, effectively prompted by the closure of the Irish Press. I believe that it is time for government to revisit this issue, in the light of developments in the regional newspaper sector, in the independent radio sector and in the national press.

Haunted by the infamous "Payback" headline in the *Irish Independent*, politicians will be reluctant to risk incurring the wrath of powerful media owners, whose power in Irish society frequently exceeds those of elected representatives. Ownership of the media is a key issue, which cannot be dodged. The dominance of a small number of media groups and the decline of small family-owned newspapers are of serious concern.

Newspapers, national and regional, are big business. So too is the independent radio sector and the NUJ is gravely concerned at the failure of the broadcasting regulatory authority to maintain the diversity of ownership of local radio stations which was said to be crucial in the development of the sector. The issue of cross-ownership is also one which needs to be addressed.

In any review of the media in Ireland these are issues that need to be tackled, but it is no surprise that they are not being addressed by the industry itself. Recent developments in the Sunday Tribune, for example, underline the extent to which effective commercial and editorial control is exercised by Independent News and Media, even where the competition authorities have sought to limit influence by restricting the shareholding.

As a trade union official I have a real concern at the anti-union stance taken by some newspapers, notably Ireland on Sunday and News International. That ideological position has an impact on editorial content but, more importantly in my day-to-day work, has serious consequences for working journalists, staff and freelances.

---

14   Report of the Commission on the Newspaper Industry, June 1996,

'Active citizenship in contemporary democracy'

by **Professor Iseult Honohan,** Department of Politics, UCD.

Introduction

I have been asked to talk about 'active citizenship: what it means and how it might be realised. Citizenship, with or without the qualifier 'active', is a currently popular concept that has recently leaped from the pages of legal and political texts into the everyday language of politicians, journalists and public servants.[15] I take it that what is of concern to us here today is active *democratic* citizenship, meaning more than just having our interests represented and getting the business of government done. Moreover, we have to think about what it may involve in the context of the realities of far-reaching social and economic change, increasing moral and cultural diversity, and significant immigration that are part of Ireland's experience of globalisation.

In this presentation, I look first at several dimensions of active citizenship, particularly those of status and practice, and at different interpretations based on these dimensions. Then I outline arguments for and against active citizenship as a sense of wider social responsibility and as participation in self-government. Finally, I look at some ways in which it may be possible to encourage these kinds of active citizenship.

Defining citizenship
If we want to think about 'active citizenship', we need first to be clear about what citizenship means. And this is not as easy as is often

---

15   The citizen thus joins the client and the consumer as a key character in contemporary society and politics.

assumed, because citizenship has a number of different dimensions, of which membership, legal status and practice are perhaps the most important.[16] On the dimension of *membership* of a state or political community, citizens are contrasted to non-citizens. The acquisition of citizenship in this sense raises important issues, as we have seen since the referendum debate of 2004, because membership is often taken to be the precondition for exercising the next two senses of citizenship, or *who gets to be* an active citizen, but I have to set it aside for the purposes of this presentation.

The two dimensions more central to the discussion of active citizenship are *status* and *practice*. In both of these senses, it may be argued that the term 'citizen' is contrasted to 'subject', rather than 'non-citizen'. Firstly, there is *legal status*, the ascription of certain rights, such as equality before the law, freedom of speech and association, etc., and certain duties or obligations, such as obeying the law, paying taxes, etc. Secondly, there is the *practice* of citizenship, including such things as participating in self-government, supporting the public good, and defending one's country. Being a citizen in the first sense is essentially a matter of laws, and of fixed rights and obligations, while in the second sense it refers to people's attitudes and behaviour.

Citizenship today

Whatever the basis for acquiring citizenship, we may still ask what it *means* to be a citizen. In contemporary terms, we may understand citizens as, minimally, people who are members of the same state, subject to the jurisdiction of a common sovereign authority, which frames their interactions in containing and structuring a multitude of practices; thus they are significantly *interdependent* with one another. This remains the case despite progressive globalisation of the economy and culture, and changing notions and practices of state sovereignty. While their association may be largely involuntary, citizens share at least common concerns and a common fate or future. To the degree that the government is accountable to them, they share a chance of determining their collective future, and a corresponding responsibility for the actions of the polity.

In the past, liberal accounts of citizenship have emphasised the

16 Citizenship is also understood as an important form of *identity*, but this is outside the scope of the discussion here.

formal rights and duties that go with legal status, while republican accounts emphasised the potential for citizens to participate actively in their own self-rule, and thus to achieve a degree of collective freedom. Different approaches to citizenship still tend to emphasise one or another of these dimensions (Kymlicka and Norman 1994).

The revival of the idea of citizenship

So it is not surprising that today the meaning of citizenship and the features emphasised in its recent revival are contested. This carries over to the way the term 'active citizenship' has been used. There are at least four different emphases in recent calls on the language of citizenship:

Individual self-reliance
First, it has been invoked in order to advocate greater individual self-reliance. This was the sense the Conservatives in Britain sought to promote in the 1980s. Norman Tebbitt's 'Get on your bicycle' remark encapsulated the argument that people should rely less on the state and be more energetic in providing for themselves.

The defence of social and economic rights
Quite a different approach, and one that comes broadly from the left, has called on the language of citizenship to argue for the defence of extensive social and economic rights against the sort of contraction implied by the Tebbitt view cited above. This draws on the idea (advanced influentially by Marshall during the building of the post-war Welfare State) that there has been a necessary development from civil to political to social and economic rights, and that these are now all complementary parts of citizenship.

A sense of broader social concern
A further meaning of citizenship takes it to refer to a broader sense of social concern. Being a citizen means not just being self-reliant, or being able to enjoy a wide range of civil, social and economic rights, but also recognising wider responsibilities to those with whom we are interdependent. This sense is encapsulated in the phrase 'being a good citizen' that is often used even in non-political contexts to

describe someone who is prepared to play their part in co-operative endeavours, indeed to do more than is strictly required of them, rather than always putting their own interests first.

Participation in the democratic process
Finally, there is the more standardly political sense of citizenship as participation in the democratic process, engaging in political discussion and decision-making, serving on juries and in public office of various kinds.

It seems fair to say that self-reliance does not in itself constitute citizenship, and the enjoyment of social and economic rights does not necessarily involve activity (even if these are a necessary precondition for it). Thus it is the last two accounts that require further examination in the context of active citizenship.

Arguments for and against active citizenship as assuming wider social concern

The best argument on behalf of the idea that citizens should be prepared to assume wider social concern stems from the extent of their interdependence, and the fact that a satisfactory society cannot be realised solely on the basis of exact and narrow adherence to the law. There are important shared goods that can be realised only if there is a significant body of citizens who have a sense of common concerns, and who are prepared to take into account in their actions the common good or wider interests of, for example, the environment and culture that they share with others. Sometimes these interests are easier to recognise in negative instances of common 'bads' or risks that face members of a community. Citizens have an interest in living in planned cities with clean air, safe transport systems, and food supplied by sound farming practices. Of course, the language of the common good can be used hypocritically, and the greater the inequalities between citizens, the less we can talk about 'common' rather than 'club' goods – that is, publicly supported goods that benefit only those with the capacities, time and resources to avail of them. The common good is a horizon of meaning or regulative idea to be taken into account in actions and decision-making, rather than a fixed goal. Rather than there being a single authoritative account of the common good, what constitutes it in different instances has to be determined through deliberation among different perspectives, and is always open to change.

Against this is it has been argued that the demand for this kind of active citizenship is oppressive, conformist and exclusive - that it makes too many demands on citizens and boils down to a call for greater obedience or loyalty to the state.

It is important first to note a distinction between one conventional idea of the 'good' citizen and the 'active' citizen. On some accounts, 'good' citizens might be seen to be simply more obedient, self-effacing or loyal to their state or fellow citizens than others. (One interpretation of what it is to be a 'good' French citizen deems it necessary for Muslim girls not to wear headscarves at school.) It needs to be made clear that adopting a broader sense of responsibility is not the same as requiring people to be more obedient to authority or to conform to existing norms or patterns of behaviour.

While democracy requires a sense of concern for the wider public good, it also centrally requires the involvement of citizens in political and social activity. Some communitarian and conservative advocates may emphasise duties and responsibility, but this is just one dimension of active citizenship. There can be different ways of being a good citizen; in any case it requires critical engagement, which may sometimes involve standing up against existing authority. Both of these dimensions are conveyed in the notion of 'engaged citizenship', expressed in the title of the Democracy Commission's May 2004 progress report: '*Disempowered and disillusioned, but not disengaged*'.

Arguments for and against active citizenship as participation

I turn then to arguments for and against active citizenship as participation in self-government.

It can be argued that there are at least three kinds of reasons why citizens need to be involved in political discussion and decision-making: (1) in order to protect their individual interests; (2) because participating is intrinsically worthwhile; and (3) because decisions to which more people contribute are likely to be better decisions, and ones to which people are more likely to adhere. The arguments advanced against extensive participation include (1) the impossibility of accommodating the large numbers of citizens in modern societies in decision-making; (2) the lack of competence of most people to judge complex political decisions; and (3) the danger of majority tyranny.

In response to these objections, we may argue firstly that citizens may be extensively involved in decision-making, not in a single forum, but at many levels in various kinds of process. Large numbers can be accommodated in various kinds of participatory structure in regions, localities, neighbourhoods or workplaces. These kinds of assembly may be united in some kind of pyramidal structure, and mesh in with a system of representation. While this calls for considerable imagination and experiment, the problem of numbers alone is not a decisive objection to a more participatory politics. It is true, secondly, that political decisions are complex, and require considerable information. But the contrast that critics of participatory democracy imply between passionate, ignorant and sectionally interested citizens and rational, informed and disinterested representatives may well seem overdrawn in the light of contemporary scandals. The way to address the problem is in part through encouraging better-informed citizens. Thirdly, it must be said that the problem of majority tyranny is not a problem of participation, but of a particular interpretation of democracy as majority rule. Majority tyranny can be imposed through representative forms of government without extensive participation.

The right to vote in regular elections for representatives is only one dimension of participation, but the alternative is not continuous instant direct democracy. What democracy requires is not that everyone be the author of every decision, but that people can make their voices heard in areas that affect them. Political equality may aim at giving citizens an equal chance to influence decisions, rather than an equally weighted vote in a mechanical decision process. This points towards a more participatory deliberative politics, in which decisions are taken on the basis of discussion and reflection. What is at stake in politics is not just distributing individual goods but also shaping shared goods. Bargaining or compromise between interests or preferences taken as fixed, is not the most appropriate way to realise these. The point of active citizenship is to bring about deliberative participation among those who, while having many different interests and perspectives, share a public sphere and common future.

Aspects of active citizenship

Thus active citizenship does not amount to a general sense of identi-fication or belonging, a meek assumption of social responsibilities, or a more vocal promotion of individual or sectional interests. We might say that there are three aspects of active citizenship that are desirable - an awareness of interdependence, an attitude of civic self-restraint, and an openness to deliberative engagement.

a)   There is the cognitive dimension through which citizens become *aware of their interdependencies* and common economic, social and environmental concerns. They recognise how they are related to others in being dependent on practices supported by them, and in affecting them by their actions. Since the possi-bility of self-government depends on the equal opportunity of all to be self-governing, they inform themselves of the social conditions of their fellow citizens, and pay *attention* to political issues, contributing to policy decisions directly or indirectly.

b)   There is the dispositional dimension, concerning attitudes and behaviour. Citizens need to *exercise some level of civic self-restraint.* This is less a matter of deferring gratification than of giving more weight to common interests than prevails in the contem-porary culture of individualism. But it may be understood as an expansion, or re-identification, of the self or individual interest in a broader sense, rather than as self-denial, or as a calculation of the balance of interests. Those who recognise interdepend-ence are more likely to accept, for example, redistributive measures that maintain political equality, individual costs incurred in taking time to recycle, limiting their own pursuit of material wealth, engaging in activities of care, and giving time and energy to political concerns ranging from voting and jury-service to attending hearings right up to serving in office. Active self-restraint implies an orientation to challenge infringements not only of one's own rights, but also those of others.

c)   Thirdly there is the practical dimension of *deliberative engage-ment.* Citizens form their own judgements, are prepared to explain their own positions, to listen to other points of view, and to revise their opinions in deliberation. But this does not presuppose consensus; there will be strong differences on how to interpret, prioritise and realise common goods. Learning to deal with conflict is itself an important part of civic virtue. Citizens need to be able to exercise independent judgement, but accept decisions when made in a fair public procedure. But they are vigilant with respect to abuses of power, public or private. They are prepared to raise, and support others who raise, issues of concern in the public arena, and to defend the interests of fellow citizens subject to injustices as well as defending themselves. This may involve opposing laws that undermine freedom, including civil disobedience and direct action.

Promoting active citizenship

It should be clear that promoting active citizenship is not just a matter of exhorting people to be more concerned, more selfless or more involved. It requires the creation of institutional frameworks that make it possible, and the provision of education and resources that make it practicable. As John Baker has addressed the issue of resources and institutions more generally, I will briefly address the question of institutions and education specifically with reference to the two dimensions of active citizenship under discussion here.

Institutions
What kinds of institutions for participation might we envisage? Active citizenship should not be envisaged in terms just of participation in civil society, but in the public sphere of politics. The focus needs to go beyond membership of social and community groups to include participation in public interaction that can have an impact on policies that affect people's lives. (See also Honohan 2002: 233-5)

If active political participation is desirable, does this mean we should introduce compulsory voting? There are several arguments in favour of compulsory voting. At a basic level, the greater the range of participants, the wider range of interests politicians will need to consider; thus compulsory voting addresses the problem that politicians can be elected by proposing policies which appeal to the classes most likely to vote, even if these are not in the interest of the majority or of the common good.

In practice, however, whether there should be compulsory participation, even at the level of voting for representatives, may depend on whether it will elicit genuine engagement and deliberation. In some circumstances - if, for example, it creates strong resentment, or is not deliberative enough - it may be justified but undesirable. If active citizenship is to be taken seriously, it might be more relevant to require people to participate more extensively in more deliberative forms of political practice, on the grounds that this would extend citizens' awareness of interdependence, give them a common experience, confront them with the views of citizens who hold different views, and engage them in deliberation with immediate implications for policy.

A number of recent institutional experiments are designed to promote informed and deliberative participation of just this kind. 'Deliberative polling' and 'citizens' juries' are variations of a procedure in which representative groups of people are given the opportunity to spend one or more days gaining information and discussing the issues before expressing their opinion on a particular question. Recently, a detailed suggestion for a publicly organised 'deliberation day' on a wider scale - to be held before elections in the USA - has been advanced (Ackerman and Fishkin, 2003). John Baker has talked about the example of the more systematic 'participatory budget' introduced in Porto Alegre, which has been the focus of considerable interest. (See also Fung and Wright, 2003). The need for people from different groups to engage with one another, rather than forming separate parallel societies, indifferent to, suspicious of, or hostile to one another has been addressed in schemes of cross-cutting constituencies, where members of different social groups have to vote for representatives who are drawn from groups other than their own (Carens 2000; Van Parijs 2000). Such experiments need examination and are doubtless subject to critique and capable of improvement, but they point to the range of ways in which more participation may be possible for citizens.

Civic education

If we are interested in these aspects of citizenship we need to bear in mind that, as Rousseau remarked, 'citizens are not made in a day'.

Social awareness, attitudes and practical capacities need time and practice to develop. Thus education is central to active citizenship.

Right now there is a great deal of interest in and emphasis on providing formal citizenship education. But we need to remember that education for – or against – active citizenship may also take place informally through practice and experience. In particular, the structure, culture and wider curriculum of schools will affect people's attitudes and behaviour as much as formal education for citizenship. The effects of school structure (hierarchical or participatory), size (large or small), and culture (orientation to exams/points or student development) need to be addressed. (See also Honohan 2005)

In any case, if the elements of active citizenship are awareness of interdependence, civic self-restraint and inclination to engage deliberatively, this suggests certain guidelines for formal citizenship education that it is not confined to conveying knowledge, but also develops dispositions, attitudes and practice.

The introduction of civic education at secondary level in Ireland has been a step forward. The underlying principles, syllabus, and universal requirement of CPSE are all positive features. Its shortcomings in practice include lack of commitment by many schools, who treat it as the last subject to be allocated, so that it suffers from incursions on class time; the reallocation of trained and committed teachers; rapid turn over among teachers; and limited scope and variety in the projects submitted.

The proposal to introduce Citizenship Studies at Leaving Certificate raises additional issues that need to be addressed. In its favour is the need to extend citizenship education beyond 15, the age at which students are likely just to be beginning to develop some level of political awareness. Again, the proposed syllabus appears to be based on well-thought out principles (Ward 2002). However, if it becomes a Leaving Certificate subject (giving it more weight in the curriculum) it will be taken only by those who remain at school up to that level and is likely to be taken only by a subset of even those students, not by all future citizens. Secondly, as the Leaving Certificate is still largely an academic examination, it may develop the *cognitive* dimension of citizenship - awareness of interdependence - but will not address the other two dimensions - civic self-restraint and inclination to deliberative engagement. A practical element addressing these two dimensions would be essential.

An alternative - or supplement - to academic studies of citizenship is some kind of community project. Two points should be made here. Firstly, while worthy in itself, not all community service or voluntary activity involves both dimensions of active citizenship - responsibility and deliberative engagement. Secondly, it has been observed that community service is more effective in creating a sense of effective participation when it is linked to curriculum subjects, rather than when it is treated as an independent activity. Thus, for example, a project to clean up a local stream that is co-ordinated with a biology or environmental science class has a greater impact than a clean-up project carried out alone.

The potential limitations of a Leaving Certificate programme could be addressed in a number of ways - through Garret FitzGerald's proposal to require Citizenship Studies as a Fifth Year subject, for example, and through building a substantial element of practice on these dimensions into Transition Year activities. Likewise, political literacy and skills may be developed through various kinds of school council and of classroom deliberation. A more radical suggestion is the requirement or encouragement of a period of civic service - during school or college years, offering a variety of alternative contexts in which this could be taken, in order to suit the varied interests of students. This might be compared to the community service (often overseas) that forms part of the 'gap year' that some British students take. Once again, such proposals need a great deal of further consideration, but point to ways in which active citizenship may be encouraged.

Conclusion

I have outlined what we may understand as two complementary dimensions of active citizenship - the sense of wider social concern and the capacity to participate deliberatively in self-government.

An emphasis on responsible citizenship does not have to be oppressive or unrealistically demanding. It represents the voluntary commitment of citizens who see the value of their contributions to society. The point is not just to exhort citizens to be concerned about the common good; the other side of this is to allow citizens to shape their individual and collective lives. People cannot reasonably be criticised as apathetic or politically ignorant if they do not have the conditions and opportunities for effective participation. We should be wary of exhortations to be more active or civic spirited, or to join voluntary associations in order to strengthen social capital, unless ordinary citizens are given a larger voice in decision-making, opportunities for meaningful participation and the material conditions necessary for active citizenship in the two senses outlined here.

References

Ackerman, B. and J. Fishkin, 2003: 'Deliberation Day' in Fishkin and Laslett (eds), *Debating Deliberative Democracy*. Oxford: Blackwell.

Carens, J., 2000: *Culture, Citizenship and Community*. Oxford: Oxford University Press.

Crick, B., 2002: 'A note on what is and what is not active citizenship'. http://www.citizen-shippost-16.lsda.org.uk/files/033 BernardCrick WHAT IS CITIZENSHIP.pdf [13-06- 2005] Democracy Commission, 2004: *Progress report*: 'Disempowered and disillusioned, but not disengaged.'

Fishkin, J. and P. Laslett (eds), 2003: *Debating Deliberative Democracy*. Oxford: Blackwell.

Fung, A. and E.O.Wright (eds), 2003: *Deepening Democracy: Institutional Innovations in Empowered Participatory Governance*. The Real Utopias Project IV. London and New York: Verso.

Honohan, I, 2002: *Civic Republicanism*. London: Routledge.

_____, 2005: 'Educating citizens: nation-building and its republican limits' in I. Honohan and J. Jennings (eds), *Republicanism in Theory and Practice*. London: Routledge.

Kymlicka, W. and W. Norman, 1994: 'The return of the citizen'. *Ethics* 104 1994 352-81

K. McDonough and W. Feinberg (eds), 2003: *Citizenship and Education in Liberal-Democratic Societies*. New York: Oxford University Press.

Van Parijs, P., 2000: 'Power-sharing versus border-crossing in ethnically divided societies', in I. Shapiro and S. Macedo (eds), *Designing Democratic Institutions*. New York: New York University Press.

Ward, E., 2002: *Citizenship Studies*. Dublin: CDVEC Curriculum Development Unit.

'Democracy and the Media'

Presentation to the Democracy Commission Media
Seminar

by **Mr. Patrick Kinsella,** School of Communications, DCU
17 May 2005

The Media and Freedom

One thing distinguishes our civilization from those which have gone before – more than anything else except our technology – and that is simple numbers. Billions of us on the planet, hundreds of millions sharing sovereignty in the European Union, millions on our island. A far cry from the city square of ancient Greece or the village council of more recent history. Clearly, sustaining these numbers would be impossible without mass media – to the extent that it is almost impossible to imagine how we would go about organizing all this complexity without the means of conveying information and opinion to large numbers of people in a short space of time.

I say this because debates about mass media usually proceed as if the media are separate from society, and are in some sense to blame for whatever social or political changes we do not like. But the media are neither monolithic nor autonomous; like every other social institution, they are a field for contest of ideas, and are subject to the same technical, economic and cultural tensions that somehow have got us where we are.

The circumstances of life in our mass society have created a separation of citizens from each other, and from the organs of power which more or less depend on popular consent. From the point of view of freedom – which is our common purpose here – the relative anonymity in which we work and play can be seen either as a loss of community, or as a gain of privacy compared to more intimate and public societies.

But this distance between the public and the structures of

government has already begun in many states to turn the formality of the Republic into the reality of rule by closed elites, with all the potential for corruption, injustice and oppression implied by outright tyranny.

The Democracy Commission is addressing the disconnection of citizens from power across a range of policy areas, but I will follow Thomas Jefferson in saying that free media – in his day only the printed press, of course – comprise the one indispensable condition for a free society.

"Where the press is free," Jefferson wrote, "and every citizen able to read, all is safe."[17] [18]

Like Jefferson, I take for granted that we have free speech: but the freedom of the media must be more than a freedom to express ideas: if citizens are to be equipped to hold power accountable, they must have independent and trustworthy sources of information; and that raises issues wider than the freedom to publish.

Note how Jefferson also stipulated that citizens must be able to read, and for us today, this goes beyond mere literacy, to access – a vital current issue as the Irish government considers changes to public service broadcasting, and as the EU tries to advance the rights of corporations to make profits by eroding the rights of states to regulate or fund media businesses. Even for Jefferson, freedom of expression and information was of little value unless is was permitted "to penetrate the whole mass of the people".[19]

Freedom requires diversity: as a condition and as a consequence of choice. And that means competition. Competition between ideas, competition between versions of reality, and between media enterprises and products.

I am sure my colleagues from the newspapers and from the National Union of Journalists will address the implications of this, for we know that the technology required to reach large numbers of people is expensive, and that the market, unattended, tends to

---

17 Jefferson to Charles Yancey, 1816. Sources at
    http://etext.virginia.edu/jefferson/quotations/jeffbibl.htm. I have changed
    'man' to 'citizen', so as not to be distracted by the need to say explicitly
    that the 19th century version of democracy is no longer acceptable in some
    important respects.
18 It is clear that Jefferson was referring to a diverse, non-monopoly press.
19 Jefferson to Edward Carrington, 1787, sources as before.

monopoly or partial monopoly. And monopolies do not tend to produce diversity of ideas.[20]

I agree that a media market with more and smaller enterprises – in the sense of ownership and control rather than titles – tends to produce diversity, but it is no guarantee. Different enterprises which share a common motive tend to compete in the same way with similar products and similar market orientation; furthermore where profit is the motive we see today in some sections of our media what Jefferson described nearly two hundred years ago, when he deplored

> ...the putrid state into which our newspapers have passed and the malignity, the vulgarity, and mendacious spirit of those who write for them...These ordures are rapidly depraving the public taste and lessening its relish for sound food. As vehicles for information and a curb on our functionaries, they have rendered themselves useless by forfeiting all title to belief.[21]

Perhaps we should allow for the distemper of advancing years in that view (Jefferson was 71 when he wrote it), but there is nothing new about the coarsening of public discourse by free media, nothing new then, in the warmongering of Fox News, in Geraldo Rivera reporting from Afghanistan and threatening to shoot people, nothing new in shock speech on the radio, in demeaning TV 'reality' contests or programmes that demonstrate dangerous pranks, not to mention the intrusions, lies and vulgarity in sections of the printed press.

I am not saying here that all modern media is rubbish; far from it, there is much to treasure in print and broadcasting. But if we accept diversity, then we must tolerate a proportion of rubbish. Once we recognise that we need a free media, we cannot then put on restraints, for where would legislators stop, once started, on telling the papers and the broadcasters what to publish?

Nevertheless, some public action is surely required, if the free media neglect their duty of questioning authority and informing the public, or if lies or vulgarity cause identifiable harm.

---

20 The Irish government's record on protecting media diversity is weak, whether we look at the toleration of INM's role at the Sunday Tribune, or the routine approval by the Broadcasting Commission of changes in ownership of independent radio and TV licences.

21 Jefferson to Walter Jones, 1814, sources as before.

Ownership, Motive And Standards

I have already stated my view that diversity of ownership may be of little value if there is no diversity of motive; one possible source of difference is politics, when publishers or broadcasters (and the name Murdoch springs to mind in the case of both, but there are others) adopt political positions, support particular parties. But at the root we generally still find the profit motive, and a dependence on advertising and the corporate executives who are the real customers of commercial mass media. That common motive and dependence is what tends to degrade in all sectors of the market.

The alternative: forms of ownership which do not depend wholly on satisfying advertisers, or do not depend at all on satisfying shareholders. It is no proof of course, but nonetheless remarkable that cooperative or trust-based ownership and control is so common among the world's great newspapers, the Irish Times included.

Such trusts often find it difficult to survive in recessions: recent changes at Le Monde illustrate how difficult it is to survive as a cooperative in a shareholder environment. Direct state assistance to such forms of enterprise is problematic. Purely commercial enterprises would rightly be concerned about unfair competition, and Irish political culture is probably hostile to the Norwegian model of state subvention (except perhaps in Irish language publications or where there are very small readerships).[22]

There may be scope for greater use of tax exemptions for non-profit publishing enterprises, but it would be hard to justify in cases where senior executives reward themselves too extravagantly.

Public Service Broadcasting

Much more than the press, it is broadcasting - and particularly TV - that provides most people with information and ideas about public affairs.

---

22 The Irish public appear to regard with cynicism any distribution of state money that depends on political decisions – thus the perennial concern with the allocation of funds from the National Lottery. Suspicion is likely to be even deeper if ministers were to decide – outside of language promotion - which newspapers should get public cash.

On the face of things, the biggest challenge to diversity of owner-ship in broadcasting has passed. In recent years RTE among other public broadcasters in Europe has had to justify its very existence against the argument that there was no longer any need for state ownership of TV, because technical developments had enabled multichannel competition. In 2001, RTE was defined by statute as a free-to-air public service broadcaster, but the debate on what that meant continued. Last year the Minister for Communications settled the issue for now, when he published the Charter which sets out RTE's duties.

But in reality, the attack on public service broadcasting continues. Private interests have succeeded in redefining PSB as a certain type of programming, rather than as a service.

At the ministerial Forum on Broadcasting in 2002, the represen-tative of Sky Ireland, Mark Deering quoted with approval a 'natural' definition of PSB:

> "broadcasting which, for one reason or another is desirable, but which the market will not provide or will provide in insufficient quantities ...it is impossible to argue for a public service broad-caster unless market failure can be shown".[23]

In his view, such broadcasting does not have to come from a partic-ular type of organization, and he went on to propose that public money could be put into a fund to which any broadcaster could apply for a subsidy, suggesting that

> ...if market failure were clearly identified, public resources would go to the best provider via a competitive bidding process. For example, in the case of arts programmes or Irish children's programmes, commercial broadcasters, arts organisations, or independent producers may provide a superior product or more cost effective use of public resources.

The trouble with this definition, and this approach to PSB, is that we lose sight of motive, of the public service element in PSB; decisions on which programmes should be made, by whom, are removed from the not-for-profit broadcaster. Programme proposals are dependent

---

23   Originally taken from the report of the Davies Commission on broad-casting in the UK in 1999.

on potential private gain, and subsidies are handed out by a separate state agency.

And that indeed is what has happened: the Broadcasting Commission of Ireland, which licenses and supervises the independent broadcasters, has been directed to devise a scheme for the distribution of 5% of TV licence revenue to assist the production of TV and radio programmes under a number of worthy headings.

Thus inevitably by dissipation of the licence fee and dispersal of the power to spend it on programmes, the existing public service broadcaster is weakened. Five percent is a small step, but in that direction lies, in the far distance, a public sector broadcaster with excellent programmes, but little money and small audiences – just as we can see already in the United States of America.

Interestingly, this approach to the weakening of RTE is not supported by TV3, whose representative at the Broadcasting Forum, Rick Hetherington, instead attacked RTE for using the licence fee to bid up the prices of popular imported programmes and sports rights.

That issue is being pursued actively by the EU Commission. Although the future of EU policy on broadcasting in general (The TV Without Frontiers Directive) is under prolonged and apparently divisive review, the EU Commission has recently secured changes in the funding of public TV in France, Spain, and Italy. Now Ireland is being investigated, and there is a suggestion that millions of euro of public money spent on TG4 will have to be repaid.

The government is being asked to justify the use of subsidies aimed at public service broadcasting (narrowly defined) to support other types of programming. So for instance, TG4 (or Telefis na Gaeilge as it was), may have put out some programmes that were not in Irish, in theory depriving some private enterprise of a fair chance to make a profit. From the broad perspective of public service, it makes sense to maximise the audience for Irish language programmes by embedding them in an attractive schedule of other popular programmes, but on the narrow definition of public service programming, it may have been illegal.

The TG4 case neatly illustrates the conflict between broad and narrow views of public service broadcasting, and I urge the Democracy Commission to come down strongly on the side of the broad definition. It is little use to democratic dialogue to have objective news programmes and balanced discussion programmes on a station that nobody watches – reflecting a modern restatement of Jefferson's requirement that the press be free, and that citizens must be able to read it.

We should also encourage the continued existence of a public service broadcasting organisation that is both independent and financially strong, not least because news and investigative current affairs are expensive.

Without large, appreciative audiences for a wide range of popular programmes, not only is advertising revenue diminished (reducing the resources available for public affairs programmes), but so too is political support for an adequate licence fee.[24]

But most important of all, if RTE were weakened, would be the erosion of the public space defined by public service broadcasting. Under the extreme version of subsidies-for-programmes, with a weak state broadcaster, the likelihood is that public affairs will be either moved to the edge of the schedule or transformed into a circus. One does not need to applaud the quality or the content of RTE's Prime Time or Question Time to be grateful that they are where they are in the schedule, and grateful that citizens have the right to question it if they are removed or fail to do their job adequately.

Politics and Public Space

The Commission's progress report raises important questions[25] about whether the media is truly playing its 'integral role' as part of our democracy. It mentions frequent complaints that the activities of the Dáil are covered inadequately, that politics is being trivialized, and that reporting is partial and unfair.

Much of this is true or largely true – of some of the media or some of the time. But we absolutely must permit diversity, which includes the right of journalists to take sides; there is nothing useful

---

24 One partial solution to the conflict with current EU policy would be to end advertising on RTE. That would be unpopular with the advertisers, at least until alternative commercial broadcasters significantly improved their market share; and it is also unlikely to be popular with legislators, who would have to double the current licence fee in order to maintain approximately the existing standard of service.

25 See paragraph 2.43, Democracy in Ireland (The Democracy Commission, May 2004).

to be done to prevent the publication of trivia or biased comment. That is the price of the diversity of a truly free press. The antidote to trivia and bias is to ensure that it does not enjoy a monopoly, and that space also exists for responsible and impartial journalism.

When it comes to the level of parliamentary coverage on radio and TV, broadcasters generally are responsive to the reality of audience interest. It hardly makes sense to cover hours of Dáil debates where even the TDs do not bother to attend. Where real events unfold (for instance in the tribunals) and where parliamentary work counts for more than tired theatre (for instance in the Public Accounts Committee), the media will take interest.

The trivialisation of politics is a more difficult problem. I believe that broadcasters in particular have a duty to find means of engaging with the issues as well as the personalities of politics (though I would add that politicians themselves frequently reduce everything to comparisons of personality).

In particular the habit of reaching always for the sporting analogy, of making a fetish of opinion polls and quoting the bookies' odds on political decisions diminishes public understanding of what is at stake at election time. It is true that audiences demand a mix of information, debate and entertainment, so it is a continuing challenge for editors to design political coverage that is both significant and lively.

A further point on broadcasting: the technical capacity now exists for multiple competing broadcast channels. There may be a temptation to use it to abolish the requirement of impartiality and introduce a range of channels with different editorial positions. The danger then would be the fragmentation of the audience into different political or ideological camps, with the loss of the neutral public space where facts can be established and opinions debated across the boundaries of creed. It is vital to retain broadcasting as a neutral platform for all strands of thought.

Restrictions on Journalism

If politics is justified in demanding more from journalism, then journalists are equally justified in demanding the best legal framework in which to do their work. Unfortunately the trend is in the wrong direction.

The amendments made to the Freedom of Information Act in 2003 led to a collapse in journalistic requests for public records from almost 2,400 in 2003 to fewer than 900 in 2004. This reduction in use of the Act was the government's explicitly stated intention in requiring payment of fees, and in further restricting the range of public records that can be released. These changes should be reversed at the earliest legislative opportunity, and other amendments introduced to give freedom of information a more substantive reality.

The inability of an official inquiry to establish the full facts of how the Department of Health failed to act on advice that the charging of nursing home fees was illegal points to a decline in the keeping of proper administrative records. Successive Information Commissioners have expressed concern that some public servants may no longer be keeping proper records and minutes of meetings precisely because they might be subject to the FOI Act. It is already a criminal offence to destroy records once they have been requested; the next amendment should impose a clearer duty on public bodies to maintain proper records of their activities.

Another significant restriction in our freedom of information regime is the constitutional provision[26] that requires cabinet discussions to be kept confidential (in order to protect collective responsibility and maintain the fiction that there is no disagreement between ministers). Thus cabinet papers revealing different ministerial positions are not released under the Act until they are at least 10 years old. The absurdity of this is demonstrated by the willingness of ministers to reveal when it suits them their differences on a whole range of issues in advance of cabinet meetings – as instanced most recently in the build up to decisions on the new terminal at Dublin Airport.

One further limit on the public's right to know what is done on their behalf is the ability of local authorities to exclude citizens from meetings at will. In a recent example Clare County Council 'went into committee' to discuss aspects of a large public works contract with a company whose labour relations record is controversial.

The excuse given was that reporting of the matter might leave the

---

26 First established by the Supreme Court in 1992, and confirmed by constitutional amendment in 1997.

council open to legal action. This risk could easily be avoided by an extension to local democracy of the privileges enjoyed by parliament: the best protection against any form of misgovernment is not to conceal facts but to let in the light.

Media Regulation

The right amount of media regulation is the minimum amount, another point repeatedly made by Jefferson, on the grounds that any restriction on freedom of expression was more dangerous to democracy than any abuse of such freedom.

Already, all Irish broadcasters operate under fairly heavy prescriptions that their news be objective and impartial, that coverage of public controversy is fair, and that they always refrain from unreasonable intrusion on the privacy of citizens. The legislation now also imposes duties to maintain standards of taste and decency, standards which are increasingly being set by judgments of the Broadcasting Complaints Commission.

There are several interesting points about this form of regulation:

- It is set down in law, but in terms which are general and often undefined
- It allows RTE and the Broadcasting Commission of Ireland to draw up more detailed guidelines for day-to-day procedures
- Editorial judgments on what is fair or objective or decent are subject to correction - on complaint from a citizen - by a supervising agency (the BCC)
- The penalty is no more than a public reprimand, and occasionally a forced retraction or apology.

Broadly speaking, the system is effective in maintaining high standards and correcting errors without excessive cost.

There is no legal obligation on print or other non-broadcast media to be fair or objective, and nor can there be if we are to maintain real freedom of expression. But newspapers, like all media, are subject to penalties after the event in the case of libel, and now increasingly in the case of invasion of privacy. Here, the remedy is not complaint and reprimand, but legal action for damages.

When publishers lose, it can be hugely expensive in damages and legal costs; now after many years of complaint we have arrived at the prospect of changes to the libel law in exchange for some form of self-regulation by the press. A press council and a press ombudsman are proposed, both hugely overdue. Much will depend on the terms under which they will operate, and as the publishers have not yet released the draft code by which the industry would wish to be judged, I will not speculate.

I believe the appointment of a truly independent press ombudsman and an effective council with a strong code of editorial ethics would provide quicker and more effective redress for people who think they have been misrepresented, traduced or unfairly exposed to scrutiny. The discussion engendered by the stream of cases is also likely to encourage a more reflective and more responsible journalism, and a useful engagement by the public in a continuing dialogue on press standards.

But the proposed self-regulation will not prevent, nor even much discourage gross violations of people's privacy and reputations. Salacious tales sell papers, and as long as the press is privately owned, and profit is at stake, salacity will be printed whatever the risk of reprimand.

In a sense, the large awards for libel over the years can be seen not merely as compensation for actual damage done to reputations – we are talking about millions of euro now – but as fines imposed by juries on arrogant or avaricious editors.

Whatever reforms are brought to defamation law, it is to be hoped that citizens will still have this remedy in the courts, and that the courts will still be able to impose penalties that sting.

The same applies to privacy. The government would be well advised to legislate to bring some order to the process, but Irish law, by way of the European Convention on Human Rights and recent precedent in other jurisdictions, already provides for substantial financial compensation for citizens unjustly intruded on.

In arguing for the retention of legal remedies for defamation and invasion of privacy, I am not advocating court action as the only way to curb abuse. The first resort should be to the new procedures, which should be quicker and more effective in all but the most egregious cases.

But as well as the moral pressure of reprimand, there must be the risk of financial penalty for those that trifle with reputation or privacy for gain.

Of course, there are other changes required to lift the chilling effect of current libel law: we need a clearly stated defence of public interest, the possibility of mitigation by early apology, and a clear distinction between what can fairly be said about the actions and lives of public officials and those of private citizens.

Accountability

Whatever emerges from the libel reform process one thing will have changed: editors will have acknowledged that they are accountable to circles beyond their shareholders or the charitable trust. But it is likely to be a rather narrow accountability, restricted to those cases where an individual citizen can complain of identifiable damage from a specific story.

Something deeper is at stake when it comes to addressing the issues raised for the media in the Commission's progress report[27]. What is to be done when the media are failing generally in their duty to monitor the powerful on behalf of the weak, or when the tone of coverage has caused offence not to identifiable citizens, but to opinion generally?

The case of Kevin Myers' provocation against single parents in the Irish Times this year is instructive. Incensed citizens turned to Ireland's unofficial ombudsmen, the radio talk show hosts. Hour by hour and day by day, mounting anger was expressed to Joe Duffy, Vincent Browne and others, until The Irish Times and Kevin Myers apologized. I am sure that lessons have been learned.

My point here is that public outrage is the most powerful sanction of all against the abuse of power, whether by politicians or by writers and editors. The trouble is, citizens generally are not sufficiently engaged to question what is presented to them. There is little general discourse in Ireland about media standards, media ethics and media agendas.

There is a failure here, by press and broadcasters themselves, and by civil society generally. The newsroom culture is, or was, 'dog

---

27 See paragraphs 2.13 and 2.43 - 2.50, Democracy in Ireland (The Democracy Commission, May 2004).

does not eat dog', by which we used to mean that newspapers in particular did not pay any attention to each other's faults. The phrase 'glass houses' springs to mind.

Actually this attitude has largely disappeared now in the heat of competition. But The Spike and The Fifth Column[28] are marked more by spite and vindictiveness than by calm and rational assessment of their rivals' work.

The most obvious gap is on RTE: on radio 'What it Says in the Papers' provides a summary, not a critique, and television is bereft both of newspaper reviews and viewer feedback. A public broadcaster ought to see the provision of a regular platform for debate on media content and standards as one of its most vital services.

There is also a need for an independent source of regular critical media monitoring. I say independent, because there are some agenda-driven media watchdog groups, whose target is less the quality of the media generally than the degree to which their own viewpoints are covered sympathetically.

Is there something useful to be done here? The School of Communications in DCU is currently reviewing its research strategy, and the possibility of media monitoring work is being considered.

Our Centre for Society Information and Media has four main research themes, one of which is Media Policies, Practices and Audiences, covering:

> media texts, production processes, reception and effects; the role of media in the public sphere, particularly in multicultural, conflict and development contexts.

Obviously, this theme could well encompass a media monitoring role. It should be said that one thing in our minds during our review will be the extent to which we put the prospects of our journalism graduates at risk if our monitoring work offends the editors. Money is also a factor; some colleagues have recently been granted funding for a project on media ownership and diversity[29], and while the project is important, it will not involve assessments of content.

28   In Ireland on Sunday and the Sunday Independent respectively.
29   A benchmark study will be followed by six monthly updates of media ownership. Of course, many other projects are also underway, but none directly relevant to our business today.

Monitoring would be a significant project in its own right, and would require separate funding.

On the other hand, it may be better if there was a separate media institute, to which academics, working journalists and other concerned citizens could contribute. The Commission may wish to form a view of which is the most practical institutional model for such an endeavour.

More broadly, media monitoring is a permanent job for the whole of civil society. It is not enough for individuals to refuse to buy the papers they do not like. Just as my reputation can be harmed whether I read the article or not, if public discourse is degraded, then everyone may suffer, not just those who see or hear it.

Citizens who value their freedom have a duty to question those who exercise power, and one important seat of power in our time is the media. Even though some editors may not like it, they can be called to account, provided enough people pay attention, and speak out.

Approaches to Cultural and Ethnic Diversity

And the Role of Citizenship in promoting a more inclusive Intercultural Society in Ireland

by **Mr. Philip Watt,** Director NCCRI

This paper seeks to provide an overview and brief discourse of different approaches to cultural and ethnic diversity and seeks to consider the role of citizenship in promoting a more inclusive, intercultural society in Ireland.

The paper is divided into two parts. Part One identifies and discusses in turn the four main approaches to cultural and ethnic diversity, which are:

- Interculturalism
- Multiculturalism
- Assimilation
- Integration

Part Two of this paper looks at the complex and multi-facetted role of citizenship in promoting a more inclusive, intercultural society in Ireland

Part One: Approaches to Cultural and Ethnic Diversity

Approaches to cultural and ethnic diversity can differ widely between countries and can change over the course of time within a particular country in response to a range of factors including: The development of new approaches to the management of inward migration flows; responses to security and economic concerns; prevailing political ideologies and historical legacies, including colonialism and access to citizenship.

The four main approaches to cultural and ethnic diversity are summarised and considered in turn, beginning with the concept of Interculturalism.

Interculturalism: The approach that has been adopted in Ireland based on the underpinning principles of interaction, equality, understanding and respect. The intercultural approach seeks to move away from the 'one cap fits all approach' towards the reasonable accommodation of diversity within public policy and service provision. The five themes set out in the National Action Plan against Racism translates the concept of Interculturalism into a holistic policy framework.

Multiculturalism: The approach pioneered by Britain from the early 1970s but which is increasingly being viewed as outmoded. Multiculturalism seeks to acknowledge and celebrate diversity without necessarily promoting interaction or equality and is often perceived as glossing over issues such as racism, unemployment and poverty.

Assimilation: The 'when in Rome do as the Romans do, whether you like it or not' approach which has been largely discredited but which is enjoying a revival in newer guises in some EU countries in the reaction to events, in particular 9/11 and the perceived rise in Islamic fundamentalism. The French model of civic integration is a distinct and largely unique approach to assimilation, but with origins in the French tradition of secularism and equality. The recent debate on the law banning overt religious symbols illustrates some of the inherent contradictions in this policy and some of the diversity of opinion on cultural and ethnic diversity within Ireland

Integration: The term favoured by the EU, but which can often mean all things to all people, including assimilation. Many countries in the EU have adopted their own definitions of integration in tandem with tighter immigration control and security policies. A recent Communication by the European Commission has sought to develop greater consensus about what is meant by integration but a major weakness in the policy is that it only applies to recent migrants and it ignores questions of the type of society in which integration should take place.

Interculturalism

Interculturalism as an overall approach to ethnic and cultural diversity is becoming increasingly embedded in key policy developments in Ireland. This is a marked change in policy and is a distinct shift away from previous laissez-faire and ad hoc approaches that characterised previous Irish government policy approaches in this area.

In January 2005, the Government of Ireland published its National Action Plan against Racism, 'Planning for Diversity', which set out for the first time an intercultural framework approach to cultural and ethnic diversity in Ireland. Speaking at the launch of the Plan, the Taoiseach, Bertie Ahern T.D. said that it 'was a clear demonstration of the Government's commitment to adapt policy to the changing circumstances of a more diverse Ireland'.[30] A Strategic Management Committee has recently been established to monitor and coordinate the Plan.

The overall aim of the National Action Plan against Racism (NPAR) is to provide strategic direction to combat racism and to develop a more inclusive and intercultural society in Ireland. It states:

'Developing a more inclusive, intercultural society is about inclusion by design not as an add-on or afterthought. It is essentially about creating the conditions for interaction, equality of opportunity, understanding and respect. In taking this approach we embrace the concept that 'one size does not fit all', and that planning for and accommodating cultural diversity, everyone will benefit from the process.

There are five key themes underpinning the NPAR that seek to translate the concept of interculturalism into a coherent and multifaceted policy framework in the Irish context. This intercultural framework can be summarised as follows:

> Effective PROTECTION and redress against racism, including a focus on discrimination, threatening behaviour and incitement to hatred;
> Economic INCLUSION and equality of opportunity, including focus on employment, the workplace and poverty;
> Accommodating diversity in service PROVISION, including a focus on common outcomes, education, health, social services

---

30 Department of Justice, Equality and Law Reform, Press release 27 January 2005. www.justice.ie

and childcare, accommodation and the administration of justice;

RECOGNITION and awareness of diversity, including a focus on awareness raising, the media and the arts, sport and tourism;

Full PARTICIPATION in Irish society, including a focus on the political level, the policy level and the community level.[31]

The NPAR is not being developed in a contextual vacuum. It is being developed at a time of unprecedented expansion of cultural and ethnic diversity in Ireland, mainly as a consequence of significant inward migration. These changes can be illustrated through a few key statistics:

- Approximately 110,000 migrant workers from outside the European Economic Area arrived in Ireland between 2000 and 2004
- Approximately 45,000 applications by asylum seekers were received by the Department of Justice, Equality and Law reform between 2000 and 2004
- Over 50,000 workers from new EU Member States (in particular from Poland) took up employment in Ireland in the period May-December 2004.[32]

It is important to emphasise (in contrast to integration) that an intercultural approach to cultural and ethnic diversity seeks to be inclusive of existing majority and minority ethnic communities in Ireland, including longstanding/indigenous minority ethnic groups.

Long-standing minority ethnic communities in Ireland include groups as diverse as the Traveller community (24,000 people), the Jewish Community in Ireland, which can be traced back to the later part of the 19th century and before and the Islamic community in Ireland which began arriving in Ireland from the 1950s and which quadrupled in size to 19,000 over the period 1991-2002. As a consequence of significant and sustained inward migration into Ireland

---

31 Government of Ireland, (2005). The National Action Plan against Racism. www.justice.ie

32 Ruhs, Martin, (2005). Managing the Immigration and Employment of Non EU Nationals in Ireland. The Policy Institute at Trinity College Dublin.

from the mid 1990s, there are now significant African, Chinese and Eastern European communities in Ireland.

Intercultural Policy Initiatives
The increasing adoption of an intercultural approach to ethnic and cultural diversity is reflected in a number of recent policy developments in Ireland. For example, it is to be welcomed that for the first time Census 2006 will include a question on ethnic and cultural background, which will capture data that is not covered by the nationality, place of birth and religious questions in Census 2002.

The United Nations CERD Committee also recently welcomed the Irish Government's decision to include an ethnicity question in its concluding comments on Ireland's First and Second Progress Report under the International Convention on the Elimination of all forms of Racial Discrimination.[33]

14 **What is your ethnic or cultural background?**
Choose ONE section from A to D, then ✔ the appropriate box.

A   White
1   Irish
2   Irish Traveller
3   Any other White background

B   Black or Black Irish
4   African
5   Any other Black background

C   Asian or Asian Irish
6   Chinese
7   Any other Asian background

D   Other, including mixed background
8   Other, write in description

The Ethnicity Question to be included in Ireland's Census 2006[34]

---

33   United Nations Committee on the Elimination of all forms of Racial Discrimination, (2005). Concluding comments on Ireland's First and Second Progress Report. www.unhchr.ie
34   Central Statistics Office. www.cso.ie

The development of an ethnicity question is essential to the intercultural approach for a number of reasons, including to:

- Monitor the changing ethnic and cultural diversity in Ireland
- Track inequality and discrimination
- Facilitate local planning
- Target and allocate resources where appropriate
- Promote awareness of ethnic and cultural diversity in Ireland
- Meet reporting requirements under international human rights instruments

The categories, such as 'Black or Black Irish' demonstrates an understanding by the CSO that cultural and ethnic diversity in Ireland should be an inclusive concept; that ethnic and cultural identity does not necessarily remain static but can change over time and that ethnic and cultural diversity is not only a product of recent immigration into Ireland.

A further recent example of an intercultural policy initiative consistent with the NPAR is the development of intercultural education guidelines for the primary sector (May 2005) and the post-primary sector (forthcoming).[35] These guidelines emphasise the need for all schools to consider and to make reasonable accommodation of cultural and ethnic diversity in all aspects of the school and classroom planning process, irrespective of the extent of diversity within a particular school.

'The aim of these guidelines is to contribute to the development of Ireland as an intercultural society based on a shared sense that language, cultural and ethnic diversity is valuable'.

The adoption of 'a whole system approach', illustrated in these two recent examples, is an essential component of the intercultural framework set out in the NPAR. There are four elements of a whole system approach which are summarised as follows:

- Mainstreaming awareness of diversity into policy making processes and into the relevant policy areas
- Targeting of specific strategies to overcome the inequalities experienced by specific groups informed by an evidence-based approach to policy development

---

35 Department of Education and Science, (2005). Intercultural Education in the Primary School. Guidelines for Schools.

- Benchmarking through targets and timescales and the development of sectoral strategies
- Engagement of key stakeholders and drivers to support the implementation of the NPAR, including policy makers, specialised and expert bodies, the social partners and local communities, including groups representing cultural and ethnic minorities.

In short, developing a more inclusive, intercultural society is about inclusion by design not as an add-on or afterthought with a particular emphasis on *interaction* and *equality*. Key pieces of legislation such as the Equality Acts 1998-2004 have an important role in underpinning this process.

Multiculturalism
The major criticism of the multicultural approach, as developed in Britain and in the Netherlands in particular from the late 1960s and mid 1970s respectively, is that while it was perceived to be an advance on assimilation and neo colonial perspective, recent events have shown it only succeeded in embedding a superficial understanding and accommodation of cultural and ethnic diversity.

This multicultural approach is based on the recognition of diverse ethnic communities, which is positive, but the role of such communities and multiculturalism as a whole was seen as an 'add-on' to existing systems rather than being mainstreamed and integral to a changing society, which is advocated in an intercultural approach.

Multiculturalism has proved weak in promoting interaction or equality or in acknowledging and tackling poverty and unemployment or, for example, in developing effective health strategies to tackle the often higher levels of morbidity and mortality among minority ethnic groups.

Key policy outcomes from a multicultural approach are the promotion of initiatives that promote 'toleration' and 'better community relations' while at the same time glossing over racism. Implicit in this approach is that the State perceives itself as the neutral broker in what is essentially defined as a conflict between communities.

This is reflected in the terminology adopted in anti discrimination legislation that was couched in terms of 'Race Relations' rather than anti-racism. The McPherson Report into the death of murdered black teenager, Stephen Lawrence highlights the limited impact of multiculturalism in tackling deep-rooted problems such as systemic racism within the London Metropolitan Police Force.

While the development of multiculturalism was an important progression from assimilation, this approach has been further criticised for continuing to advocate that it was up to minorities to adapt in order to succeed without any significant focus on the role of the majority communities or the State in accommodating diversity. In its worst forms, a multicultural caricature emerged and resulted in framing cultural and ethnic diversity in terms of 'saris, samosas and samba'.

As a side note, in the experience of many of those involved in antiracism/intercultural awareness training, if sufficient care and planning are not taken what can start as a natural and legitimate curiosity about different cultures in a training session can sometimes descend into a voyeuristic examination of cultural practices and demands towards trainers from minority ethnic communities to justify their beliefs.

In response to the concerns of trainers, the National Consultative Committee on Racism and Interculturalism (NCCRI) has developed guidelines for anti-racism training. These emphasise the importance of cultural awareness and cultural competence as a strand of anti-racism and intercultural awareness training, while advocating that the key focus of training should be on majority community attitudes and practices and the translation of awareness into organisational practice and policy.[36]

In Britain, multiculturalism is increasingly being superseded by 'social cohesion'. While there are positive features within this policy, this approach has the appearance of a half way house between multiculturalism and assimilation with a renewed emphasis on the need for minority ethnic groups to integrate into British society.

Recent changes in other EU member states have resulted in a retreat from the multicultural rhetoric of the past. The Netherlands is another case in point. The views of Pim Fortuyn and his political supporters and the murder of the filmmaker Theo Van Gogh have been extensively discussed and identified as the key factors in the retreat from the support of multiculturalism. There has, however,

---

36   NCCRI, (2001). Guidelines and Anti-Racism and Intercultural Training

been less media focus on the views, fears and experience of the minority communities within the Netherlands.

While there were many attractive features of the Dutch multicultural system, it never addressed fundamental issues of social exclusion, poverty and historical legacies of exclusion. For example, unemployment rates for Turks and Moroccans stood at 21% and 36% in the early 1990s and these groups were for the most part excluded from social housing.[37] This is in large part the legacy if the *Gastarbeiter* (literally 'guestworkers') system that operated in the Netherlands up until the 1970s. Generations of migrant workers and their families were viewed as temporary residents and denied basic social and economic rights open to Dutch and other EU citizens. This factory of grievances was never adequately addressed and helped create conditions for alienation and exclusion among these and other communities, with inevitable consequences.

In short, multicultural approaches as developed in Britain and the Netherlands were a significant progression from the assimilationist and neo-colonial approaches to cultural and ethnic diversity that preceded them. It is evident, however, that the form of multiculturalism promoted failed to adequately acknowledge or address the structural inequalities created by the legacies of, for example the guest worker system in the Netherlands or the institutional racism prevalent in sectors of the British police.

Assimilation

The assimilationist approach to cultural and ethnic diversity can best be summed up as 'when in Rome, do as the Romans do, whether you like it or not'. The classic assimilationist approach views cultural and ethnic diversity as divisive and conflictual and has tended to presume that minority ethnic groups were deficient and lacking in cultural capital. This approach promoted the absorption of minorities into a 'shared' value system that was viewed as the only way forward; its aim was to make minority ethnic groups and their needs and aspirations as invisible as possible.[38] Few countries if any now openly aspire to the assimilationist approach described above, because of its overtones of racism and denial of cultural diversity.

However, assimilationist approaches can continue to inform

---

37 Bloomfield, J et al, (2004). Planning for the Intercultural City
38 Farrell, F and Watt, P. (2001) Responding to Racism in Ireland. Veritas.

policy development even in countries where a multicultural or intercultural approach is adopted as an official policy. A classic example is the persistent refusal by many local authorities in Ireland to implement their own published accommodation plans for Travellers. There continues to be very slow progress in delivering new Traveller-specific accommodation such as halting sites and group housing schemes by local authorities in Ireland. There is a range of factors involved, the most obvious reasons including opposition from local residents and the absence of an adequate enforcement agency at central Government level.

There continues to persist a mindset within some local authorities that the best way to deal with the Traveller 'accommodation problem' is to force Travellers into local authority housing estates by a process of consistent evictions and the non-delivery of Traveller specific accommodation. Over time, Travellers and their needs will become as invisible as possible. However, Traveller culture has proved resilient in the face of such action and in-action in the past.

While some Traveller families do freely chose to move into local authority housing, the usual preference is for accommodation that will allow Travellers to live together in their traditional extended family groups. This usually involves eight to ten units of accommodation that can be best facilitated in a small Traveller halting site or in a group-housing scheme.

Civic Integration: The French model of Assimilation

The French approach of 'Civic Integration' is a more complex and multifaceted form of assimilation that has significantly different origins than classic assimilationist approaches.[39]

It is based on a concept of the nation as a political community of equals and a secular state with universal rights, with an implicit assumption of the cultural uniformity and of what it means to be French. Policy dimensions of this policy include the consistent reluctance by the French State to collect data disaggregated by ethnicity and more recently the banning of overt religious symbols in schools.

Opinion writers in the Irish newspapers were sharply divided on whether the French Government was justified in its approach, with divisions appearing along diverse fault lines. The debate in Ireland

39   Entizinger, H. (1994). A future for the Dutch Ethnic Minorities Model in Lewis B et al Muslims in Europe.

highlights both the different views on cultural and ethnic diversity in Ireland and the essential contradictions within the French civic integration approach.

The debate in Ireland focussed on the passage of new legislation in France in February 2004, which banned overt religious symbols of faith such as the Muslim hijab (headscarves), Jewish skullcaps and large Christian crosses. President Chirac claimed that the aim of the ban was to protect the French Republican principle of secularism and equality but some commentators contended that the primary aim was to curb a perceived growth of Islamic fundamentalism.

In response to a protest outside the French embassy in Dublin at the new law, Fintan O Toole stated in the *Irish Times*: 'The protestors are wrong and they expose the dangers of a kind of multicultural ideology that is in fact a recipe for ghettoisation'.

As further justification for his stance, he disagreed with the view that Muslims have a specific dress code, saying 'that the only references in the Koran are vague'.[40]

On the other hand Lara Marlowe, writing for the same paper, argued that the debate on headscarves in France revealed a racist subtext and that the law is widely viewed as a means to breaking Islamic fundamentalism. She contended that one of the outcomes of the debate in France is that it stirred strong anti-Islamic prejudice on issues that went far beyond headscarves. She reported that Deputies who voted against the ban did so because the law was discriminatory, stigmatising and marginalizing the Muslim community in France.

While this debate raged in France, many schools in Ireland including national schools with either a Catholic or Protestant ethos, have for the most part quietly adopted their own pragmatic and common sense intercultural approaches to the issue of the wearing of the hijab. Without any fuss or controversy, the general policy is to allow the hijab to be worn in school, provided that it adopts the colour of the school uniform.

Integration

'Integration' is often the term used in related discourse on immigration and related diversity in the European Union. As a term it is often problematic because it is vague and usually refers to 'third country

---

40 For further discussion, see NCCRI's journal Spectrum, (March 2004), media review, p17 available on www.nccri.ie

nationals' i.e. those from outside the European Union.

The recent European Commission Communication outlines the most recent thinking on integration.[41] The Communication focuses on developing a holistic approach to the integration of 'third country nationals' including refugees and migrants, by:

- Reviewing current practice and experience with integration policy at an EU and national level
- Examining the role of immigration in relation to demographic ageing in the EU and its impact on economic growth
- Outlining policy orientations and priorities to promote the integration of migrants and refugees.

In emphasising the need for a holistic approach, the EU underlined the need for integration policies to link with a wider EU policy on employment and social cohesion, including the European Employment Strategy and the National Action Plans Against Poverty and Social Inclusion.

In short, the EU Commission's current approach to integration has some features that are consistent with the intercultural approach advocated in Ireland, including a strong emphasis on linkages with socio-economic policy and anti-poverty strategies. However, the 'draft' EU policy approach to integration lacks ambition and vision in important respects. For example, it only applies to 'third country' nationals, in particular migrants and refugees, and it excludes long-standing and indigenous minority ethnic groups.

The Irish Government's National Action Plan against Racism seeks to define the concept of integration as a series of *strategies* rather than an end in itself. In particular, the NPAR envisages the need for targeted strategies that focus on particularly marginalized groups:[42]

> 'In the context of this Plan integration simply means a range of targeted strategies for the inclusion of groups such as Travellers, refuges and migrants as part of the overall aim of developing a more inclusive and intercultural society'.[43]

---

41 European Commission, (COM (2003) 336 final). Communication from the Commission to the Council, the European Parliament, the European Economic and Social Committee and the Committee of the Regions.
42 Ibid, p66
43 Ibid,

The overall plan emphasises that cultural and ethnic diversity is inclusive of both recent and longstanding minorities in Ireland.

This overview and brief discourse highlights recent developments in Ireland in developing an intercultural approach to cultural and ethnic diversity, which is underpinned by the National Action Plan against Racism. Examples highlighted in this paper linked to an intercultural approach, include improved data collection (benchmarking) and provision - the development of an inclusive approach to service provision as illustrated by recent intercultural education guidelines.

The paper highlights key differences between an intercultural approach and the multicultural approaches that have been pioneered in Britain and the Netherlands until recent years. It contends that it was not so surprising in hindsight that the superficial form of multiculturalism described was quickly undermined by events following 9/11.

Despite positive features, the multicultural approaches described failed to address fundamental issues such as the legacy of the guest-worker system in the Netherlands or the institutional racism highlighted by the McPherson report in Britain.

There are few countries that advocate the classic form of assimilation described in this paper because of its neo-racist overtones. However the assimilationist mindset continues to persist at both a conscious and unconscious level in many countries, including Ireland.

The French form of civic integration cannot be directly equated with assimilation because it has very different origins and ambitions, but whatever the origins there is a distinct danger that the outcomes of civic integration may be the same as assimilation, as illustrated in the case of the recent law banning overt religious symbols in France.

The concept of 'integration' is widely used at an EU level in discussion about approaches to cultural and ethnic diversity, often without adequate definition of what constitutes integration or with little focus on the type of society in which integration is to take place.

While the most recently espoused EU model of integration has some progressive features, its continued focus on 'third country nationals' and the concomitant omission of existing ethnic and cultural diversity is a major weakness in this approach.

This paper advocates that 'integration' should not be seen as an end in itself, but should be more closely defined as a range of targeted strategies for the inclusion of groups such as Travellers, refugees and migrants as part of the overall aim of developing a more inclusive, intercultural society.

Part Two: The role of citizenship in promoting a more inclusive, intercultural society in Ireland

It has long been recognised that Citizenship can act as a tool for inclusion and exclusion in the context of overall approaches to cultural and ethnic diversity. In Part One of this paper there is a focus on the gastarbeiter system that prevailed in the Netherlands until the 1970s where Turks, Moroccans and others were denied citizenship rights and concomitant access to key services, including social housing provision. This acted as a factory of grievances that could not be papered over by the multicultural policies promoted in the Netherlands.

In Ireland, the recent Citizenship Referendum focussing on the rights and future of Irish-born children and their non-national parents has dominated the recent debate on the role of citizenship as a tool for inclusion or exclusion in respect of cultural and ethnic diversity.

The Citizenship Referendum, the subsequent decision to regularise the 11,000 families in Ireland with Irish born children, and the proposed Immigration and Residence Bill have largely concluded this debate. Therefore, this part of the paper focuses on the post referendum political reality in the context of continuing demographic and policy changes in Ireland.

Acquiring Citizenship in Ireland
There are three principal ways of acquiring citizenship:

- Birth
- Descent
- Naturalisation

Citizenship in most states is based on either the *jus soli* or *jus sanguinis* principles. *Jus soli* is citizenship by birth where a child acquires citizenship of the host country by virtue of being born there, irrespective of the nationality of his/her parents. This applies to some common law states such as the United States, New Zealand and Canada. Ireland as a common law state was in this category prior to the 2004 citizenship referendum. Britain ended its *jus soli* approach in 1983 in response to the political conclusion at the time that it acted as a 'pull' factor in respect of immigration.

Jus sanguinis is the principle of acquiring citizenship, whereby citizenship is by descent (literally by blood). In order for the child to be a citizen, one or both parents must be citizens at the time of the child's birth. This is the form of citizenship that exists in almost all European states, including Ireland since 2004.[44]

Citizenship by naturalization occurs in most states whereby the state confers citizenship on non-nationals who have fulfilled certain criteria. In Ireland this is generally five years of legal residence (over a period of nine years). In addition, the applicant must be of good character and in some countries is required to meet language requirements. In some cases, the person is required to renounce their previous nationality. The number of naturalisations in Ireland has, so far, been relatively small. During 2001-2004 a total of 5,387 non-nationals acquired Irish citizenship, with one commentator estimating that on the basis of nationality, most of these are people with refugee status in Ireland.[45]

According to the Department of Justice, Equality and Law Reform, there is currently a backlog of 9,000 naturalisation applications with an average waiting time of over two years. Immigration officials estimate that the 184% increase in applications between 2001 and 2004 is likely to accelerate in coming years.

There are alternatives to naturalisation that are currently the subject of consideration and reform through a consultative process on immigration and residence that concludes in July 2005.[46] The Government is committed to introducing an Immigration and Residence Bill that will provide a framework to streamline and speed up the process of obtaining residency, including long-term residency and to revise the employment permit system.

---

44 NCCRI, (2004) Advocacy Paper 2. International Perspectives Relating to the Future of Irish Born Children and Their Non National Parents in Ireland
45 Ruhs, p 27
46 Department of Justice, Equality and Law Reform, (2005). Outline Policy Proposals for an Immigration and Residence Bill.

At present there is already a residency category of 'permission to remain without condition as to time'. This is open to non-national residents who have been legally resident in Ireland over eight years but who have not applied for naturalisation.

For the most part however, residency rights for migrant workers from outside the European Economic Area is largely dependent on the type of employment permit that regulates their entry into Ireland. For those on work permits (the vast majority), residency is given for one year, renewable, and further residency is dependent on the issuing of another work permit. For those more highly skilled workers on work visas or authorisation, the period of residency granted is two years, renewable.

The Role of Citizenship in promoting a more inclusive, Intercultural Society in Ireland

Citizenship is an important though complex tool in respect of creating a more inclusive, intercultural society in Ireland. This is evident from applying the themes of the intercultural framework set out in Part One of this paper:

Protection and redress against racism	Everyone in Ireland, irrespective of their legal status, is protected by the Equality legislation (protection against discrimination) and the Criminal Law (protection against crime motivated by racism). However there are increasing indications that people with less secure/less permanent residency status in Ireland are probably less likely to come forward to vindicate their rights.[47] Irish Travellers and minority ethnic groups with EU nationality still feel the bitter sting of racism, despite their citizenship.
Economic **inclusion**	Although all people legally entitled to work in Ireland are entitled to the same employment protections as Irish citizens, for those without citizenship or long term residency rights, the process of vindicating rights may be more difficult in practice because of concerns that their

---

47 NCCRI and the Equality Commission for Northern Ireland, (2005). *Seeking Advice and Redress against Racism*, p12.

	employment or residency status might be affected. In the absence of data it is difficult to be conclusive about this issue.[48]
Accommodating diversity in service **Provision**	Existing long-term residency rights confer few additional rights to people from outside the European Economic Area. For example, they are at present required to apply and reapply for travel visas and they are required to pay full economic fees to attend third level colleges. The most significant advantage is that they are no longer required to obtain an employment permit to work in Ireland. If this situation continues, citizenship will be perceived as an increasingly attractive option.
Recognition and awareness of diversity	The concept of citizenship has the potential to be an inclusive or an exclusionary concept. Increasing the access to citizenship or to long-term residency certainly sends out a positive message about cultural and ethnic diversity in Ireland (see discussion below on this issue). The inclusive approach to framing the ethnicity question in Census 2006 is a further example of inclusiveness that is not simply based on citizenship.
Participation in Irish society, including a focus on the political, policy and community level	The symbolic and legal entitlement of citizenship, which confers reassurance of residence and, for example, the expectation of protection when travelling abroad. It also can confer greater access to key services (including social housing) and the right to vote in all elections. It should be noted that all legal residents in Ireland have already the right to vote in local elections, irrespective of citizenship.

The increasing numbers of people both applying for and acquiring naturalisation demonstrates that an increasing number of recent migrants to Ireland see the value in Irish/EU citizenship. However, it is worth noting that to date it is mostly people with refugee status rather than labour migrants who have been granted citizenship, even though Refugee status confers almost all the rights of Irish citizen-

---

48   The Labour Inspectorate in the Department of Enterprise, Trade and Employment does not collect statistics on the proportion of migrant worker cases in their case files.

ship. The desire for naturalisation among the refugee community may be a legacy of people who have lived in the vulnerable position of asylum seeker, sometimes for many years, or who have been unable to obtain passports from their country of origin for obvious reasons.

Although the number of applications for naturalisation is rising, it is unclear how many of the thousands of people coming to Ireland as labour migrants will eventually become or even want to become Irish citizens. There is an implicit assumption, which was also evident in the 2004 citizenship debate, that the ultimate goal of all migrants coming to Ireland, whether as asylum seekers or labour migrants, is to remain here indefinitely and become an Irish/EU citizen.

Yet the changing patterns of inward migration to Ireland and our own experience of emigration suggest that this is not necessarily the case. In the context of increasing globalisation and emerging labour shortages in many OECD countries, migrants now have the option to stay a few years in Ireland, to remit money to relations and to either return to their home country or to move on to better conditions in a third country. In this context, it is worth noting that until recently almost half of all inward migration to Ireland was comprised of returning Irish emigrants (see Table One). This demonstrates that when economic conditions improve, the natural inclination of many people is to return to their home country.

Table One

Pattern of Inward Migration into Ireland
Origin (% of Total) Inward
Migration into Ireland in 1996 and 2002 (CSO)[49]

Origin	1996	2002	2003
Returned Irish	45%	40%	35%
UK	21%	11%	14%
Rest of EU	13%	12%	14%
USA	10%	4%	3%
Rest of world	11%	32%	35%

Others migrants will want to stay and make Ireland their home and bring over partners and immediate family members or will make

49   Adapted from Central Statistics Office (10 December 2003). Population and Migration Estimates, April 2002.

families in Ireland. For this group the issues of access to long term residency and citizenship will be more important than those who are here on a temporary basis.

A further factor to be considered is that prior to EU enlargement in 2004, 40% of labour migration into Ireland was from what now constitutes the new European Union States. With newly acquired EU citizenship and the present absence of a ceiling on inward migration into Ireland from the new EU countries, there are few additional rights that would be conferred by such EU nationals taking out Irish citizenship.

The difficulties in accessing long-term residency and the few rights that are conferred by this status have, for the time being, increased the attractiveness of Irish citizenship. However, should the forthcoming Immigration and Residency Bill tackle the administrative delays and end petty rules, such as having to apply and reapply for visas for foreign travel, then it may be the case that long-term non-EEA nationals who wish to make their homes in Ireland will be happy to be long-term residents rather than Irish citizens. Only time will tell on this issue.

In conclusion, it is clear that access to citizenship and the associated concomitant rights is an important element in promoting a more inclusive, intercultural society in Ireland. In particular, for those people from outside the EEA who want to make Ireland (or another EU country) their permanent home. The biggest demand for citizenship is from those in previously very vulnerable positions, particularly asylum seekers who have acquired refugee status and those with humanitarian leave to remain. The ambition of labour migrants from outside the EEA to take out Irish citizenship will greatly depend on the detailed administrative arrangements that will follow in the wake of the forthcoming Immigration and Residence Bill. The present uncertainties in respect of the EU constitution may also be a factor if these uncertainties are not resolved in the near future.

If access to and rights conferred from the forthcoming legislation in respect of long-term residency are generous and the administrative arrangements efficient, then the present upward trend in naturalisation applications, particularly by labour migrants, may be reduced. An analogy could be drawn to employment. There are fewer employees or employers who now advocate the need for permanent jobs for life. Many people will want to move on to another employer/another form of employment at regular intervals in their career, while others will not. The key for those who move is that they can protect their employment rights, their future after retirement (pension rights) and improve their standard of living. Migrants will also want similar assurances that if they do not take out citizenship, their long-term rights will be protected and their contribution to Ireland's economy acknowledged.

In an optimistic scenario and in the context of continued inward migration into Ireland, which will in large part be determined by prevailing economic conditions, the ability to access residency and rights that are almost on a par with citizenship is likely to suit the many who may not want to relinquish their own citizenship/national identity.

In a more pessimistic scenario, with poorer economic conditions and the introduction of tighter immigration controls in Ireland and across Europe, the importance of citizenship as a tool for inclusion and exclusion will increase. A further factor in the equation is that in other parts of Europe the increase in support for ethno-centric forms of nationalism and the worrying, though fluctuating, fortunes of movements opposed to cultural and ethnic diversity are added factors in the broader equation of whether an inclusive, intercultural approach to cultural and ethnic diversity can develop and thrive in Ireland.